97B
COUNTERINTELLIGENCE
AGENT
COURSE:
Volume 1

Counterintelligence Operations

UNITED STATES ARMY

ISBN: **1500735825**
ISBN-13: **978-1500735821**

DEDICATION

To those who aspire to the ranks of the men and women serving our country in the ranks of the United States Army Military Intelligence Corps this book is dedicated.

Table of Contents

Counterintelligence Operations..**1**

Intelligence Support Missions...**86**

Counterintelligence Operations Appendix A **227**

Counterintelligence Operations Appendix B..**247**

Counterintelligence Operations Appendix C..**259**

Intelligence and Electronic Warfare Appendix A...**261**

1 COUNTERINTELLIGENCE OPERATIONS

LESSON 1

'

CI INVESTIGATIONS: PURPOSE, SCOPE,

JURISDICTION AND AUTHORITY

CRITICAL TASK: NONE

OVERVIEW

LESSON DESCRIPTION:

In this lesson, you will learn the rationale and applicable doctrine concerning the conduct of counterintelligence (CI) investigations to include the authority, jurisdictional constraints, scope, and the administrative functions for all phases of an investigation.

TERMINAL LEARNING OBJECTIVE:

ACTIONS: Describe the functions of the Personnel Security Central
                  Clearance Facility (CCF) and other applicable control offices;
                  identify and perform the administrative responsibilities for
                  all phases of a CI investigation; and state the doctrine,
                  scope criteria, and purpose for the initiation of an
                  investigation

CONDITIONS: You will be given narrative information and illustrations from
               FM 34-60.

STANDARD: You will initiate, perform all administrative functions, and
               properly record the results of both favorable and unfavorable
               CI investigations IAW with the provisions of FM 34-60.

REFERENCES: The material contained in this lesson was derived from the
               following publications:

AR 380-5,
AR 381-10,
AR 381-20,
AR 380-67,
FM 34-60,

This lesson has two parts:

Part A: Purpose, Scope, Jurisdiction and Authority for CI investigations.

Part B: Source of Investigation Requests, Control Offices, and Function of The Personnel Security Central Clearance Facility (CCF).

PART A: PURPOSE, SCOPE, JURISDICTION AND AUTHORITY

FOR CI INVESTIGATIONS

PURPOSE OF CI INVESTIGATIONS. CI investigations are aimed at the detection, prevention, and neutralization of actual or potential threats to the security of the command and the Army, regardless of whether criminal activity is involved. Although prosecution of the offenders may be the natural consequence of some CI investigations, the primary objective is the security of the command. Many operations of CI units must be coordinated carefully with those of military police (MP) investigative units and other intelligence and security agencies. This coordination will prevent operations of one agency from having a negative effect on or compromising the operations of another.

SCOPE OF INVESTIGATIONS. It is Department of the Army (DA) policy that a CI investigation will be limited in scope to the minimum amount of assets necessary to obtain adequate information on which to base an adjudication or decision. Special care and minimum use of covert investigative techniques will be used, particularly when authorized to investigate nonaffiliated United States (US) citizens and organizations. When the use of such techniques is contemplated, the legal officers of the US Army Intelligence and Security Command (INSCOM) must be consulted to ensure the action is in conformance with Army Regulations (AR), federal statutes, and if applicable, the laws of the host foreign country. When any legal doubt exists, prior approval must be requested from the Deputy Chief of Staff for Intelligence, DA (DCSINT, DA).

All CI investigators and supervisors must understand that a legal distinction exists between an investigation involving foreign intelligence agencies and a routine investigation involving US citizens or allied foreign nationals. As a general rule, use of covert techniques is prohibited in routine investigations involving citizens of the US or allied foreign nations.

Information developed during the course of any CI investigation that indicates involvement by a foreign intelligence service must be reported by the fastest secure means available, consistent with the "need to know" principles, to Army Case Control Officer (ACCO).

ARMY JURISDICTION. An agreement was entered into in 1949 by DCSINT, DA; the Office of Naval Criminal Investigative Service (NCIS) US Navy; the Office of Special Investigations, (OSI), Inspector General, US Air Force; and the Federal Bureau of Investigation (FBI). This agreement is commonly known as the "Delimitations Agreement". It establishes the responsibilities of the signatories for investigating all activities coming under the categories of espionage, counterespionage, criminal subversion, and sabotage. This agreement is binding upon all US Army investigative agencies.

NOTE: ONI has been redesignated as the Naval Criminal Investigative Service (NCIS).

DCSINT, DA is responsible for:

* The investigation and disposal of all cases of espionage, counterespionage, criminal subversion, and sabotage involving active and retired Army military personnel.

* The disposal, but not investigation, of all cases in these categories involving Army civilian employees in the US, Puerto Rico, and the Virgin Islands.

* The investigation and disposal of all cases in these categories involving Army civilian employees stationed in areas other than the US, Puerto Rico, and the Virgin Islands, except part of such investigations as have ramifications in the US, Puerto Rico, or the Virgin Islands.

* The investigation of all cases in these categories involving civilians and foreign nationals who are not employees of the other subscribing organizations, in areas where the Army commander has supreme jurisdiction over the Armed Forces stationed therein, including possessions of the US other than Puerto Rico and the Virgin Islands.

* Informing the other subscribing organizations of any important developments.

PART B: SOURCE OF INVESTIGATION REQUESTS,

CONTROL OFFICES, AND FUNCTION OF CCF

SOURCE OF INVESTIGATION REQUESTS. The mission of CI elements and units is "the detection, identification, assessment, counter, neutralize, or exploit threat intelligence collection efforts.

In fulfillment of this mission, CI personnel and units engage in a broad range of operations with direction and guidance from higher authorities within their areas of operations. Some of those activities which may be termed "force protection", include the following:

* Safeguarding defense information.

* Assessing vulnerabilities and recommending solutions for Army facilities which have classified defense contracts or have been designated as key defense installations.

* Conducting CI surveys, inspections and services.

* Conducting two types of investigations.

* CI Investigations (Aka: SAEDA) and personnel security investigations (PSI).

A Counterintelligence Investigation (CII) is one in which sabotage, espionage, spying, treason, sedition, or subversion, FIS directed sabotage, activity is suspected or alleged because of the receipt or development of credible derogatory information. The primary purpose of each CII is to identify, neutralize and exploit information of such a nature form and reliability that may determine the extent and nature of action, if any, is necessary to counteract the threat and enhance security. CII may have various origins, but generally originate from four common sources:

Signal Scope Background Investigation (SSBI). During the conduct of a routine SSBI by the Defense Investigative Service (DIS), credible derogatory information reflecting on subject's loyalty is investigated.

As a result, the investigation classification will be changed from that of a SSBI to CII. DIS will dispose of the case IAW its charter, Department of Defense (DOD) Directive 5105.42. DIS has the option to run the investigation or refer the case to the appropriate investigative agency. CI has investigative jurisdiction, as well as case dispositions, for CII involving active or retired members of the U.S. Army and DOD civilians working overseas. The FBI has jurisdiction for DOD civilians employed within the Continental United States (CONUS).

NOTE: The SSBI will NOT be changed to a CII if the information reflects adversely on subject's suitability; that is, integrity, discretion, morals, or character.

CI Walk-In Interview. A walk-in is an individual who seeks out CI Agents to volunteer information which is believed to be of intelligence value. When an individual reports activity that falls within the scope of a CII to an intelligence unit or other military organization, this information is immediately reported to sub-control offices who have authority to initiate a CII. The CII would be

conducted by the appropriate investigative agency having jurisdiction over the individual being investigated. DIS could be requested to conduct all or part of the military components of the investigation.

Reports From Other Intelligence and Security Agencies.

Leads Obtained Directly From Sources Used in Special Operations.

CII's are generally incident investigations concerning acts or activities which are committed by, or involving known or unknown persons or groups.

Initiation of a CII.

CII on individuals under the jurisdiction of the Army will be initiated only by:

* US Army Intelligence and Security Command (INSCOM) ACCO.
* Sub-control offices overseas.
* Direction of higher authority.

CONUS Investigations. Within CONUS, major commands, agencies, and activities will forward requests for initiation of CII to INSCOM. When a CI, which was not requested by a major command (MACOM), agency, or activity, is initiated by one of the services, the appropriate command will be notified through intelligence channels. During the course of a CII, the control officer will keep the MACOM informed of the progress of the case.

NOTE: The Delimitations Agreement of 1949 emphasizes that each military service will be responsible for its own internal security. CII on individuals under the jurisdiction of the U.S. Army will be initiated only by U.S. Army agencies.

Overseas Investigations. In overseas areas, the responsibility for investigation of the agreed categories rests with the military service that is in supreme command of the area. This procedure is subject to coordination with the Central Intelligence Agency (CIA) and agreements with other DOD intelligence components and host government agencies, IAW AR 381-20. Normally, the Army will be the supreme authority in an area of operations or postwar zone of occupation and will have the investigative responsibility of espionage, sabotage, and subversion committed by any individual in the area. The one exception is personnel under the jurisdiction of other military services in the area. This exception is based upon the assumption that the CI agencies of the Navy and Air Force are operational in the area and will be able to take care of their own personnel. If they are not, by prior agreement with such services, the Army will become responsible for and conduct all such investigations.

"What is derogatory information?"

Para 1-304.3, AR 380-67, defines derogatory information as:

"Information that constitutes a possible basis for taking an adverse or unfavorable personnel security action."

    a. Adverse loyalty information (see para 2-200 a-f, 2-200k and Appendix E, para 3, AR 380-67).

    b. Adverse suitability information (see para 2-200g-j and 2-200 1-q, Appendix E, para, 1, 2, 4, 5, and 6, AR 380-67).

    c. Appendix I, AR 380-67 discusses the adjudication policy. It provides "Disqualifying Factors" - some types of serious conduct that can justify a determination to deny or revoke and individuals eligibility for access to classified information.

If the individual is a member of the U.S. Army, action may be taken to suspend favorable personnel action concerning him until the investigation is completed. This action will be initiated under the provisions of:

    Paragraph 6, AR 600-31, Suspension of Favorable Personnel Actions for Military Personnel in National Security Cases and Other Investigative Procedures.

Chapter 4, AR 604-10, Military Personnel Security Program.

Under the individual flagging action, many personnel actions will be suspended: promotions; appointment, enlistment, reappointment or reenlistment; discharge or normal release from active duty; entry on active duty; awards, decorations, or commendations; retirement; security access; attendance at service education or training programs; requests for excess leave; and reassignment, except when cogent reasons exist and then only within the command.

Significant derogatory information:

SUB-CONTROL OFFICES (SCO). Within DA, the DCSINT has staff responsibility for all CI investigative activities. DCSINT formulates policy for the conduct, management, direction, and control of CI operations.

Administration and control of CI investigations - special operations, and counterespionage project are exercised by INSCOM, through ACCO. The ACCO exercises overall control and coordination of MI Army CII, and ultimate case control. Within a geographic area or region, INSCOM maintains control of CI, investigative activities through the SCO established in theater support brigades.

CII are initiated only by the responsible SCO. The following SCOs are responsible for all Army CII investigations and operations within their geographic areas:

* Deputy Chief of Staff for Intelligence (DCSINT), US Army Europe (USAREUR), for the Commander-in-Chief USAREUR area of responsibility (G2, USAREUR).

* 501st Military Intelligence (MI) Brigade (Bde), for the Commander, Eight US Army (EUSA) area of responsibility.

* S2s for the Commanders, 470th, 500th, and 902nd Military Intelligence Brigades.

* Commander, FCA, USAINSCOM, for all other areas.

Major commands (MACOM), agencies, and activities within CONUS will forward requests for initiation of CII to the appropriate SCO.

When a CII, which was not requested by another MACOM, agency, or activity is initiated by a SCO, the appropriate command is notified through intelligence channels.

During a CII, the SCO will keep the major commander informed concerning the progress of the case.

CENTRAL PERSONNEL SECURITY CLEARANCE FACILITY (CCF).

Jurisdiction. The Secretary of the Army delegated the authority to grant, deny, or revoke security clearances for access to classified defense information to the Commander, U.S. Army CCF, under the provisions of DA General Order Number 14, dated 27 July 1977.

The DCSINT, DA, delegated the authority to grant, deny, or revoke access to Sensitive Compartmented Information (SCI) to the Commander, U.S. Army CCF, under CCF, in DAMI-DOS letter, dated 3 October 1977.

This authority applies to the following DA personnel:

1.   US Army, DA and contractor personnel affiliated with the Department of Defense and the Army.

2.   Persons employed, hired on an individual basis, or serving on an advisory or consulting basis for whom Army personnel security clearances are required, whether or not such persons are paid from appropriate or nonappropriated funds.

3.   Employees of the Army National Guard, Army-Air Force Exchange Service (AAFES), American Red Cross, United Service Organization (USO) who are required to have Army personnel security clearance.

4.   Reserve Components and National Guard personnel not on active duty.

5.   Members of the Reserve Officers Corps.

The above includes U.S. citizens who are native born, naturalized, derivative birth and derivative naturalization.

Responsibilities. The commander, CCF, is the only person designated to deny, revoke, or restore access when suspended by the local commander. CCF monitors the progress of all actions taken concerning the revocation of security clearances and stores all reports relating to the security clearances of personnel under its jurisdiction.

Whenever derogatory information is developed or becomes available to any DOD element, it shall be referred to the commander or security offices at the organization to which the individual is assigned for duty. The commander or security officer shall review the information in terms of its security significance and completeness. If further information is needed to confirm or disprove, additional investigation should be requested.

When the Commander learns of derogatory information on a member of his/her command that falls into the scope of para 2-200, AR 380-67, the commander will immediately forward DA Form 5248-R to Commander CCF. DA Form 5288 will be submitted in a timely manner and will indicate detail information and actions being taken by the commander or appropriate authority (i.e., conducting an inquiry or investigation). Follow-up will be submitted at 90 day intervals if the commander has not taken final action. At the conclusion of the command action, a final report will be forwarded to CCF that must contain results of any local inquiry, investigations, or board actions and recommendations of the command concerning restoration or revocation of the individuals security clearance. Commanders will not delay any personnel actions while waiting final action by CCF. Actions should proceed with CCF being informed by DA Form 5248-R.

* If a personnel file does not indicate the existence of a security clearance, commanders must still report information that falls into the scope of para 2-200, AR 380-67, since the person may require a security clearance at a later date. Only a final report is required.

* Suspend individual's access on an "informal" basis while gathering information to determine a formal suspension is warranted and forward all derogatory information to CCF on DA Form 5248-R with the commander's recommendation. If the commander does not suspend access, CCF will review available information and may advise the commander to suspend.

* If the commander decides on formal suspension of access, DA Form 873 will be removed from individuals personnel file and attached to DA 5248-R and reported to CCF. Once this is done, the commander may not restore access until a final determination is made by Commander, CCF.

When CCF receives derogatory information and denial or revocation of a security clearance and or access to SCI is deemed appropriate, CCF will:

* Forward a Letter of Intent (LOI) through the command security manager to the individual. The LOI will outline the derogatory information and explain the proposed actions. The LOI will offer the individual the chance to reply in writing the chance to explain, refute or mitigate the incidents.

* The LOI will direct suspension of access to classified material. If the LOI addresses SCI access, only, collateral access may continue.

The individual will acknowledge receipt of the LOI by signing and dating the enclosed form letter. The person will indicate his/her intention of submission of a rebuttal. The form letter will be submitted to CCF immediately.

The commander will ensure that the person is counseled as to the seriousness of CCF's contemplated actions and will offer advice and assistance in forming a reply. The individuals response must address each issue raised in CCF LOI. Any written documentation may be forwarded as well as letters of recommendations from supervisors. The response will be forwarded to CCF through the representative who provided the LOI.

All replies to Letters of Intent will be endorsed by at least one commander. Endorsements should include commander's recommendation(s) to deny, revoke or restore the individual's security clearance. The commander should provide a rationale addressing the issues outlined in the LOT. Responses without commander's recommendation will returned for comment.

When the Commander, CCF, receives the response to the LOI, a final determination is made. The final determination is furnished through the security officer to the individual. IAW AR 600-7-, CCF provides unfavorable information to the DA Suitability Evaluation Board (DASEB), USAR Personnel Center, or National Guard Personnel Centers on all E6 and above, commissioned and warrant officers. A copy of the LOI, individual rebuttal and CCF final letter will be provided. DASEB will determine which information will remain in the military personnel file.

When an individual is incarcerated by military or civil authorities on a conviction of a criminal offense, or when a person is dropped from the rolls as a deserter, his commander will take the following actions immediately.

* Withdraw the DA Form 873 from the individual's Military Personnel Records Jacket (MPRJ) GR GPF and stamp or print across the face, "Revoked by authority of Commander, CCF, Deserted-(Date)," or "Revoked by authority of Commander, CCF, incarcerated as a result of civil conviction or court martial (date)."

* Forward the DA Form 873 - and DA Form 5248-R explaining the circumstances to the Commander, CCF, (PCCF-M), Fort George G. Meade, MD 20755-5250.

* If no DA 873 is in the MPRJ or OPF, DA 5248 explaining the circumstances will be forwarded to Commander, CCF (PCCF-M).

* If the person has transferred, endorse the LOI, to the gaining command and forward an info copy to CCF (PCCF-M). If released from active duty, with a Reserve Obligation forward the LOI to the U.S. Army Reserve Personnel Center, ATTN: DARP-SPI, St. Louis, MO 63121-5200. Forward a copy to CCF (PCCF-M).

* If released from active duty without a reserve obligation, endorse the LOI to CCF (PCCF-M) with copy of discharge orders.

CONDUCT OF A CII. CI Agents conducting CII investigations must have a thorough understanding of the objectives and operations of foreign espionage, sabotage, and subversive organizations: CI investigative training; and training and/or experience in counterespionage

operations. This is necessary because it is critically important during the conduct of a CII that all information is fully developed and properly presented, regardless of whether or not the information is favorable to the subject. Also, all data obtained must be factually presented to eliminate any need for presumptive evaluation during the adjudication of the case.

The most important fundamental that should be remembered concerning the conduct of a personal subject CII is that the CI Agent must attempt to prove or disprove the allegation against the subject.

The CI Agent must remember to use caution during the investigation, especially when interviewing the immediate supervisor of a subject, so as not to compromise the investigation or cast a stigma on the subject.

When interviewing a source, the CI Agent will attempt to obtain a sworn statement in the sources own handwriting, if derogatory information reflecting on the subject's loyalty arises, or if information is obtained which refutes previously obtained information concerning the subject's loyalty. If illegible, prepare a typewritten sworn statement for the source to review and sign. Include the original handwritten statement as an attachment to the IMFR. Never destroy the original statement.

For Record. When conducting a CII, the CI Agent's objective of the investigation is to determine the nature and extent of damage to national security. The intent is to develop information sufficient enough to permit its use in a civil or military court or to initiate Counterespionage (CE) procedures. However, the investigation should not be limited to collecting only evidence which is admissible in court. The investigation reports should include all relevant and material information. The CI Agent must remember that hearsay and opinions expressed by sources during an interview may serve a further use as leads in continuing the investigation. The CI Agent must also remember to limit his investigation to the allegation.

Often during the course of an investigation, information relevant to other areas of possible CI interest develop. This information will generally concern the suitability of the individual as regards his morals, character, and integrity. This information will be reported by the CI Agent but not pursued unless specifically tasked.

In accordance with the provisions of AR 381-20, it is the policy of the DA to afford the subject of a CII every reasonable opportunity to explain, refute, or mitigate any adverse information directly involving him. This is accomplished through a subject interview. A subject interview is advantageous to both the subject, by affording him the opportunity to tell his side of the story, and to the government. A CI Agent must get permission from his control officer prior to interviewing a subject of a CII.

LESSON 1

PRACTICE EXERCISE

The following items will test your grasp of the material covered in this lesson. There is only one correct answer for each item. When you have completed the exercise, check your answers with the answer key that follows. If you answer any item incorrectly, study again that part of the lesson which contains the portion involved.

1.   There are four signers of the Delimitations Agreement. They are the DCSINT, DA; the Office of Naval Criminal Investigative Service (NCIS), US Navy; the Office of Special Investigations (OSI), Inspector General, US Air Force; and which of the following?

        A.   Central Intelligence Agency.

        B.   Defense Intelligence Agency.

        C.   Defense Investigative Service.

        D.   Federal Bureau of Investigation.

2.   The authority to grant, deny, or revoke personnel security clearances to classified defense information has been delegated to the Commander, CCF, by which of the following?

A.   Secretary of the Army.

B.   Commander, USAINSCOM.

C.   Commander, DIS.

D.   DCSINT, DA.

3.   Adverse information in which of the following areas would be justification for changing a SSBI to a CII?

    A.   Morale.

    B.   Loyalty.

    C.   Integrity.

    D.   Discretion.

4.   Special Agents conducting a CII will limit the investigation strictly to the production of evidence which is admissible in court.

    A.   True.

    B.   False.

5.   From whom is prior approval requested from concerning the use of covert investigative techniques if legal doubt exists?

    A.   Commander, USAINSCOM.

B.   FBI.

C.   Secretary of the Army.

D.   DCSINT, DA.

LESSON 1

PRACTICE EXERCISE

Answer Key and Feedback

Item	Correct Answer and Feedback
1.	D. Federal Bureau of Investigation. (page 1-2).
2.	A. Secretary of the Army. (page 1-6).
3.	B. Loyalty. (page 1-4).
4.	B. False. (page 1-10).
5.	D. DCSINT, DA. (page 1-2).

LESSON 2

CONDUCT CI INVESTIGATIONS OF SABOTAGE, ESPIONAGE, TREASON,

SEDITION, AND SUBVERSION

CRITICAL TASKS: 301-340-1001

301-340-2009

OVERVIEW

LESSON DESCRIPTION:

In this lesson, you will learn how to plan, prepare for, and conduct sedition, subversion, sabotage, espionage, and treason investigations; the legal constraints involved with this type of CI investigation; and how to properly record results of the investigations.

TERMINAL LEARNING OBJECTIVE:

ACTIONS: Plan, prepare for, conduct, and record the results of sedition, subversion, sabotage, espionage, and treason investigations.

CONDITIONS: You will be given narrative information and illustrations from FM 34-60 and FM 34-60A.

STANDARDS: You will plan, prepare for, conduct, and prepare properly formatted reports for the conduct of designated CI investigations IAW the provisions of STP 34-97B4-SM-TG.

REFERENCES: The material contained in this lesson was derived from the following publications:

AR 380-5

AR 381-10

AR 381-12

AR 381-20

FM 34-60

FM 34-60A

STP34-97B4-SM-TG

This lesson has five parts:

Part A: Sabotage.

Part B: Espionage.

Part C: Treason.

Part D: Sedition.

Part E: Subversion.

PART A: SABOTAGE

ELEMENTS OF SABOTAGE. The elements of sabotage are set forth in title 18, US Code, Sections 2151-2156. It is summarized in FM 34-60 as

"An act of which is to damage the national defense structure;

Sabotage is also a form of "subversive warfare" which can be used to impair the will of the populace to resist. Sabotage is an effective weapon designed to damage or destroy a nation's capacity to defend itself. It is indispensable to warfare, and used by all nations. It is not a recent innovation of modern warfare. During Biblical times, armies destroyed the enemy's fields, crops, cities, and towns.

At the turn of the 18th century in France, peasants were angered by the fact that machines were replacing workers. A French workman angrily threw a shoe into the machinery when he was working. Consequently, the term "sabotage" is accredited to the French word "sabot", a wooden shoe. Regardless of the origin of the word, the fact exists that sabotage has been used in one form or another through the centuries. It was used extensively and effectively during the last two World Wars and in other outbreaks of hostilities and armed conflict.

We expect acts of sabotage, both in overseas area of operations(AO)/and in CONUS, to increase significantly in wartime. Sabotage is an effective weapon of guerrilla and partisan groups operating against logistical and communication installations in occupied hostile areas, and during insurgencies.

Sabotage may be conducted by trained saboteurs sponsored by hostile guerrilla, insurgent, or intelligence organizations or by individuals operating independently who are motivated by revenge, hate, spite, or greed. In internal defense or limited war situation where guerrilla forces are active, we must be careful to distinguish between acts involving clandestine enemy agents and armed enemy units or dissatisfied friendly personnel. The threat posed to DOD by this hidden army of potential saboteurs is a challenge to CI personnel. Ferreting out individuals in the Army establishment who are members of this hidden force is a continuous, direct effort of CI. For that reason, the CI investigator must be acquainted with the saboteur's potential targets; methods; and capabilities. Equipped with this knowledge, he is better prepared to detect, prevent, and neutralize sabotage conducted against or within the Army establishment.

Sabotage or suspected sabotage are normally categorized by the means employed. The

traditional types of sabotage are incendiary, explosive and mechanical. Decline of communism, sabotage can take on a new form with nuclear, biological chemical, magnetic or electromagnetic means. With the rise and dependency of computers sabotage can take on a new means.

Types of Saboteurs. Saboteurs are classified into two main categories: independent saboteurs and enemy agents. Both are dangerous because their actions can have a serious effect upon wars or the national defense.

* Independent Saboteurs. While not in the employ of any foreign power, but for reasons of their own, they commit acts of sabotage that aid the enemy. An example would be the individual who sets fire to an installation or activity as an act of defiance against an unwanted reassignment. As stated earlier, this type is normally motivated by revenge, hate, spite, or greed. Actions committed by the independent saboteur would probably not be considered sabotage in the CI sense; however, each case must be considered on its own merits.

* Enemy Agents. More dangerous, the enemy agent is recruited, trained, and directed from a sabotage organization which is expert in covert operations. The agents are carefully selected and trained to perform all types of missions. The sabotage effort can be a constant threat to the security of the target nation when coordinated with other weapons and measures used by the enemy.

Sabotage Targets. Sabotage targets are virtually limitless. Many likely sabotage targets are readily accessible to the average citizen during the course of his daily activities. However, CI investigative responsibility is limited to countersabotage measures within the Army establishment and areas over which it has jurisdiction.

23

Types of Targets. Sabotage targets will be at any echelon.

Example targets are those that must be reduced for tactical reasons, or could make the continuances of war difficult if not impossible.

    *   Bridges.

    *   Tunnels.

    *   Supply storage areas.

    *   Railway systems.

    *   Communication facilities.

    *   National level economics, political, geographical, and military
         resources.

    *   Industries.

Target Analysis. The factors considered by the saboteur in his target analysis are:

    *   Criticality: Items needed for national defense.

    *   Vulnerability: The degree of susceptibility of a target to damage.

    *   Accessibility: The degree of ease or difficulty in infiltrating the
         target area.

    *   Recuperability: Restoration of a target to a point where the
         original purpose is served.

The last factor, recuperability, is most important to the saboteur. The target must be reduced to a state of incapability for a reasonable period of time to be worth the risks involved.

SABOTAGE METHODS. There are many different methods to commit sabotage, some of which are neither physical nor violent. Passive Sabotage is a nonviolent means or indirect action directed at morale. It involves passive resistance on the part of the populace. It is not organized to the extent that individuals or groups are given specific tasks.

Active Sabotage is the method of sabotage of primary interest to the CI investigator. It has the physical forms of sabotage as expressed in Title 18, US Code. They are classified as:

*   Incendiary.

*   Explosive.

*   Mechanical.

The saboteur decides which form he will use based on type of target; vulnerability; security; desired effects; time element; and availability of sabotage materials.

The question of which form is more effective against specific types of targets is relatively easy to decide. However, the ability to properly use the various methods depends upon the training of the saboteur.

Incendiary Sabotage. Is the use of a combustible material to maliciously start a fire to destroy property. Normally, this constitutes arson. **(Arson becomes an act of sabotage when there Is an Intent to hinder defense efforts and reason to believe the act may hinder the war effort.)**

Explosive Sabotage. Violently destructive and, when properly used, can neutralize or destroy targets which are resistant to fire. The saboteur will use explosives on selected targets when speed of destruction is desired, or when he wants to instill fear among the populace or employees of an installation.

Mechanical Sabotage. The easiest to perpetrate and is usually directed against industries, railroads, and ships. No special tools are required; the main requirement is the saboteur must have access. The five basic classifications of mechanical sabotage are--

*   Breakage.

*   Use of abrasives.

*   Acts of omission.

*   Substantiation.

*   Contamination.

These acts cover a wide field and may be committed by the saboteur either singly or in combination.

SABOTAGE BY NUCLEAR, BIOLOGICAL, AND CHEMICAL (NBC) MEANS. We are aware of the immense destruction capability of nuclear weapons and also of the fact that the U.S. has no monopoly over the manufacture of these weapons. With respect to biological and chemical agents, we know other nations have exhibited an interest in these areas. The former Soviet Union has experimented with and standardized some of these agents. Suffice to say, small nuclear weapons and controlled biological and chemical agents have definite sabotage potential.

Biological Agents. Biological warfare (BW) is the military use of living organisms or their toxic products to cause death, liability, or damage to man, domestic animals, or crops. BW has never been used on a large scale with modem weapons. However, throughout history there are documented cases wherein diseases were used in attempts to reduce an enemy's ability to fight.

Chemical Agents. Chemical warfare (CW) agents can produce effects ranging from highly lethal to mildly incapacitating. There are many chemical compounds, producing various effects, available to the saboteur. Such compounds could include:

* Agents which produce a deep sleep for several hours.

* Lethal poisons which enter the body through a small break in the skin.

* Chemicals to contaminate drinking water.

Whatever chemical or agents the saboteur uses, all can be disseminated by means of aerosols, capsules, vials, special dispersal containers, or spread in areas to be carried by wind and dust.

Nuclear Devices. An important factor when discussing the potential use of nuclear devices for sabotage is the destructive capability of an atomic explosion. Some atomic demolition devices destroy indiscriminately. Others, like biological and chemical warfare agents, destroy only personnel. Buildings, machinery, and equipment all remain unharmed. We must not rule out the possibility that, should the enemy launch a major attack against the U.S., all three sabotage means-nuclear, biological, and chemical-will be used to the fullest extent.

ARSON. Arson is one of the saboteur's most effective weapons. He may apply flames directly to combustible material or he may employ mechanical timing devices for delayed ignition. For

* Breakage.

* Use of abrasives.

* Acts of omission.

* Substantiation.

* Contamination.

These acts cover a wide field and may be committed by the saboteur either singly or in combination. any case in which sabotage is a possibility, the following are accomplished by MP and/or criminal investigators:

* Protect the scene from mutilation by removing all unauthorized people from the area, roping off the area if necessary, and posting guards to deny entrance and prevent removal of any items.

* Locate witnesses, record their names and addresses, and, if feasible, hold them for questioning. Witnesses held should be segregated. Notify MI.

Burning Factors. Combustion or burning is the rapid oxidation of substances accompanied by generation of heat and light. Burning occurs only when three essential ingredients are present-fuel, oxygen, and a temperature sufficiently high to maintain the process of combustion. Withdrawal of the fuel, elimination of oxygen, or lowering of the temperature will extinguish the burning.

Although fuels may be gaseous, liquid, or solid, combustion usually occurs when they are in a finely divided vaporous state. With many materials, oxidation takes place slowly at room temperature. However, for oxidation to reach the point of combustion, the materials must be heated. When heated, an oxidizing agent gives off oxygen, which in turn has an intense attraction for any fuel. If the ignition temperature is reached, a violent reaction occurs.

Most ordinary combustibles are compounds of carbon and hydrogen with the frequent addition of mineral matter and oxygen. When they burn completely and freely in air, the carbon reacts with the oxygen to form carbon dioxide, the hydrogen combines with the oxygen to form water vapor, and the mineral matter remains behind as ash.

Several factors contribute to the spreading of a fire. Drafts and air supply directly affect behavior of fire. A fire started in a completely closed space will soon become extinguished due to use of the available oxygen and generation of noncombustible gases which smother the fire.

Conversely, the combustion rate is greatly increased if the slightest chimney action exists where the hot gases and flame from the fire contact combustible material. Disastrous fires have resulted in large buildings where the elevator shafts or stairways served as a chimney to direct the uprushing flames and gases.

Other factors that may influence the spread of fire include:

* Dryness of surrounding vegetation or the structure itself.

* Presence of rain or amount of humidity.

* Temperature of the surrounding air.

* Building construction, to include wooden partitions, unprotected doors and window, elevator shafts and stairways, overhanging eaves, and wooden shingles.

EXPLOSIONS. An explosion is the rapid and violent combustion of a material (solid, liquid, or gas) with resultant pressure and heat. Explosions are generally classified as low- or high-order, according to the speed in feet per second of the expansion caused by the combustion.

Low-order explosions (diffused). An explosion in this category is characterized by a slow expansion over a relatively wide area into a combustion known as deflagration. Most explosives causing this type of explosion have a pushing rather than a shattering effect which results in a twisting and tearing type of deformation.

In a building, walls are forced outward, causing the roof to fall into the interior. Objects are scattered in erratic directions with no semblance of pattern. Other normal characteristics are absence of local shattering, craters, and a clearly marked area of special damage or discoloration. Such explosions result from gas, liquid fuel, solvents, dust, and chemicals.

High-order explosions (concentrated). An explosion in this category is characterized by an extremely rapid combustion, known as detonation reaction, occurring through the action of explosives such as dynamite, TNT, nitroglycerine, penta erythritol tetra nitrate (PETN), and various "plastic" explosives.

No atmospheric oxygen is required since the explosive carries its own oxygen supply in the form of compounds of high oxygen content. An explosion of this nature produces a large volume of gas, heated and expanded by the heat of the reaction.

Its origin can be considered a point where the forces produced radiate equally in all directions. Near the center, there will usually be shattering or fragmenting of material with evidence of small, high- velocity fragments. Movable objects and debris will be blown out in a radiating pattern from the center of the explosion. Suction effect or deflection of forces by objects may after this pattern, but identification of the pattern should still be possible.

X-ray films of cadavers, burned by the explosion, may reveal foreign objects which are helpful in the identification of the explosive device used.

The difference between the two types of explosions is significant to the investigator because the first type is ordinarily accidental while the second is more likely to be deliberate or planned.

Explosive Accessories. Safety fuse. Usually consists of a train of black powder in waterproof casing. The fuse is the medium for carrying a flame to the explosive charge.

Detonating cord. An example would be PETN explosives which are wrapped in a protective casing that makes them insensitive to shock. Detonating cord and fuses are used to detonate main charge explosives.

Blasting caps and detonators. Are copper or aluminum cases filled with an initiating and a detonating charge. They may be nonelectric or electric. Blasting caps and detonators are ignited in one of two ways:

```
*    Ignition by safety fuse.  Crimpers must be used to clamp the detonator to
         the fuse.  Tool marks left by the crimpers on detonator case
         fragments found at the scene of the explosion may aid in making
         positive identification of suspect tools.

    *    Electrical ignition.  Detonators are wired to an electrical source.
         Closing the circuit will result in instantaneous or timed (interval)
         explosions.  Connecting wires usually remain intact after explosion
         which may provide valuable trace evidence.
```

Boosters. An explosive charge is sometimes used to amplify or boost the shock provided by detonators or blasting caps in order to detonate main charge explosives.

Timing devices. Electrical, mechanical, or chemical devices may be used to trigger an explosive charge at a predetermined time.

Handling Explosives. Ordnance detachments (explosive disposal) are strategically located through out CONUS and overseas commands. Members of these detachments are qualified explosive disposal technicians.

In cases where the use of explosives is suspected, the explosive ordnance disposal (EOD) control detachment nearest the scene should be notified immediately for support.

The EOD technicians can provide invaluable assistance not only in disarming explosive devices, but also in the identification of residue of devices that have exploded. These remnants may give excellent clues concerning the type of explosive used, how it was detonated, and how and where it was manufactured (commercially or homemade), and the approximate amount of explosive used.

Undetonated explosive residues (in the area, in safelocks, keyholes, and so on), spilled explosives, and explosive charges left behind by the perpetrator must not be touched. Even a small amount of explosive residue can be detonated and cause a serious explosion.

The explosives technician provided by the EOD detachment will decide whether the bomb will be disarmed or destroyed. If the expert decides to destroy the device, the investigator may be able, beforehand, to photograph its outer surfaces, or, if it is packaged, photograph the writing or postage data on the wrappings. If the device is destroyed, the investigator should carefully collect all remaining evidence.

Do not photograph bombs or explosive charges with a flashbulb since the heat may cause detonation.

The search for remaining explosives at the scene must be supervised by an EOD technician. In case of suspected sabotage, local MI personnel are notified. If the incident takes place within CONUS, the FBI must be contacted.

CONDUCT OF SABOTAGE INVESTIGATIONS. U.S. Army Criminal Investigation Division Command (CIDC) will assume investigative lead for actual or suspected sabotage. CI elements will monitor the CIDC investigation and attempt to ascertain the existence of hostile, enemy, or foreign Government involvement or intent of the sabotage. CI elements will not conduct their own investigation until foreign Government involvement or intent of the sabotage. CI elements will not conduct their own investigation until foreign Government involvement is evident or suspected. If foreign Government involvement is determined, then a Joint (CI/CIDC) investigation may be conducted, with CIDC normally retaining investigation lead.

As a CI Agent, you are not expected to be a technical expert in the chemistry of fires and explosives or to be fully knowledgeable of machinery and complicated equipment. You are, however, encouraged to obtain the assistance of technical experts during the planning stage of a sabotage investigation.

Fundamental Investigative Rules. Three fundamental investigative rules should be foremost for the CI Agent investigating a sabotage incident. They are as follows:

* Sabotage investigations require immediate action.

* The saboteur may still be near the scene, so other military targets may require immediate additional security protection to preclude or limit further damage.

* The incident scene must be preserved and analyzed before evidence is altered or destroyed.

General Investigative Guidelines. When conducting investigations of sabotage, the CI Agent must proceed with objective, and logical thoroughness. The standard investigative interrogatives apply:

WHO: Determine a list of probable suspects and establish a list of persons who witnessed or know about the act.

WHAT: Determine what military target sabotaged and the degree of damage, to the target (momentary and operational).

WHEN: Establish the exact time when the act of sabotage was initiated and when it was discovered; from as many sources as possible.

WHERE: Determine the precise location of the target and its relation to surrounding activities.

WHY: Establish all possible reasons for the sabotage act through the investigation of suspects determined to have had a motive, ability, and opportunity to accomplish the sabotage act.

HOW: Establish the type of sabotage (such as, incendiary, explosive, mechanical, chemical) and determine the procedures and materials employed through investigation, technical examination, and analysis.

Special Investigative Actions. The following outline of possible investigative actions may be used as a guide for investigating most incidents in which sabotage is suspected:

Obtain information and analyze the details surrounding the initial reporting of the incident to the CIDC unit. Establish the identity of the person reporting the incident and his reason for doing so. Determine the facts connected with the reported discovery of the sabotage and examine them for possible discrepancies.

Examine the incident scene as quickly as possible. The CI Agent will attempt to reach the scene before possible sources have dispersed and evidence has been disturbed.

* Assist the MP protect the scene from disruption. The MP will remove all unauthorized personnel from the area, roping off the area if necessary, and post guards to deny entrance and prevent anything from being removed.

* CI Agents should help MP investigators at the crime scene; they should not interfere with the crime scene investigation.

* CI Agents may help CIDC personnel process the crime scene, to include locating all possible sources for questioning. CI keep sources separate only in the sense that they are identified to MP or CIDC. CI Agents should not physically separate sources.

* Preserve the incident scene by taking notes, making detailed sketches, and taking pictures. See appendix A for a more detailed explanation of crime scene processing.

* Arrange for technical experts to search the scene of the sabotage act; collect and preserve physical evidence; and obtain all possible clues. Arson specialists, explosives experts or other types of technicians may be required.

* Take steps necessary to prevent further damage to the target and safeguard classified information or material.

* Interview sources and obtain sworn statements as soon as possible to reduce the possibility of forgetting details or comparing stories.

* Determine the necessary files to be checked. These will be based on examination of the incident scene and by source interviews. CI conducts such action only in coordination with CIDC. CIDC has the crime scene expertise and responsibility; CI has the modus operandi (MO) expertise to identify to CIDC. Source file of particular importance may include:

1. Friendly unit MO file.

2. Partisan, guerilla, or insurgent activity file.

3. Local police files on arsonist.

4. Local police MO files.

5. Foreign intelligence agency MO files.

6. Terrorist MO files.

7. Provost Marshal files.

File checks should include background information on sources and the person who discovered and reported the act of sabotage.

Interrogate suspects. Study all available information such as evidence, technical and laboratory reports, statements of sources, and information from informants in preparation for interrogation of suspects.

PART B: ESPIONAGE

ELEMENTS OF ESPIONAGE. Unlike sabotage cases, most espionage investigations will be personal subject rather than incident-type cases; that is, they will originate with allegations regarding the activities of known individuals. There are instances, however, when CI personnel will be directed to conduct investigations of incidents in which espionage is suspected, but the identity of suspect(s) has not been established.

Leads in espionage investigations may originate from a wide variety of sources, prominent among which are the following:

* Reports from sensitive sources.

* Reports from other intelligence, security, and law enforcement agencies.

* Evidence of espionage discovered during inspection and surveys, of classified document handling and storage procedure.

* Reports submitted by military and civilian personnel IAW AR 381-12.

* Evidence of espionage discussed during screening of refugees, line crossers, displaced persons, civilian interns, enemy prisoners of war (EPW), detectors, and similar groups in areas of armed conflict

* Information developed during the course of routine PSI.

There are five elements of espionage:

* Contact or communications.

* Collection.

* Tradecraft.

* Reward or Motive.
* Travel.

All of these elements are identifiable during the course of a counter espionage (CE) investigation. Examples of the elements of espionage are that:

(1) The accused communicated, delivered, or transmitted any document, writing, code book, signal book, sketch, photographic negative, blueprint,

34

plan, map, model, note instrument, appliance, or information relating to national defense.

(2) This matter was communicated, delivered, or transmitted to any foreign Government, or to any portion or party or military or Naval Force within a foreign country, whether recognized or unrecognized by the US, or to any representative, officer, agent, employee, subject, or citizen thereof, either directly or indirectly.

(3) The accused did so with the intent or reason to believe that such matter would be used to the injury of the US or to the advantage of a foreign nation.

Federal Espionage Statutes. The espionage statutes encompass many kinds of activities. They have as their ultimate goal to prevent defense information from falling into the hands of a foreign nation. The outstanding aspects of the Title 18, US Code, Sections 793-796, are summarized in FM 34-60 as follows:

"The Act, either directly or indirectly, of obtaining, delivering, transmitting, communicating, or receiving information in respect to national defense with the intent or reason to believe that the information may be used to the injury of the U.S. or to the advantage of any foreign nation. The offense of espionage applies in time of peace or war."

Investigative Guidelines in Espionage Cases. Analysis of the statute and pertinent court decisions permit the following conclusions to be drawn about proof of espionage:

*   "National defense information: is information of military significance which has not been published for public consumption; that is, not distributed in public channels. It need not be classified defense information as defined in AR 380-5. The critical points are if it relates to the national defense and has been restricted to authorized channels.

*   "Any foreign nation" means the nation involved need not be a declared enemy.

*   Loss through gross negligence requires no positive act because it is a crime of omission.

*   Each facet, "loss through gross negligence" and "failure to promptly report," is a separate and distinct crime.

The espionage investigation must be directed toward the collection of information and evidence to show national defense information was involved, and there was an intent or reason to believe the US would be injured or a foreign nation would benefit.

<u>Spying, Article 106, Uniform Code of Military Justice (UCMJ).</u> Spying is strictly limited to a wartime military situation. This is governed by international law, particularly the provisions of the Geneva Conventions. Although the crime of spying as defined in Article 106, UCMJ, differs from espionage, CII based on Article 106 are categorized as espionage cases for reporting and statistical purposes. There are five elements that must be present to constitute the crime of spying:

* It only occurs during time of war.

* It is committed in a U.S. military AO.

* The accused must be caught while seeking information to communicate to the enemy.

* The accused must have the intent of communicating the information to the enemy.

* The accused must have been acting in a clandestine manner.

<u>Conduct of Espionage Investigations.</u> No single set of investigative procedures Is applicable to the conduct of espionage investigations. Espionage is made up of many different elements; espionage investigations are not always aimed at the arrest and prosecution of the offender. Prosecution of espionage case may be deferred to the Department of justice, CONUS or to the host country OCONUS. CI Agents responsible for such an investigation must have a thorough and up-to-date knowledge of all espionage and counterespionage methods and procedures as discussed in FM 34-5(S).

In any espionage case, use any or all types of investigative techniques and tools described in FM 34-60 AND 34-5(S).

* Determine what specific techniques to use on a case-by-case basis.

* Get proper authorization to utilize investigative techniques.

* Conduct the investigation IAW current laws and regulations.

Records examinations may break the cover story of an espionage suspect. CI Agents may use properly authorized physical or technical surveillance to obtain leads or evidence. They may use confidential or sensitive source or undercover operations to locate and identify suspects. Investigative photography may provide evidence of an attempt to transmit national defense information to a foreign nation.

The following quotation from testimony in February 1950 by the late J. Edgar Hoover, who was then FBI director, explains why arrest and prosecution are not always the objectives of espionage investigations:

"In a criminal case, the identification and arrest of the wrongdoer are the ultimate objectives. In an espionage case, the identification of the wrongdoer is only the first step. What is more important is to ascertain his contacts, his objectives, his sources of information and his methods of communication. Arrest and public disclosure are steps to be taken only as matters of last resort. It is better to know who these people are and what they are doing, and to immobilize their efforts, than it is to expose them publicly and then go through the tireless efforts of identifying their successor."

PART C: TREASON

ELEMENTS OF TREASON. Treason is the only crime defined in the US Constitution. Historically, those in power passionately desired to remain in power. In order to do so, any opposition was usually severely punished. Thus, treason (the historical name for violent opposition) was regarded by those possessing autocratic power as the most heinous crime, punishable with swift, harsh, and extraordinary punishment. The laws regarding treason were greatly abused because of their application in struggles for retention of power.

The framers of the American Constitution had every right to be apprehensive about the improper application of the concept of treason. The turmoil-ridden history of English treason and seditious libel had been carried to the American colonies. Prior to the American expression of treason, punishment was not limited to the perpetrator of the act of treason. An adverse effect was felt by the close kin and heirs of the convicted enemy of the state. Corruption of blood and forfeiture of estates, existing or inheritable, were popular forms of secondary punishment and state enrichment. Thus, aware of a need to limit the scope of such punishment, Article III, Section 3 of the U.S. Constitution was written. An extract is as follows:

"Treason against the United States, shall consist only in levying war against them, or in adhering to their enemies, giving them aid and comfort. No person shall be convicted of treason unless on the testimony of two witnesses to the same overt act, or on confession in open court. The Congress shall have power to declare the punishment of treason, but no attainder of treason shall work corruption of blood, or forfeiture except during the life of the person attainted."

Investigations in which treason is suspected or alleged are rare. Most cases occur during wartime, or upon conclusion of hostilities.

Allegations of treason may originate with:

-Liberated Prisoner of Wars

-Interned US Civilians

-Examination of Captured Enemy Records

-Interrogation of Enemy Military and Civilian Personnel

Federal courts have recognized two distinct types of treason: Levying war and aiding and comfort.

Elements of Treason Under Federal Statute. Interpretation by the federal courts in treason

cases leads to the following generalities concerning the legal elements of the crime of treason under federal statute:

* The accused must owe allegiance to the U.S. A U.S. citizen owes permanent allegiance whether in the U.S. or on foreign soil (unless an effective renunciation of citizenship was made). An alien in the U.S. owes temporary allegiance to the U.S. because he enjoys the protection of U.S. laws.

* A levy of war must be an actual waging of open hostilities against the government with specific intent to cause its overthrow.

* Adherence to the enemy means, in general, any act committed after a state of war exists which indicates a want of loyalty to the U.S. Government, and sympathy with its enemies, and which, by fair construction, is directly in furtherance of their hostile designs.

The investigative burden for a treason case consists of proving the following:

* The individual owed allegiance to the US when the act was committed.

* During the levy of war, there were open hostilities against the US and there was a specific intent to overthrow the US Government.

* The individual provided tangible or intangible aid to the enemy.

* Two witnesses to the same overt act must testify or it must be established that the accused intends to confess in open court.

Aiding the Enemy, Article 104, UCMJ. Investigations conducted by CI personnel to prove or disprove charges brought against an individual subject to the UCMJ under Article 104, Aiding the Enemy, may in some cases be categorized as treason cases. The article provides that "any person who (1) aids, or attempts to aid, the enemy with arms, ammunition, supplies, money, or other things or (2) without proper authority knowingly harbors or protects or gives intelligence to, or communicates, or corresponds with or holds any intercourse with the enemy, either directly or indirectly, shall suffer death or such other punishment as court-martial or other military commission may direct."

Physical Acts Which Constitute Aiding the Enemy. From the wording of the article and interpretation by the Court of Military Appeals, there are three physical acts which constitute the crime of aiding the enemy. Any one of these acts, with general criminal intent, is a violation of the article:

* Aids, or attempts to aid the enemy with arms, ammunition, supplies, money or other things.

* Without proper authority, knowingly harbors or protects or give intelligence to or communicates or corresponds with or holds any intercourse with the enemy, either directly or indirectly.

Proof Requirements Under Article 104. It is necessary to prove only that one or more of the prohibited acts actually occurred. The enemy need not be a declared enemy but may be a "substantial" enemy as in the case of the communist forces in the Korean or Vietnam conflicts.

The requirements of proving allegiance and proving the overt act by two witnesses which are essential under the federal treason statute do not apply.

Korean Conflict Cases Under Article 104. Article 104 was used in the majority of the courts-martial cases arising from the Korean prisoner of war incidents. Most of the specifications in these cases concerned the third act listed above and specifically that part of the act making correspondence, without proper authority, a crime. The Court of Military Appeals established in these cases that there are only three types of communication with the enemy which may be made with "proper authority" under military law, regardless of the motives which prompt the communication:

* A communication disclosing name, rank, Social Security Number (SSN), and date of birth.

* A communication concerning the necessities of life.

* A communication concerning regulations and orders of the place of confinement.

Conduct of Treason Investigations (CTI). Counterintelligence CTI cases in which treason is alleged or suspected during times of war are more apt to be opened immediately upon the conclusion of hostilities. Allegations of treason may originate with liberated prisoners of war, interned U.S. civilians, examination of captured enemy records, or interrogation of enemy military and civilian personnel. Treason cases will almost always be personal subject rather than incident-type cases. Unlike most other CTI, the investigation of a treason case will be primarily concerned with obtaining evidence of the past rather than current activities of the suspected or accused person.

Records examination, interview, and interrogation normally will be the principal investigative techniques. The CI Agent must give particular attention to the legal requirement governing the collection and preservation of evidence, especially the taking of statements from witnesses and suspects. The CI Agent must be careful to sort out fact from rumor or hearsay when taking testimony and reporting the results. In many cases, it will be necessary for the investigator to consult regularly with legal authorities during the course of the investigation to ensure the elements of proof are being fulfilled and all applicable legal conditions and restrictions are met.

PART D: SEDITION

ELEMENTS OF SEDITION. Sedition may be generally defined as "conduct or language inciting to rebellion against the authority of the state." CTI regarding alleged or suspected sedition may be based either on Section 2385, Title 18, USC (also know as the Smith Act), or Article 94, UCMJ, Mutiny or Sedition.

Sedition cases may be classified as either incident-type cases, such as the discovery of literature advocating the violent overthrow of the US government, or personal subject cases, such as the distribution of such literature by a known person. Leads by control offices may originate from several sources, reports from other agencies, or information developed during the course of routine Background Investigation. CTI involving sedition may occur with equal frequency in either peacetime or wartime.

Anyone who conspires to overthrow the U.S. government commits a specific crime under the provisions of Section 2384, Title 18, USC. Unlike the general conspiracy statute, which makes it a crime to conspire to commit any federal crime, the seditious conspiracy stature does not require the commission of an overt act toward fulfillment of the conspiracy's objective. The crime of seditious conspiracy is complete when two or more persons have

40

entered into an agreement to overthrow the U.S. government, or to prevent, hinder, or delay the execution of any U.S. law. It should be noted seditious conspiracy is a conspiracy to <u>actually</u> overthrow as distinct from a conspiracy to advocate overthrow.

The Smith Act enumerates the specific types of prohibited activity which, if done with "intent to cause the overthrow of the government by force or violence," constitute sedition:

*   Advocating action or teaching the duty or necessity of such overthrow.

*   Using words to incite imminent lawless action with the specific intent of overthrowing the U.S. government.

Court decisions relative to advocacy or overthrow have established that advocacy must be calculated to incite persons to take action toward the violent overthrow of the government. Mere advocacy or teaching of forcible overthrow of the government as an abstract principle, divorced from any effort to instigate action to that end, does not constitute the crime of sedition under the Smith Act. The requirement for the advocacy to "incite persons to take action" is of particular significance to the CI Agent. In cases alleging violation of the Smith Act, it can be expected considerable effort will be directed toward proving the oral or written material involved was intended to incite listeners or readers to take action.

Article 94, UCMJ, pertains to both sedition and mutiny. Article 94 makes it a crime for "any person to this chapter who, with the intent to cause the overthrow or destruction of lawful civil authority, creates in concert with any other person, a revolt, violence, or other disturbance against such authority is guilty of sedition." The investigation of charges of sedition under Article 94 will usually be assigned to CI personnel.

Mutiny charges under Article 94 may include a collective effort to overthrow lawful military authority, or the individual creation of a riot or disturbance with the intent to overthrow lawful military authority. The offense of mutiny may be committed in either of two ways: by several persons acting in concert to refuse to obey orders from proper authority with the intent to override military authority or by a person, with similar intent, acting either alone or in concert with others, creating a violence or disturbance. The investigation of mutiny incidents normally will not be assigned to CI personnel unless the mutiny is believed to be related to hostile intelligence or subversive activity.

During the conduct of sedition complaint-type investigations, several principles apply. These include the facts that covert investigative techniques are usually most applicable, but that standard interview and interrogation techniques should also be used. Also, the CI Agent should be thoroughly knowledgeable of the complaint area as it is related to subversive activities, subversive individuals, and subversive organizations. Such knowledge will greatly facilitate the sedition investigations concerning methods of operation, identity of personnel and organizations.

Additional techniques which may be applied during the conduct of sedition investigations can be found in FM 34-60A(S).

Enlistment to serve against United States - Title 18, USC Section 2390.

> "Whoever enlists or is engaged within the United States or in any place subject to the jurisdiction thereof, with intent to serve in armed hostility against the United States . . ."

PART E: SUBVERSION

ELEMENTS OF SUBVERSION. Under neither constitutional nor statutory law does the U.S. recognize subversion as a punishable offense, unless the subversive act is directed against members of the U.S. forces. What is often called subversive activity is not illegal and could be defended under the First Amendment to the Constitution which guarantees the right of free speech.

Although subversion is not "clearly illegal", it is not any less of a threat to our national security than the crimes of espionage or sabotage. Both of these illegal acts are criminal offenses because the exact nature of these activities is contained in federal criminal statutes and the UCMJ. Accordingly, an investigator knows exactly what constitutes these crimes and can judge his course of action. However, the obscure nature of subversion makes it difficult to detect, and to decide on a course of action once its presence is suspected or detected. The threat from subversion assumes greater proportions when the connection between subversive activity and the crimes of espionage and sabotage are considered. By subverting the loyalty of the citizens of a nation, a hostile power can achieve the objective of weakening that country's resistance to aggression and can provide itself with a pool of potential espionage agents and saboteurs.

From the CI point of view, the CI Agent must remain constantly alert to such activities, as well as the activities of any foreign power which pose a threat to military security, operations, and personnel. Subversion covers a broad spectrum of activity, all of which is clearly inconsistent with the best interest of national security.

Section 2387(a), Title 18, USC defines criminal subversion as:

> "Whoever, with intent to interfere with, impair, or influence the loyalty, morale or discipline of the military or naval forces of the United States:

(1) Advises, counsels, urges, or in any manner causes or attempts to cause insubordination, disloyalty, mutiny, or refusal of duty by any member of the military or naval forces of the United States; or

(2) Distributes or attempts to distribute any written or printed matter which advises, counsels, or urges insubordination, disloyalty, mutiny, or refusal of duty by any member of the military or naval forces of the United States."

American constitutional law requires that any penal statute fix ascertainable guilt, either forbidding specific acts or in some cases placing an obligation to perform some specific act. The offense and the elements instituting the act must be sufficiently clear so the ordinary person can intelligently choose in advance which course he may lawfully pursue.

On the surface, Section 2387(a), Title 18, USC is very clear, but upon analyzing the law, there is no clear standard for judging exactly what subversion is. One important question remains constant concerning the obscure treatment of the term subversion: "At what point does an individual exercising his right to free speech influence the loyalty, morale, or discipline of a member of the armed forces?

As Assistant Chief of Staff for Intelligence, Department of the Army (ACSI, DA), Major General Harold R. Aaron probably best described the current position of CI in investigating subversive activities:

> "The Army wholly endorses the Constitutional principle of freedom of expression. Furthermore, the Army has undertaken very practical measures to ensure that nothing curtails the soldier's right to express any opinion he desires through whatever legal means he chooses.

> On the other hand, Army counterintelligence would be derelict in its duty if it did not remain alert to detect security threats from those who would abuse the constitutional right of freedom of expression, by promoting aims and objectives meant to undermine the soldier's loyalty and respect for authority and to reduce the Army's capability to fulfill its mission."

AR 381-20, based on federal statutes, specifies that the suspect must be actively attempting to undermine a soldier's loyalty and respect with willful intent. The burden of proof to meet this requirement is extremely difficult to fulfill. Also, under the UCMJ, no specific article addresses subversion. The armed forces would have to invoke Article 92 and/or Article 134, UCMJ, if one of its members were to be punished for subversive activities.

The element of intent and the statutory standards of individual conduct in areas of subversive activity are not clear cut. As a result, the CI investigator must be diligent, perceptive, and precise in his efforts and findings.

Many subversion cases will be based on adverse loyalty information developed during a routine BI, Subversion and Espionage Directed Against U.S. Army (SAEDA) reports submitted by military or civilian personnel under AR 381-12, reports from other intelligence and security agencies, and leads obtained directly from sources used in CI special operations. Note the terminology "criminal subversion," "subversive activity," and "subversion' are clues to the CI Agent to turn to Section 2387 of Title 18, USC, for detailed elements of the crime. The objective of such CTI will usually be to determine if there is a need for some type of administrative action;

for example, removal from a sensitive assignment to protect the security of the military command.

Other statutes and laws pertaining to acts of subversion. Sections 2387 and 2388 of Title 18, USC, prohibit speeches and acts made to cause mutiny, cause insubordination, lower the morale in the military forces, or interfere with recruitment. Section 2388 additionally prohibits, during wartime, the spreading of false rumors to interfere with the war effort. Under these statutes, the government is not required in criminal prosecutions to prove the acts intended by the accused actually occurred. The government would have to show two things:

* An intent on the part of the accused to bring about the criminal objective.

* The speeches and acts were of such a nature that one could reasonably infer such speech or acts would cause mutiny, insubordination, or the lowering of morale.

A CI investigation of subversive activity must determine conclusively what act occurred; establish that the activity was detrimental to the national security, based on evidence of prohibitive nature; and establish that the activity did not rise to the level of treason, espionage, sabotage, or sedition.

OTHER ACTIVITIES WHICH MAY WARRANT INVESTIGATION. When a person, who is considered by the major commander concerned to be knowledgeable of classified information (as defined by AR 380-5), is in the absent without leave (AWOL) status (special category absentee (SCA)) the absentee's commander will submit an electrical message through intelligence channels. Investigative action in such cases is directed toward determining the circumstances surrounding the absence and what, if any, classified information could be compromised. Inquiry into the circumstances will seek to learn if there was any intent to defect and if any subversive elements, hostile propaganda, or an intelligence recruiting effort were involved.

A CI debriefing of returned SCA is required. Upon return of an absentee/deserter, the intelligence officer of the individual's unit will report his presence to the nearest supporting CI unit. The CI units will, in turn, determine if the individual is a SCA and, if appropriate, conduct the debriefing.

When a military person absents himself from his unit and seeks asylum in a foreign country, he is identified as Military Absentees in, or Attempting to go to, a Foreign Country or Embassy (MAFOR). MAFOR is defined as "any person who absents himself from his unit and seeks political asylum in a foreign country or embassy, or is voluntarily residing in a foreign country." This includes persons who have attempted to take this action. It also includes those instances where credible information is reported or developed that the individual intends to take such action. It does not include a person stationed in a foreign country who absents himself in the same country unless he seeks political asylum in that country. Although primarily applied to military personnel, DA civilians who meet this definition are also considered MAFOR.

While a MAFOR may not be a SCA, investigating and debriefing procedures and objectives are the same as for SCA. If the MAFOR seeks asylum in a foreign country with interest harmful to those of the U.S., he is considered a defector.

LESSON 2

PRACTICE EXERCISE

The following items will test your grasp of the material covered in this lesson. There is only one correct answer for each item. When you have completed the exercise, check your answers with the answer key that follows. If you answer any item incorrectly, study again that part of the lesson which contains the portion involved.

1.   Which is an example of a sabotage target?

        A.   Bridge.

        B.   Tunnel.

        C.   Supply dump.

        D.   All of the above.

2.   Are CI Agents tasked with investigating incidents of possible sabotage expected to be technical experts in the chemistry of fires and explosives?

        A.   Yes.

        B.   No.

3.   The objective of all espionage investigations is to obtain sufficient evidence to arrest and prosecute the offender.

        A.   True.

        B.   False.

4.   Loss through gross negligence and "failure to promptly reports is considered a crime of what?

        A.   Omission.

        B.   Remission.

        C.   Commission.

        D.   Submission.

5.   When would an investigation, in which treason is alleged to have occurred, most likely be conducted?

        A.   Immediately prior to hostilities.

        B.   During hostilities.

        C.   Immediately after hostilities.

        D.   As soon as the crime of treason is alleged.

6.   CII involving sedition will occur only during wartime.

A.   True.

B.   False.

7.   Which article of the UCMJ covers mutiny?

A.   5.

B.   28.

C.   94.

D.   137.

8.   The definition of subversion included in Section 2387 of the <u>United States Code</u> is clear and specific; therefore, CI Agents would have no problems obtaining sufficient evidence to obtain a conviction of any person charged with the offense of criminal subversion.

A.   True.

B.   False.

LESSON 2

PRACTICE EXERCISE

Answer Key and Feedback

Item   Correct Answer and Feedback

1.   D.   All of the above. (page 2-3).

2.   B.   No. (page 2-8).

3.   B.   False. (page 2-13).

4.   A.   Omission. (page 2-12).

5.   C.   Immediately after hostilities. (page 2-16).

6.   B.   False. (page 2-16).

7.   C.   94. (page 2-17).

8.   B.   False. (page 2-18/2-19).

LESSON 3

PHYSICAL EVIDENCE

CRITICAL TASKS: 301-340-1002

301-340-1100

OVERVIEW

LESSON DESCRIPTION:

In this lesson, you will learn how to identify physical evidence of CI interest; to preserve a crime scene through photography and/or sketches; and to fulfill all requirements for the handling of physical evidence to include admission before a judicial proceeding.

TERMINAL LEARNING OBJECTIVE:

ACTIONS: Identify physical evidence of CI interest; prepare sketches; take photographs; prepare evidence tags; account for, store, release, and dispose of evidence; and process a crime scene.

CONDITIONS: You will be given narrative information and illustrations from FM 34-60 and FM 19-20.

STANDARDS: You will process physical evidence of CI interest IAW the provisions of STP 34-97B14-SM-TG.

REFERENCES: The material contained in this lesson was derived from the following publications:

AR 55-355

AR 190-22

AR 195-2

AR 195-5.

AR 380-5

AR 710-2

FM 19-20

FM 34-60

STP 34-97B1

This lesson has two parts:

Part A: Physical Evidence of CI Significance.

Part B. Account for, Store, Release, and Dispose of Evidence.

PART A: PHYSICAL EVIDENCE OF CI SIGNIFICANCE.

Physical evidence is tangible in nature and recognizable in form. It tends to prove or disprove a fact in dispute. It includes all articles and materials collected in connection with an investigation to establish the identity of the perpetrator and the circumstances under which an incident occurred. The articles and materials are used to aid in the prosecution of the offender or to terminate the case.

The importance of physical evidence, which may be encountered in any type of CI operation, is not limited to those investigations likely to result in a trial. Physical evidence of probative value is often essential to the proper determination of administrative actions such as the granting of a security clearance, the issuance of a visa for entry into the U.S., or the admission of an alien into the armed forces.

CI Agents are not expected to be experts on physical evidence. The analysis of various substances normally will require the services of one or more specialists such as ballistics experts, chemists, and fingerprint technicians to fully identify the substance and its relationship to the crime. However, as a CI Agent, you should have a general knowledge of the value, limitations, and characteristics of physical evidence and be able to recognize, collect, handle, and preserve evidence encountered during the course of an investigation.

Documentary Evidence. Documents are the most common items of physical evidence encountered by CI. Manuscripts, magnetic tapes, records, files, reports, sworn statements, photographs, video tape movies, pamphlets, maps, sketches, passports, identity papers, and similar documents are likely to be collected in CI operations.

Questioned Documents. Questioned documents are those whose validity is disputed. Chapter 21, FM 19-20, Law Enforcement Investigations, describes various categories of questioned documents and types of assistance available for criminal investigation experts and laboratories. This assistance may be obtained through liaison with the appropriate provost marshal's office.

Documents Containing Codes and Ciphers. Codes and ciphers (cryptography) are often used in communication between operational elements of espionage agencies. Unless the key to the system has been obtained, the investigator should not expend any time attempting to decrypt the message. The investigator should provide along with a history of the circumstances under which it was obtained and a brief summary of the related investigation, the document should be processed in accordance with the unit standing operating procedures (SOP).

You should also be familiar with the procedures of your unit for obtaining the assistance of appropriate experts and laboratory facilities. It should be noted that some of the information presented in this lesson pertains to strictly criminal investigations. However, as a CI Agent, you should be familiar with the overall procedures for handling evidence.

Documents Suspected of Containing Secret Writing. Secret writing or the concealment from visible detection of written material by means of invisible inks, specially treated papers, microphotography, and similar systems are also important facets of espionage communication systems. Documents taken from espionage suspects, or otherwise obtained under conditions indicating the possible presence of secret writing, should be tested for indications of secret writing. No attempts should be made to recover any secret text. The material should be forwarded to a facility or agency where the expertise is available.

Other Types of Evidence. Traces and clues often may be found in the form of latent fingerprints; firearms and ammunition; indentations made by tools, tires, or shoes; and from deposits of foreign substances such as fibers, soils, and stains.

Fingerprints. Fingerprints evidence is the most positive means of identifying individuals, since they never change throughout a person's lifetime. Surface fingerprints can be transferred, photographed, and developed by various techniques, thus providing invaluable evidence for purposes of identification. Detailed consideration of fingerprint patterns and methods of collection and preservation are included in chapter 7 of FM 19-20.

Indentations and Fractures. Physical impressions and indentations left in various media are often of value as evidence. Examples would be footprints, tool marks, and tire imprints. Collection and preservation methods are included in Chapter 8, FM 19-20.

Tire imprints may identify a particular vehicle by association of the brand, amount of wear, and unique scars. Direction of travel can often be determined from the direction in which sand, soil, or water was thrown; speed of the vehicle from the distinctiveness of the track; and the weight of the load from the depth of the track.

Footprints may reveal direction and speed of movement, sex, approximate height and weight, and physical deformities. In addition, the brand of footwear may be apparent and provide additional leads.

Firearms and bullets have individual characteristics subject to scientific examination for identification purposes. Each firearm and bullet fired therefrom have individual characteristics which may be detected by expert examination under a microscope. The weapon will have on it the name of the manufacturer, a trademark, serial number, and possibly fingerprints or distinctive features. When discharged, a cartridge casing and bullet will have such characteristics as scratches or indentations associating them specifically with a particular weapon. Collection and preservation methods are discussed in Chapter 9, FM 19-20.

If examined by an expert, glass fractures may reveal the direction of the blow or the type of instrument used to break the glass. The nature of a projectile which pierced the glass can sometimes be identified. Since each type of glass has peculiar characteristics, examination may serve to identify the glass manufacturer and thus provide leads in some investigative situations, Chapter 10, FM 19-20.

Trace Evidence is evidence which is examined and attested to, by laboratory examiners to be admissing in court. Trace items include:

Fibers. Hairs and fibers have distinctive characteristics which may be useful in identification. They may be classified as animal, vegetable, mineral, and synthetic.

Animal fibers include hair, wool, silk, and fur. Each type can be distinguished from another, and many types have individual characteristics which permit further differentiation. By study of the diameter and texture of a human hair, for example, determination can sometimes be made of the race, sex, and general age of the individual.

Vegetable fibers include cotton, linen, Jute, and sisal, each of which has its own distinctive characteristics such as color of dye and number of strands per thread.

Mineral fibers include glass and asbestos.

Synthetics have expanded much beyond the well-known rayon and nylon, but can be distinguished from one another by laboratory analysis.

Soil and Stains. Samples of soil can provide information of value when examined microscopically and chemically. Study may indicate a difference between soil and dust, the latter being composed chiefly of vegetable fibers. Soil analysis may reveal the geological source or general origin, and at times a specific area of origin. Stains resulting from any cause are susceptible to analysis in a laboratory. They may be identified as food, vegetable matter, grease, oil, paint, rust, or body fluids.

Laundry Marks. Dry cleaning, laundry, and other clothing or linen marks, whether they be made with indelible or invisible ink, may provide valuable clues in identification. Police usually maintain records which can help with this type of identification.

Detective Dyes. Police at times use dyes and florescent powders which can be dusted or sprayed on items likely to be handled by suspects. Some of these are virtually indelible; others are invisible, but susceptible to detection under ultraviolet light for prolonged periods after contact.

Collection and preservation methods are outlined in Chapter 11, FM 19-20.

PART B: ACCOUNT FOR, STORE, RELEASE, AND DISPOSE OF EVIDENCE.

HANDLING EVIDENCE. Physical evidence is one of the CI Agent's most valuable assets in pursuing the investigation to a successful conclusion. It produces leads for the investigative action during conduct of the investigation. It aids in establishing guilt or innocence of an accused person in a court. To achieve the maximum benefit from physical evidence, the investigator must not only be skilled in its collection, but he must also know how to handle and care for it. The evidence must be preserved for the development of leads, for laboratory examination, and/or for presentation in court.

Such handling and care involves:

*   Storing the evidence to retain the integrity of the item in its original condition as nearly as possible.

    *   Maintaining a chain of custody for the item to assure responsibility and ensure its evidentiary value.

    *   Transmitting the item properly to the laboratory for analysis.

    *   Disposing of the item when it is no longer of evidentiary value.

DEFINITIONS.

Evidence. Anything that helps to ascertain the truth of a matter or gives proof of a fact. (AR 195-5). Evidence may be physical or testimonial.

* Physical Evidence - evidence like identified weapons and fingerprints that is obtained by searching crime scenes, tracing leads, and developing technical data.

* Testimonial Evidence - like sworn statements of eyewitness accounts and admission of guilt is obtained through communication with people.

This lesson addresses only physical evidence. Physical evidence is divided into two general categories:

* Movable evidence can be picked up at a crime scene or any other location and transported. Examples are tools, weapons, clothing, glass, and documents.

* Fixed or Immovable evidence cannot be readily removed from a scene because of its size, shape, or makeup. Examples would be walls, telephone poles, and floors.

Fragile evidence is physical evidence which, if special care is not taken to preserve its state, can deteriorate to a point where it is no longer of evidentiary value. It may be movable or immovable. A footprint in the snow is actually immovable, but a cast of it can be taken and preserved so as to be admissible as evidence. Fingerprints can be "lifted" or removed; body fluids can be preserved in their natural state or close thereto.

NOTE: The remaining portion of this lesson addresses the general precepts of handling, packaging, and caring for an item of physical evidence after it has been collected and until it is disposed of.

EVALUATING EVIDENCE. The question invariably arises as to whether an object is or is not evidence. The investigator resolves this question by evaluating the object, in light of the circumstances and conditions you find at the crime scene. You evaluate each piece of evidence, individually and collectively, in relation to all other evidence. Support your evaluation with common sense and sound judgement enhanced by your past experience. If doubt exists, the object is secured and processed as evidence. Later evaluation can determine the worth of such evidence to the investigation and its ultimate disposition.

IDENTIFICATION. The investigator who first receives, recovers, or discovers physical evidence must be able to state positively at a later date that the specific article or item was obtained in connection with a specific investigation. Identification is accomplished when the investigator marks and tags the evidence as it is obtained or collected. The investigator should form the habit of marking and tagging evidence promptly.

Marking. The person initially assuming custody of evidence marks it by inscribing his initials and the military date and time directly upon individual item(s) of physical evidence. Care must be exercised to place the markings so as not to destroy any latent characteristics of the item(s) or to reduce its value as evidence. The investigator should use Judgment and common sense when determining where to mark such item(s). He should first consider how an item is normally handled and how it may have been handled during the crime.

The purpose of marking is to enable the investigator to positively identify the object at a later date. The markings should be inconspicuously placed, especially when the evidence is recovered stolen property and will be returned to the rightful owner. By placing identifying marks in inconspicuous locations, unnecessary marring of personal property is avoided.

When an item of evidence cannot be marked without marring, it is placed in a suitable container, which is sealed with a cover and then both the container and cover marked for identification. Since evidence such as hair, soil, and fluids cannot be marked, they are also placed in suitable containers, which are then sealed and marked.

A carborundum or diamond point pencil is recommended for marking on hard surfaces and ink on other items. The investigator then records the marking and its location in his notebook.

Tagging. Tagging further serves to help the investigator to identify evidence. DA Form 4002, Evidence/Property Tag, contains pertinent data about the evidence and is attached to the article or container (see figure 3-1).

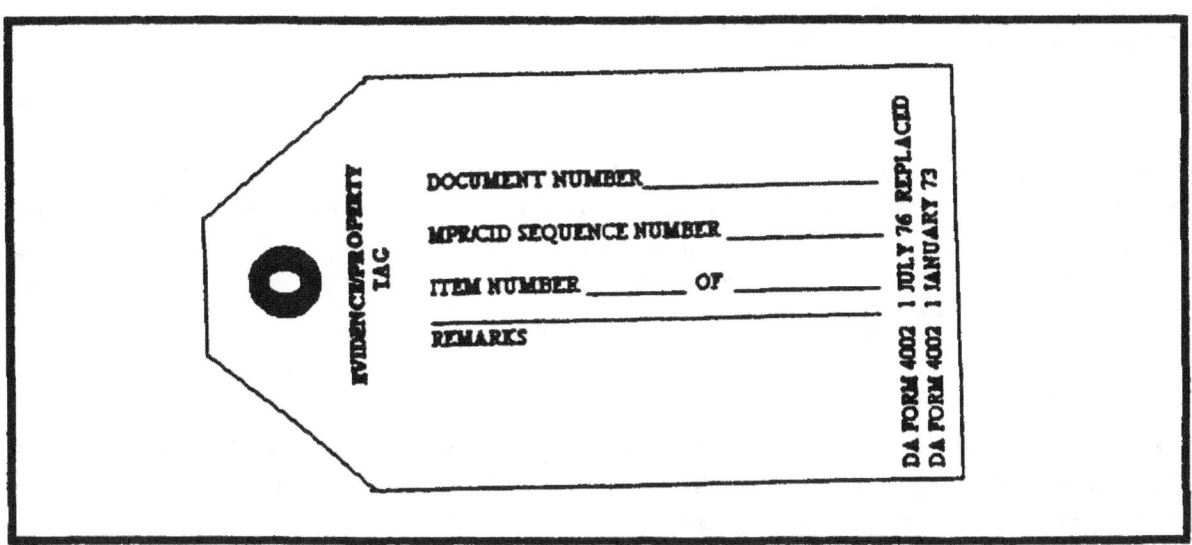

Figure 3-1. DA Form 4002, Evidence/Property Tag.

Evidence must be tagged before it is submitted to the evidence custodian. It should be done at the crime scene when the evidence is collected.

The evidence tag should be completed in ink. The tag aids in the processing and handling of evidence by the evidence custodian and the laboratory examiner. Some of the information needed to complete DA Form 4002, such as document number or MPR/CID sequence number, is extracted from DA Form 4137, Evidence/Property custody Document (See Figure 3-2).

CHAIN OF CUSTODY. The chain of custody begins when an item of evidence is collected and maintained until that evidence is disposed of. The chain of custody assures continuous accountability. If it is not properly maintained, an item may be inadmissible in court.

Chain of custody is a chronological written record of those individuals who have had custody of the evidence from its initial acquisition until its final disposition. Those persons in the chain of custody must be identified on the DA Form 4137, Evidence/Property Custody Document, which is initiated when the evidence is acquired by the CI Agent.

Responsibility. Each Individual in the chain of custody is responsible for that item of evidence. This includes it care, safekeeping, and preservation while under his control. Because of the sensitive nature of evidence, an evidence custodian is provided copies of DA Form 4137 to assume responsibility for the evidence when it is not needed by the investigator or other competent authority such as a lawyer involved in the investigation.

Evidence/Property Custody Document DA Form 413. This form is used to record acquisition, chain of custody, and disposition of evidence. This form is hereafter referred to as the custody document. It is a multiple-purpose form designed to be used as a receipt and record the chain of custody, authority for final disposition, and witnessing of destruction. The form is normally prepared with an original and three copies. Entries should be typed or printed legibly in ink. (Figure 3-2)

The last or third copy is used as a receipt when evidence is received from a person. The original and first two copies go to the evidence custodian. He keeps the original and first copy for his records. The second copy is returned to the CI Agent for inclusion in the case file.

Individual blocks on the Evidence/Property Custody Document should contain the following information:

MPR/CID SEQUENCE NUMBER and CID ROI NUMBER blocks are completed LAW local unit SOP.

RECEIVING ACTIVITY block contains the name of the office or organization conducting the investigation.

LOCATION block contains the installation or base where the office or organization conducting the investigation is located.

NAME, GRADE, AND TITLE OF PERSON FROM WHOM RECEIVED block is completed when evidence is received from an individual rather than from a crime scene. When evidence is obtained from an individual, the OWNER or OTHER block is checked.

When evidence is not received from an individual, an appropriate term such as "crime scene" or "found" is entered in this block, and the OTHER block checked.

ADDRESS block holds the address of the individual from whom the evidence is obtained. If the evidence is not received from an individual, this block is annotated "NA".

LOCATION FROM WHERE OBTAINED block holds the location of the evidence at the time it was acquired by the CI Agent. It may be further augmented by a crime scene sketch.

REASON OBTAINED block is completed by the word "Evidence" when the item is obtained as possible evidence.

TIME AND DATE OBTAINED block contains the military date and time the evidence was acquired by the CI Agent such as "2150, 4 May 90".

ITEM NUMBER block contains a chronological numbering of the separate items appearing on the form which corresponds with the item number shown on the evidence tag. Each item should be assigned a separate item number. When similar items pertaining to the same investigation are not grouped together, it is advisable to list them as separate items. An example would be cartridge casings of the same caliber found in separate locations within the same room. This will facilitate identification by matching the specific item number on the evidence custody document with the evidence tag attached to the item. In cases where like items are found at the same place, but are already grouped when received by the CI Agent, one entry number is sufficient.

QUANTITY block contains the number of items included in each entry.

DESCRIPTION OF ARTICLES block holds a description of each item of evidence. It is detailed accurately and in detail based upon what is actually observed about the object at the time it is acquired. The item's physical characteristics and condition, especially if the item is valuable, are described. The value of articles is never estimated or listed, nor is the type of metal or stone (in the case of jewelry or similar items) stated beyond giving color, size, and configuration. For example, an article appearing to be gold is listed as "gold colored metal". Serial numbers are listed whenever possible. The words "LAST ITEM" are placed in capital letters after the last item listed. These words are centered on the page and solid lines are drawn from the words to the margin on each side of the form.

CHAIN OF CUSTODY block has item numbers, date, released by, received by, and purpose of change of custody. The first entry under RELEASED BY is the name and signature of the individual from whom the property was taker Should the individual refuse or be unable to sign, the individual's name is entered in lieu of signature. When the evidence is obtained directly from a crime scene or found by the CI Agent, the first RELEASED BY block contains "NA". The first entry under RECEIVED BY is the CI Agent receiving the property. The purpose of change of custody is described briefly, such as "Evaluation as Evidence" or "Release to Evidence Custodian". This procedure is followed each time there is a custody change. When the CI Agent initially receiving the evidence is also the evidence custodian, the first RECEIVED BY block is completed by the custodian (CI Agent) and the purpose of the change of custody block is, "Received by Evidence Custodian". An original signature is not necessary on all copies of an evidence custody document; however, when signing through carbons, be sure the signature is legible on all copies. If and when any change of custody occurs, it is the responsibility of the person in control of the evidence at that time to ensure that entries of the change are made on the original DA Form 4137, and all appropriate copies. The importance of keeping accurate and complete custody documents cannot be overemphasized.

FINAL DISPOSAL ACTION block is used by the evidence custodian and approving authority in making final disposition of the evidence. This section will normally be completed by the evidence custodian prior to requesting final disposal authority. However, the CI Agent, initially acquiring the evidence, may enter this information in pencil if such disposal action can be anticipated. Any penciled entries must be verified by the evidence custodian and be printed in ink or typed before requesting approval for disposition.

The CI Agent assists the custodian's later disposition of the evidence by completing this section. This is especially helpful in cases of release to an owner when the owner's name does not appear elsewhere on the form. The item number and name and unit of the person to receive evidence are entered after the RELEASE TO OWNER OR OTHER line, such as "Item 1-Owner-SPC Charles Smith, B Co, 2d Bn, 1st Tng Bde". For evidence which will be destroyed, such as controlled substances, the item number and method of destruction are indicated, such as "Item 3 - released to US Secret Service, Final Disposition".

FINAL DISPOSAL AUTHORITY is completed when the evidence is of no further value. The first portion of this section is completed by the evidence custodian, and the second portion is completed by the individual authorized to grant final disposal.

WITNESS TO DESTRUCTION OF EVIDENCE is completed for any evidence destroyed. A witness attests to the destruction by placing his name, organization, and signature in this section. In the CHAIN OF CUSTODY section, the evidence custodian enters the item number of the evidence destroyed, date destroyed, and his name and signature. The word "Destroyed" is placed in the RECEIVED BY column.

The location of evidence while in the depository is written in pencil in the bottom margin, such as "Safe 1, Shelf 1." The document number, a two-part number, assigned chronologically, is reflected in the space provided such as "1-90" and represents the first evidence custody document received by the evidence custodian for the year 1990.

After final disposal of the evidence, the original copy of the evidence document is mailed or hand carried to the official who authorized the final disposal.

A sample of the custody document is shown in figures 3-2 and 3-3.

	EVIDENCE/PROPERTY CUSTODY DOCUMENT	MPR CID SEQUENCE NUMBER
	For use of this form see AR 195-45 and AR 195-5; the proponent agency is US Army Criminal Investigation Command	CID REPORT/CID ROI NUMBER

RECEIVING ACTIVITY	LOCATION	
NAME, GRADE AND TITLE OF PERSON FROM WHOM RECEIVED ☐ OWNER ☐ OTHER	ADDRESS (Include Zip Code)	
LOCATION FROM WHERE OBTAINED	REASON OBTAINED	TIME DATE OBTAINED

ITEM NO	QUANTITY	DESCRIPTION OF ARTICLES (Include model, serial number, condition and unusual marks or scratches)

CHAIN OF CUSTODY

ITEM NO	DATE	RELEASED BY	RECEIVED BY	PURPOSE OF CHANGE OF CUSTODY
		SIGNATURE	SIGNATURE	
		NAME, GRADE OR TITLE	NAME, GRADE OR TITLE	
		SIGNATURE	SIGNATURE	
		NAME, GRADE OR TITLE	NAME, GRADE OR TITLE	
		SIGNATURE	SIGNATURE	
		NAME, GRADE OR TITLE	NAME, GRADE OR TITLE	
		SIGNATURE	SIGNATURE	
		NAME, GRADE OR TITLE	NAME, GRADE OR TITLE	
		SIGNATURE	SIGNATURE	
		NAME, GRADE OR TITLE	NAME, GRADE OR TITLE	

DA FORM 4137   Replaces DA FORM 4137   DOCUMENT

Figure 3-2. DA Form 4137 (continued).

ITEM NO	DATE	RELEASED BY	RECEIVED BY	PURPOSE OF CHANGE OF CUSTODY
		SIGNATURE	SIGNATURE	
		NAME, GRADE OR TITLE	NAME, GRADE OR TITLE	
		SIGNATURE	SIGNATURE	
		NAME, GRADE OR TITLE	NAME, GRADE OR TITLE	
		SIGNATURE	SIGNATURE	
		NAME, GRADE OR TITLE	NAME, GRADE OR TITLE	
		SIGNATURE	SIGNATURE	
		NAME, GRADE OR TITLE	NAME, GRADE OR TITLE	
		SIGNATURE	SIGNATURE	
		NAME, GRADE OR TITLE	NAME, GRADE OR TITLE	
		SIGNATURE	SIGNATURE	
		NAME, GRADE OR TITLE	NAME, GRADE OR TITLE	
		SIGNATURE	SIGNATURE	
		NAME, GRADE OR TITLE	NAME, GRADE OR TITLE	
		SIGNATURE	SIGNATURE	
		NAME, GRADE OR TITLE	NAME, GRADE OR TITLE	

FINAL DISPOSAL ACTION

RELEASE TO OWNER OR OTHER (Name 'Unit) _____
DESTROY _____
OTHER (Specify) _____

FINAL DISPOSAL AUTHORITY

ITEM(S) _____ ON THIS DOCUMENT PERTAINING TO THE INVESTIGATION INVOLVING _____ (Name)

_____ (Name) _____ (Organization) _____ (IS ARE) NO LONGER

REQUIRED AS EVIDENCE AND MAY BE DISPOSED OF AS INDICATED ABOVE (If original was no request, so not sign, he signs in inactive correspondence.)

(Typed Printed Name, Grade, Title) _____ (Signature) _____ (Date)

WITNESS TO DESTRUCTION OF EVIDENCE

THE ARTICLE(S) LISTED AT ITEM NUMBER(S) _____ (WAS WERE) DESTROYED BY THE EVIDENCE CUSTODIAN IN MY PRESENCE ON THE DATE INDICATED ABOVE

(Typed Printed Name, Organization) _____ (Signature)

Figure 3-3. DA Form 4137 (Concluded).

EVIDENCE LEDGER. This is a bound record book (FSN 7530-00-286-8363) kept by the evidence custodian to provide double accountability and to cross-referenced custody documents. Ledgers will be destroyed three years after final disposition has been made of all items entered in each ledger. The ledger is prepared with the following six columns (see Figure 3-4).

* Document number and date received. Contains the document number assigned to the evidence custody document. The date the DA 4137 was received in the evidence room is entered below this number.

* MRP number or CID sequence number. The number assigned to the investigation the evidence pertains to. For CI officers maintaining their own evidence facility, utilize the column IAW local SOP.

* Brief description of evidence. A brief description is entered. Include the item number from the DA 4137.

* Date of final disposition. Date the evidence as disposed of, as shown in "Chain of Custody" section of DA 4137. When several items are not disposed of on the same date, the date of disposition should be shown opposite its description.

* Final disposition. A brief note on the means of final disposition is entered.

* Remarks. Evidence custodian can record any information he/she thinks is necessary.

Document No Date Received	CID Seq/ MPR No.	Brief Description Of Evidence	Date of Final Disposition	Final Disposition	Remarks
1- 93 2 Jan 93	76-005	1. .22 CAL PISTOL SN 12345 W/ MAGAZINE. 2. .22 CAL EXPENDED CASING "NE" 3. .22 CAL Expended CASING "T" 4. EMPTY .22 CAL AMMO BOX	2 FEB 93 ALL ITEMS	REL TO ATF DESTROYED DESTROYED DESTROYED	

Figure 3-4. Evidence Ledger Sample.

PHOTOGRAPHY AS EVIDENCE. A photograph may be valuable as evidence since it presents facts in pictorial form and creates mental impressions more vivid and realistic than those achieved by words alone. It presents evidence more accurately than the verbal description and permits consideration of evidence which, because of size, bulk, weight, or condition, cannot be brought into the courtroom. A photograph also reduces the need for lengthy descriptions and explanations.

Rules Pertaining to Photographs as Evidence. In order to qualify for admissibility as evidence, photographs must have been made in accordance with the following general rules:

*   The represented object must be material to the case under trial.

*   The photograph must be free of distortion.

*   It must be verified by a person who is personally acquainted with the locality, object, person, or thing represented and who is able to state that the photograph represents the appearance of the subject matter in question.

*   Nothing must be removed or altered at the scene of an incident prior to the taking of the photograph unless absolutely necessary; then, a note should be made indicating the reason for the removal or alteration.

 *   Although not a prerequisite for admissibility as evidence,
      photographs should be supported by notes made at the time of
      photography. The notes provide a description of what the photograph
      includes: case number or name of the subject; time and date;
      lighting and weather conditions; plate, film, lens, and type of
      camera; time of exposure and stop used; specific reason for taking
      the photo; location of the camera; compass direction; and specific
      reference to all important objects portrayed. Any one of these
      details may be important during a trial, particularly if the
      photograph is challenged. The notes should be retained by the
      investigator (photographer) in format similar to the Photo Data Card
      shown in figure 3-5.

Further information on the use of photography is found in appendix A.

PHOTO DATA CARD

Case number: _____ Subject: _____ Photographer: _____

Location: _____ Date: _____

Time of Day: _____ Weather Conditions: _____

Camera: _____ Negative Size: _____

Lens (Type): _____ Focal Length: _____

Diaphragm Setting: _____ Shutter Setting: _____

Film: _____ Filter: _____

CAMERA POSITIONS

A. Compass Reading: _____ B. Height: _____

C. Lateral Position: _____ D. Tilt: _____

Artificial Light Used: _____ Developer: _____

Developing Time: _____ Temperature: _____

Agitation: _____ Method of Printing: _____

Contrast: _____ Enlarger Lens: _____

Paper: _____

Distance between Important Objects in View: _____

_____

Description of Area: _____

_____

Remarks: _____

_____

Figure 3-5. Photo Data Card.

EVIDENCE TRANSMITTAL.

Transmittal Methods.

The method used to transmit evidence to the crime labs depends on the type of evidence and how urgently the results are needed. There are three methods: first class registered mail, handcarry, transported by Government carrier.

Wrapping, Packaging, and Transmitting.

A package wrapped for shipment to the laboratory consists of evidence from only one investigation. Each item of evidence within the shipping container should be in its own separate package. Violation of this procedure can result in contamination of evidence and problems in chain of custody.

Pack each item of evidence that will minimize friction and prevent shifting, breaking, leaking, or contact with other evidence. Pack in cotton or soft paper items that are particularly susceptible to being broken, marred, or damaged.

Items such as glass fragments, evidence in glass containers, impressions, casts, ammunition, bullets, cartridge cases, tablets, and capsules particularly susceptible to breaking, should be packed in cotton or soft paper.

Fingerprints. When evidence is to be examined for fingerprints, each item of evidence should be packed in a manner that prevents damage to the fingerprints. This is accomplished by fastening the object in the container so it will not shift. No other object may come in contact with the object suspected of containing fingerprints. Items should be dry before packaging.

The nature of the evidence will govern the use of warning notices to be affixed to the outside wrapper or box, such as "Fragile", "Expedite", or "Corrosive".

Stains. Items that contain stains, such as clothing with stains of blood or other body fluids, should not be placed in airtight plastic containers, 'sweating" and moisture accumulation may result within such containers, contaminating the evidence. Such items must be dry before packaging.

Liquids. Liquid evidence, with the exception of explosives, oils, and gasoline, should be packed in all-glass, sterile bottles or other containers and sealed with wax or other suitable material.

Small Objects. In general, small solid items, such as bullets, fibers, hair, paint scrapings, powder, powder patterns, and threads should be placed upon a piece of plain paper; the paper folded. This should be packed in separate pill or powder boxes, paper containers or druggist folds and sealed with adhesive tape, wax, or other suitable material.

Paper or String. Documents, string, twine, and rope should be placed in an inner cellophane envelope and an outer manila envelope. Cellophane is not suitable for packing any item which will rust or corrode.

Materials bearing traces of accelerants like those recovered in an arson or sabotage investigation should be sealed in a vapor tight container such as a mason jar. They should not be sent in plastic bags because accelerants will leak through plastic.

Growing plant material should not be placed in airtight plastic containers as moisture accumulates, making examination difficult. Growing plants should either be dried before shipment or wrapped in porous paper. The laboratory should be notified in advance of the shipment.

Packages containing items of evidence that require careful or selective handling while in transit label "Corrosive", "Fragile", "Keep Away From Fire", or "Keep Cool".

Federal laws prohibit transmitting certain items through postal channels. If there is any question of mailing, the nearest postmaster should be consulted.

Chemicals, gases, unexploded bombs, detonators, fuses, blasting caps, and other explosive or inflammable materials cannot be sent by mail. Transmittal of these items of evidence must conform to the provisions of AR 55-355, Military Traffic Movement Regulation; Interstate Commerce Commission regulations; and appropriate state laws and municipal ordinances.

Before such items are forwarded, the laboratory must be notified the shipment is planned and must acknowledge receipt of notification. In your notification give details of how the materials are packed. This will reduce the danger involved in unpacking those items at the laboratory.

NOTE: More details can be found in appendix B of this manual or refer to the appendix in FM 19-20 for further details.

Transmittal of Classified Evidence. For transmittal of classified evidence three wrappers should be used:

* Inner wrapper. The sealed container is wrapped and property sealed. The full address and return address of the transmitting agency should be placed on the wrapper. When appropriate, the notation "evidence-to be opened by laboratory personnel only" and the classification of contents are placed on all six sides of the package. An envelope containing two additional copies of the evidence receipts, plus two copies of DA Form 3655, Crime Lab Examination Request, should be affixed to the inner wrapper.

* Middle wrapper. The package is then wrapped and sealed a second time. The markings are the same as for the inner wrapper, except no notation is made that the package contains evidence.

* Outer wrapper. The package is then wrapped a third time and again sealed. The outer wrapper bears only the two addresses; however, a special handling notation must be made if the evidence is perishable, flammable, fragile, explosive, corrodible, or corrosive.

Submitting Evidence to a Crime Lab. The following steps must be followed when preparing evidence for submission to a crime lab:

* DA Form 3655, Crime Lab Examination Request (Figures 3-6 and 3-7), is completed in an original and two copies. One copy is maintained in the investigative case file.

* Each item of evidence is labeled to correspond with the entries on DA Form 3655 and packed securely in a box. Documentary evidence may be placed in an envelope or series of envelopes which are in turn placed in another envelope. Each item of evidence must be wrapped separately.

* The box or envelope containing the evidence is sealed with tape or glue.

CRIME LAB EXAMINATION REQUEST for use of this form, see AR 196-6 the proponent agency is the United States Army Criminal Investigation Command		LAB USE ONLY REFERRAL NUMBER	
TO (include zip code) Commander US Army Criminal Investigation Laboratory Ft Gordon, GA 30905	FROM (include zip code) Commander Ft Benning Field Office Third Region, USACIDC Ft Benning, GA 31905	RECEIVED	RETURNED
		Regis Mail	Regis Mail
		RV EXP	RV EXP
		HAND	HAND
		Date	Date
		Received By	
ATTN: Chemistry Division		EVIDENCE RECEIPT	
		RECEIVED	RECEIVED
1.Contributor Case Number	2. Investigator's Name	3. Autovon & Phone Number	
4. SUSPECT (S) (Last, First and middle names)			
5. VISTIM (S) (Last, First and middle names)			
6. Type of Offense	7. One Copy of Evidence Receipt inclosed Yes No	8. Other evidence Previously Submitted Yes No	
9. If "YES" in items, list other suspect, date submitted, unit case and laboratory referral number.			

Figure 3-6. DA Form 3655, Crime Lab Examination Request. (Continued)

* The sender should place his initials or signature across the sealed flap of the inner envelope or across the paper tape used to seal the inner box and cover his initials or signature with transparent tape.

*   The original and one copy of DA Form 3655 plus the original evidence custody document are placed in an envelope, which is sealed and addressed to the laboratory with an attention line to the specific division (document, fingerprint, firearm, and so on).

    *   The sealed envelope is securely taped to the box or envelope containing the evidence.

    *   The box containing the evidence is than wrapped in heavy paper and sent via first class or registered mail, express, or hand-carried to the laboratory. If postal or express channels are used, the evidence is accompanied by a request for a return receipt from the laboratory (Postal Form 3811).

NOTE: In the case of classified evidence, investigators must comply with the provisions of AR 380-5.

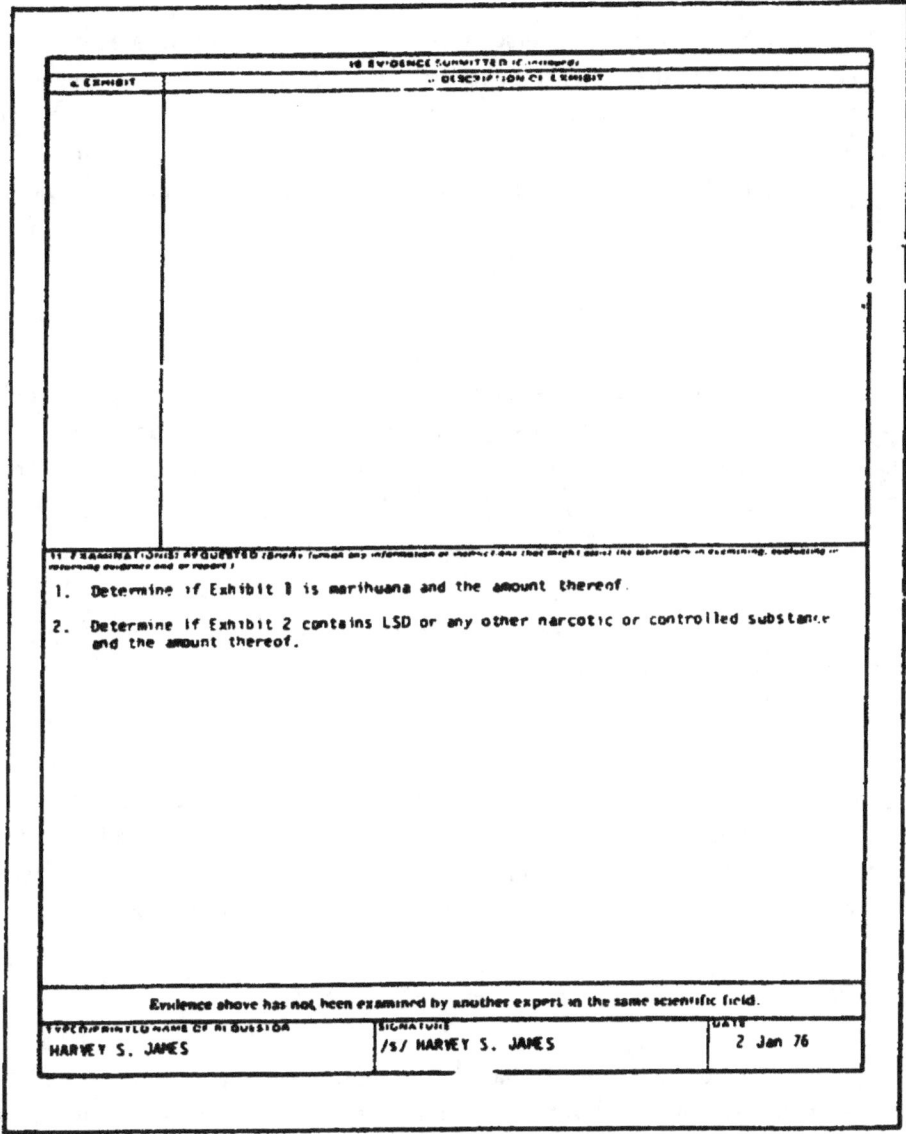

Figure 3-7. DA Form 3655 Crime Lab Examination Request (Concluded).

<u>Temporary Release of Evidence</u>. Evidence may be removed from the evidence room only for permanent disposal or temporary release for specific reasons. The most common reasons for temporary removal are:

* Transmittal to a crime laboratory for forensic examination.

* Presentation at a courts-martial or hearing conducted under Article 32, UCMJ.

75

The person evidence is released to will sign for it in the "Received By" column on the "Chain of Custody" section on the original and first copy of DA Form 4137. The person receiving the evidence must safeguard it and maintain the chain of custody until it is returned to the evidence custodian. The evidence custodian will release the original DA Form 4137 to the person who assumes temporary custody, or to first class mail or other transmittal channels, along with the evidence. He will then put the first copy of the DA Form 4137 in a suspense folder. When the evidence is returned, the original DA Form 4137, properly annotated by the custodian and the person returning the evidence, will be put in the evidence document file. The first (suspense) copy, with the chain of custody properly annotated, will be refiled with the original DA Form 4137.

When items on the same DA Form 4137 must be temporarily released to more than one agency or person at the same time, additional copies will be used and processed as above. A note will be made on the original and first copy indicating that additional copies have been made. The chain of custody for all evidence will be recorded on the first copy of the DA Form 4137.

Personnel receiving evidence, either on a temporary or a permanent basis, will be required to present identification to ensure evidence is only handled by authorized persons.

Transmittal to US Army Criminal Investigation Laboratory (USACIL). Requests for USACIL analysis should be coordinated with and made by the local CIDC elements. This will ensure that items of material value or physical evidence in an investigation are not mishandled, improperly accounted for, or contaminated. It will also ensure USACIL elements are aware of incidents of suspected criminal activity as defined in paras 3-1 through 3-3, AR 195-2.

Even when CID personnel have no direct interest in materials being shipped to USACIL, they can still be of assistance by providing proper laboratory request forms, addresses, and advice on packaging and transmittal. The date, name, and unit of the CID representative coordinated with will be entered in Item 11 of DA Form 3655. More detailed instructions pertaining to the release of various items of evidence may be found in AR 195-5.

FINAL DISPOSITION OF EVIDENCE. Evidence will be disposed of as soon as possible after it has served its purpose or is determined to be of no value as evidence. Evidence released to a trial counsel for judicial proceedings will be returned as soon as possible to the custodian for final disposition. If an item of evidence is made part of the record of trial, the trial counsel will immediately notify the custodian so the DA Form 4137 can be properly annotated. This will be considered final disposition.

When final action has been taken in known subject cases, the original custody document will be sent to the Staff Judge Advocate (SJA) of the commander with general courts-martial jurisdiction over the subject. The SJA will complete the final disposal authority part of the DA Form 4137 if the evidence is no longer needed. When evidence must be retained, this part of the form will not be completed; a brief statement giving the reason for keeping the evidence will be furnished to the evidence custodian on separate correspondence. In unusual cases, where there is a high risk of losing the original DA Form 4137, (for example, isolated units that must mail the DA Form 4137 to the servicing SJA for disposition approval), a letter or memorandum for record may be substituted for disposition approval. When this method is used, enough information will be furnished to allow the SJA to make a decision. The return correspondence from the SJA giving disposition approval will be attached to the original DA Form 4137 for filing.

Evidence in an investigation for which no subject has been identified may be disposed of 3 months after completion of the investigation without SJA approval; it may be disposed of earlier with SJA approval. However, care must be taken with serious crime, when it is possible a subject may later be identified. In such a case, it may be advisable to keep the evidence longer than 3 months. When the subject is not known, evidence custodians will obtain the approval of the commander, SJA, provost marshal, or representative, as appropriate. This approval will be given by completing the final disposal authority section of the original DA Form 4137.

When evidence is permanently released to an external agency, the final disposal authority part of the DA Form 4137 will be completed. This will be considered final disposition of the evidence.

Items in the evidence room that, after laboratory analysis, seem to have no value as evidence may be disposed of after consulting with the proper SJA. Items of possible evidence that are determined to have no value as evidence by the CI Agent before being sent to the evidence custodian, may be disposed of by the agent; this is done only after consulting with the immediate supervisor and getting approval. This does not include found controlled substances. In unusual cases, oral approval may be obtained followed by written approval.

When it is not practical or desirable to keep items of evidence, (eg. automobiles, serial numbered items, items required for use by the owner, undelivered mail, large amounts of money, and perishable or unstable items) disposal action may be taken immediately. If such items can be immediately disposed of, it will not be necessary to enter them into the evidence room. This will be coordinated with SJA. The SJA will complete the final disposal authority portion of the DA Form 4137. If it is not possible to get written approval of the SJA before the disposal of the evidence, oral permission will be obtained, followed by written approval.

The guidance below on evidence disposal will be followed. When a legal question on methods of disposal comes up, the SJA will give legal advice.

    *   (1) U.S. government property will be released to the organization to which issued.

*   (2)   Personal property that is legal to own will be released to its rightful owner.

*   (3)   U.S. government treasury checks and money orders from any APO money order facility will be returned to the issuing APO.

*   (4)   Other types of negotiable instruments (eg. money orders, travelers checks, and checks) owned by a business firm will be released to the firm. If the firm does not want them returned, they will be destroyed.

*   (5)   Except as provided for in (3) above, US postal money orders that cannot be identified as the property of a specific person will be sent to the Military Money Order Division, Postal Data Center, P.O. Box 14965, St. Louis, MO 63182. A letter of transmittal that has the investigative case number, date of final report of investigation, offense, and complete identification or both subject and victim will be included. The letter will also state that information on the ROJ. If it is foreseen that postal money orders will be kept as evidence for more than 120 days from the date received by the evidence custodian, a first class letter will be sent immediately to the Military Money Order Division, Postal Data Center; it will list the serial number and symbol number of each money order and the reasons for retention. This may prevent the issue of duplicate money orders.

*   (6)   Negotiable instruments and other documents obtained from a person will be retuned, unless the owner does not want them. In this case, they will be destroyed.

*   (7)   Known document standards will be released to the agency or person from whom received or the rightful owner, unless they are not wanted. In this case, they will be destroyed.

*   (8)   Exemplars and other documents of no value to the person or agency from whom received will be destroyed.

*   (9)   Items of personal property that belong to deceased or missing Army personnel will be released to the summary court officer appointed to dispose of the descendent's effects.

*   (10)   Controlled substances will be destroyed in the presence of a witness who is a CID Special Agent or in the grade E-6 or above. The witness must not be involved in the chain of custody. Destruction will be by burning or by a method that will make it permanently useless.

*   (11)   Normally, counterfeit currency and coins, counterfeiting equipment will be released to the nearest office of the US Secret Service (USSS), unless the USSS directs otherwise.

*   (12)   Firearms and ammunition may be disposed of as follows:

        (a)   U.S. government firearms and ammunition kept as evidence will be returned to the-proper military unit. If the unit cannot be identified, they will be released to the installation accountable officer, IAW paragraph 2-5, AR 710-2.

(b) Contraband firearms and ammunition kept as evidence will be released to the nearest office of Alcohol, Tobacco, and Firearms (ATF) Divisions, U.S. Treasury Department (18 USC 924d). This includes firearms and ammunition that were used or intended to be used in committing a crime. U.S. Government property is excluded. ATF Form 4631 (Request for Forfeiture), available at local ATF offices, must be filled out and sent to ATF along with a copy of the investigative report.

When ATF does not accept such weapons, they will be released to the supporting DPDO for destruction, per DOD 4160.21-M and DOD 4160.21-M-1. ATFs refusal will be documented; this will be attached to the proper DA Form 4137. In all cases, the evidence custodian will witness the destruction of weapons at DPDO facilities. Ammunition refused by ATF will be released to the nearest ammunition supply point or depot.

(c) In oversea areas, weapons described above will be turned in to the servicing DPDO. The DPDO will demilitarize them on a mutually agreed upon date. Ammunition described above will be turned in to the nearest ammunition supply point or depot.

(d) Legal personal weapons impounded for minor infractions, (eg. failure to register per local laws), must be returned to the rightful owner when the requirements have been met and they are no longer needed as evidence.

* (13) When evidence is of obvious value and the owner is unknown or cannot be located, it will be turned in to the Defense Property Disposal Office (DPDO) per DOD 4160.21-M.

* (14) items of evidence found at crime scenes that have no known owner and are of no obvious value (eg. match books, beer cans, bottles, glass fragments, and wooden sticks) will be destroyed in the presence of a witness. Crushing, burning, or other methods will be used to render the items useless and harmless.

* (15) When the owner of the money is not known or cannot be located after reasonable attempts, the money will be turned in to a U.S. Army Finance Officer. A DD Form 1131 (Cash Collection Voucher) will be used. A copy of the DD Form 1131 will be attached to the original custody document.

* (16) Post exchange Items, commissary items, and items illegally Introduced into a host country, that are connected with black market, customs, and postal investigations, will be disposed of per--

    (a) Local regulations.

    (b) Status of forces agreements, and

(c) Law or customs of the host country.

LESSON 3

PRACTICE EXERCISE

The following items will test your grasp of the material covered in this lesson. There is only one correct answer for each item. When you have completed the exercise, check your answers with the answer key that follows. If you answer any item incorrectly, study again that part of the lesson which contains the portion involved.

1.   You have a document containing cryptography, for which you do not have the key. What is your action?

    A.   Attempt to decrypt the message.

    B.   Process it in accordance with the unit standing operating procedures (SOP).

    C.   Take it to the nearest cryptofacility for decryption.

    D.   Forward it to the CCO.

2.   What are the most common items of physical evidence encountered by CI personnel? (Write in your answer)

3.   Which may reveal the sex, approximate height, and weight of an individual?

      A.   Fingerprints.

      B.   Footprints.

      C.   Hair.

4.   If the items of evidence are small, is it permissible to consolidate the evidence from two or more investigations into one package to ship to the laboratory?

      A.   Yes.

      C.   No.

LESSON 3

PRACTICE EXERCISE

Answer Key and Feedback

Item   Correct Answer and Feedback

1.   B.   Process it in accordance with the unit standing operating procedures.

         (page 3-2).

2.   Documents are the most common items of physical evidence encountered by CI. (page 3-2).

3.   B.   Footprints. (page 3-3).

4.   B.   No. (page 3-15).

PART 2: INTELLIGENCE SUPPORT MISSIONS

LESSON 1

INTELLIGENCE AND ELECTRONIC WARFARE

SUPPORT TO OPERATIONS

CRITICAL TASKS: 301-372-2014

301-372-2015

301-372-2406

301-372-2602

OVERVIEW

LESSON DESCRIPTION:

In this lesson you will learn the fundamentals for Electronic Warfare in support of military operations.

TERMINAL LEARNING OBJECTIVE:

TASKS: Conduct IEW operations in support of all types of military operations.

CONDITIONS: You will be given narrative information and illustrations from FM 34-1.

STANDARDS: Identify the fundamental information needed for conducting IEW operations.

REFERENCES: The material contained in this lesson was derived from the following publications:

FM 34-1   FM 34-130

FM 34-2   FM 34-10-2

FM 34-8   AR 381-10

INTRODUCTION

The mission of Army intelligence is to provide timely, relevant, accurate, and synchronized IEW support to tactical, operational, and strategic commanders across the range of military operations. In war, IEW operations support the winning of battles and campaigns. In Stability and Support Operations (SASO), IEW operations support the promotion of peace, the resolution of conflict, and the deterrence of war. These operations reduce uncertainty and risk to US forces and permit the effective application of force.

IEW IN THE FORCE PROJECTION ARMY

Today's Army is a force projection Army. Continental United States (CONUS)-based with a limited forward presence, the Army must be capable of rapidly deploying anywhere in the world, operating in a joint or combined environment, and defeating regional threats on the battlefield or conducting SASO. IEW is fundamental to effective planning, security, and execution of force projection operations. IEW operations have changed fundamentally from those of the Cold War model. The environment in which the Army now operates requires IEW support based on the mission rather than on a monolithic threat. During the Cold War era, intelligence developed into a threat-based system upon which the Army based its doctrine, training, and modernization. For over four decades, the "threat" was the former USSR now known as the Commonwealth of Independent States (CIS). The Army developed organizations, systems, tactics, and procedures needed to conduct defensive operations against CIS and Eastern European forces attacking through central Europe. Our defense was built upon the movement of heavy corps from in-theater garrisons to general defense positions with follow-on forces arriving later from CONUS. Movement and support of the corps would occur within a robust communication zone containing extensive communications and logistics infrastructures. From alert through the termination of hostilities, tactical IEW units were to be the principal sources of tactical intelligence flowing up to divisions, corps, and theater. Intelligence, in general, would flow from the ground up to higher echelons. And, because the US focused the national intelligence effort on our Nation's most likely threat, we possessed in-depth, continuous, and nearly automatic intelligence on the forces of the CIS.

In the force projection Army, mission-based intelligence focuses on developing broad baseline knowledge of potential threats and operational environments supporting numerous plans and likely contingency missions. From this broad baseline, commanders possess the capability to prioritize, focus, and surge the intelligence system supporting force projection operations. The commander plays a key role in mission-based intelligence and intelligence readiness. Since there is no longer one threat facing the US, command involvement is essential in ensuring that the intelligence system is focused on the commander's top contingencies. Force projection operations build force levels from the bottom up versus top down as during the Cold War. IEW assets are tailored to meet the requirements of the mission and deployment sequence. In force projection operations, commanders depend on small, deployable teams with access to national and joint intelligence. Intelligence in the initial stages of the operation will flow from higher to lower. The situation and the commander's concept of operation will dictate the size and capabilities of follow-on IEW assets. Figure 1-1 illustrates the transition from Cold War era to force projection intelligence. The nature of force projection operations and mission-based intelligence requires commanders to redefine intelligence readiness. Intelligence readiness means that MI must develop broad knowledge on priority contingency areas, update those databases daily, and be prepared to surge in support of emerging missions. Commanders and G2s (S2s) must direct the intelligence effort daily to ensure the databases will be there upon alert to support contingency planning and execution. If our divisions, corps, and theater forces stand ready to project force anywhere in several potential contingencies, then it is essential that their intelligence support be at the same or

higher level of readiness. To maintain that level of readiness, MI must provide commanders with routine, direct, and habitual links into the intelligence system to provide and, perhaps more importantly, to focus intelligence on their tactical and operational needs early.

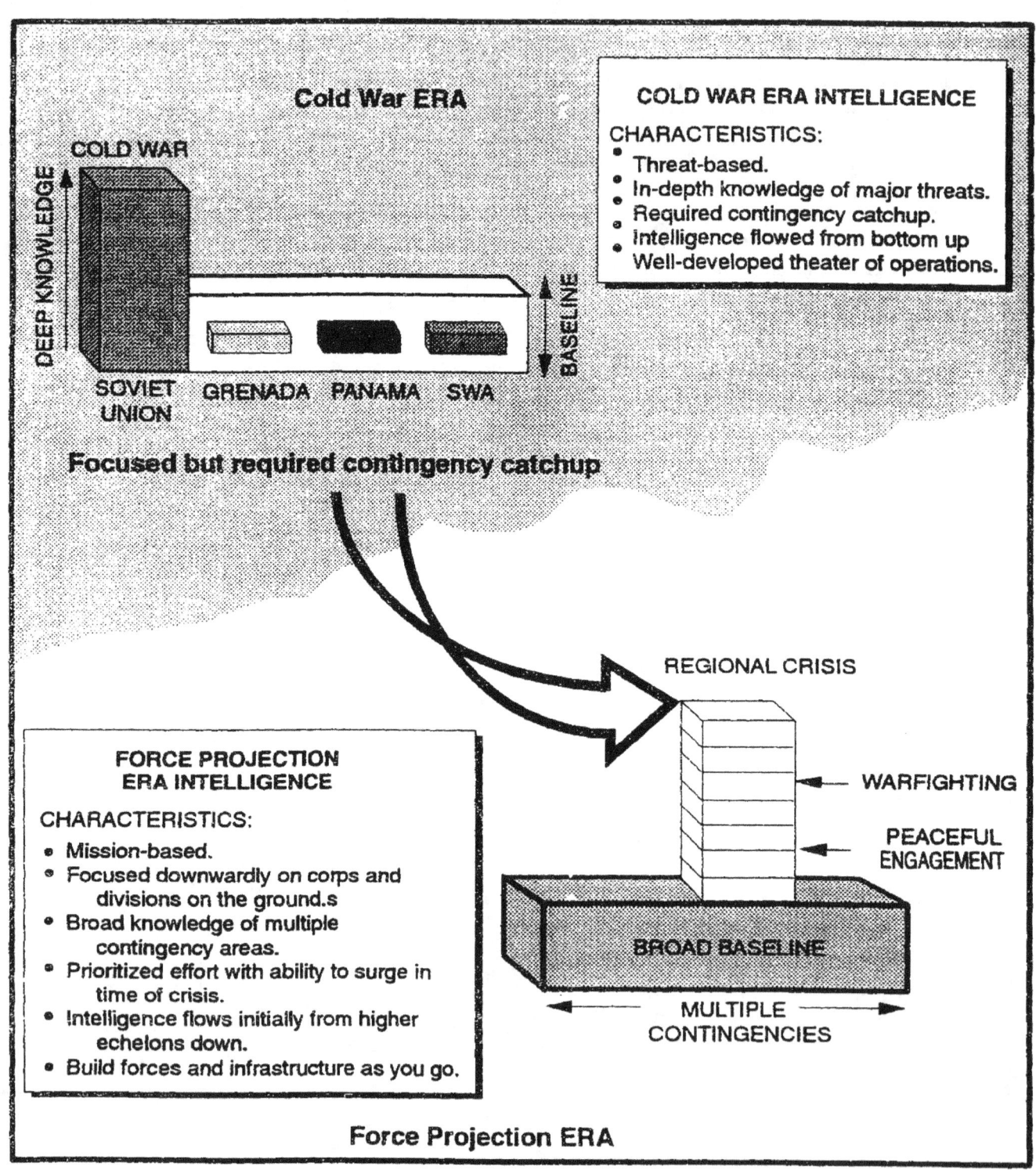

Figure 1-1. Transition from Cold War era to force projection era intelligence.

PRINCIPLES OF FORCE PROJECTION IEW

Successful force projection IEW support is based on understanding five key principles: the commander drives intelligence, intelligence synchronization, split-based operations, tactical tailoring, and broadcast dissemination. See Figure 1-2.

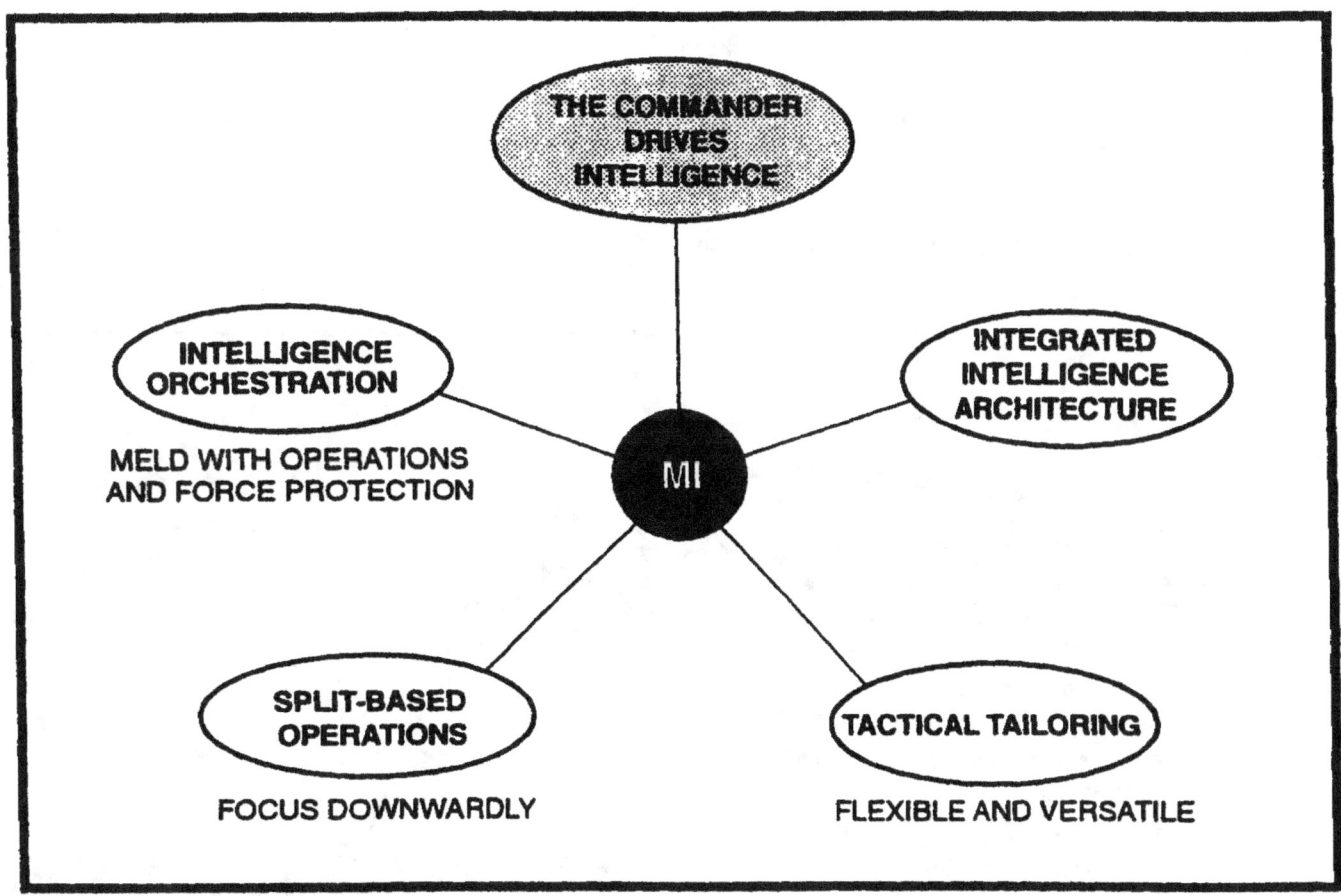

Figure 1-2. Principles of force projection IEW operations.

The Commander Drives Intelligence

The commander's role in EW is not just when the crisis begins, but well before and throughout the operation. It is central to the success or failure of EW support in force projection operations. The commander must take an active role in focusing, integrating and training the intelligence system. He must focus the effort and ensure it is responsive to his information requirements (IR) and those of his subordinates. As shown in Figure 1-3, the commander must -

- Identify, clearly articulate, and prioritize intelligence and targeting requirements.

- Understand the capabilities and limitations of the Intelligence BOS.

- Know how to leverage and employ the intelligence system to its full potential.
- Broker subordinates' information and resource requirements.

- Meld the Intelligence BOS into the total combined arms effort.

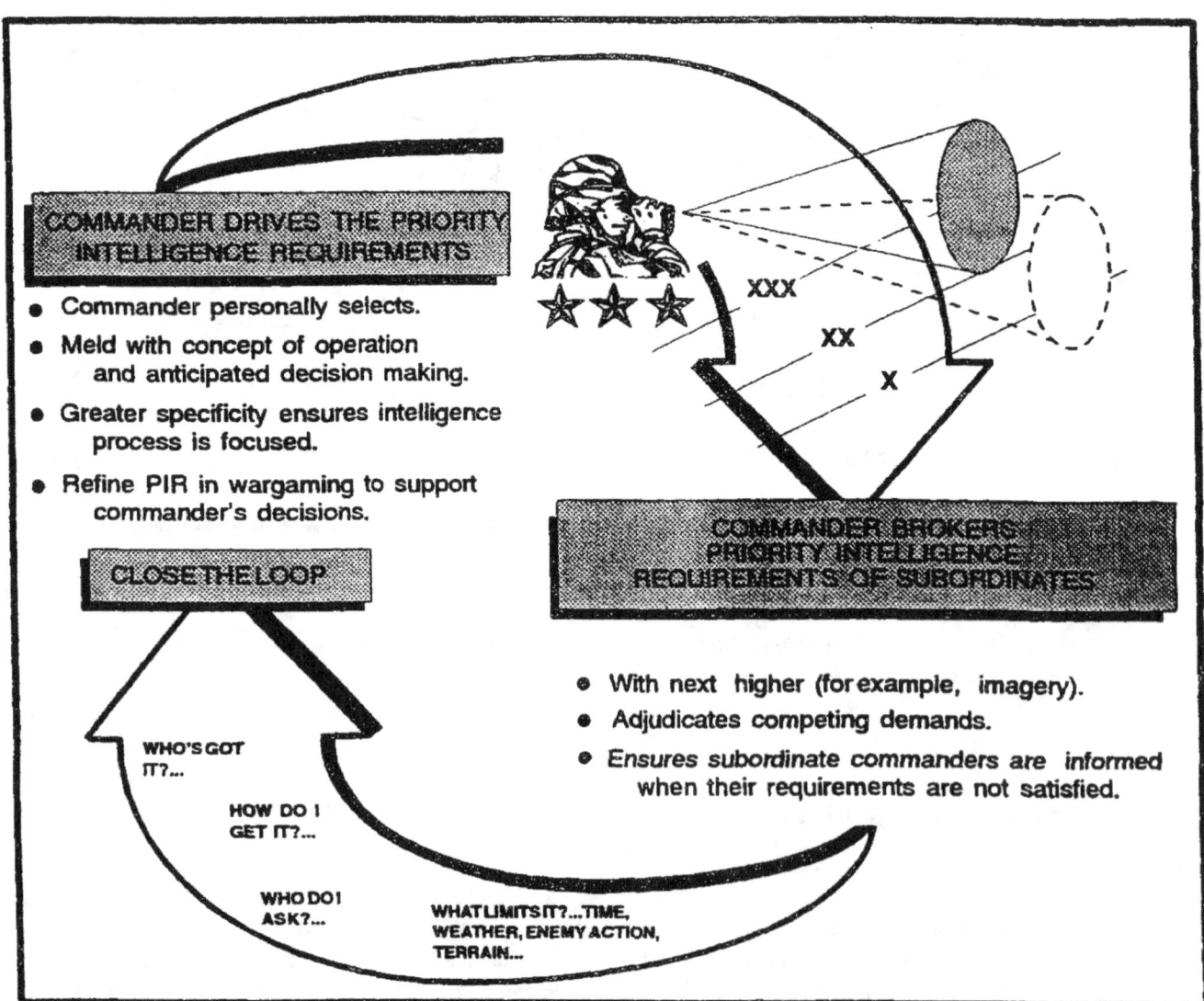

Figure 1-3. The commander drives intelligence.

Intelligence Synchronization:

Intelligence synchronization ensures IEW operations are linked to the commander's requirements and respond in time to influence decisions and operations. In the synchronization process, the G2 (S2) takes the commander's priority intelligence requirements (PIR) and backward plans to ensure that collection and production efforts are orchestrated with the operation, and deliver intelligence when required. The collection manager ensures specific orders and requests (SORs) fully support all PIR and IR. The collection manager also synchronizes collection and reporting to deliver relevant information, on time, to support operational decisions. Intelligence synchronization ensures the MI unit commander has the time, guidance, and resources to execute IEW operations. Intelligence synchronization is a continuous process, which keeps the

intelligence cycle and IEW operations tied to the commander's critical decisions and concept of operations. See Figure 14. For more information on intelligence synchronization, refer to FM 34-2 and FM 34-130.

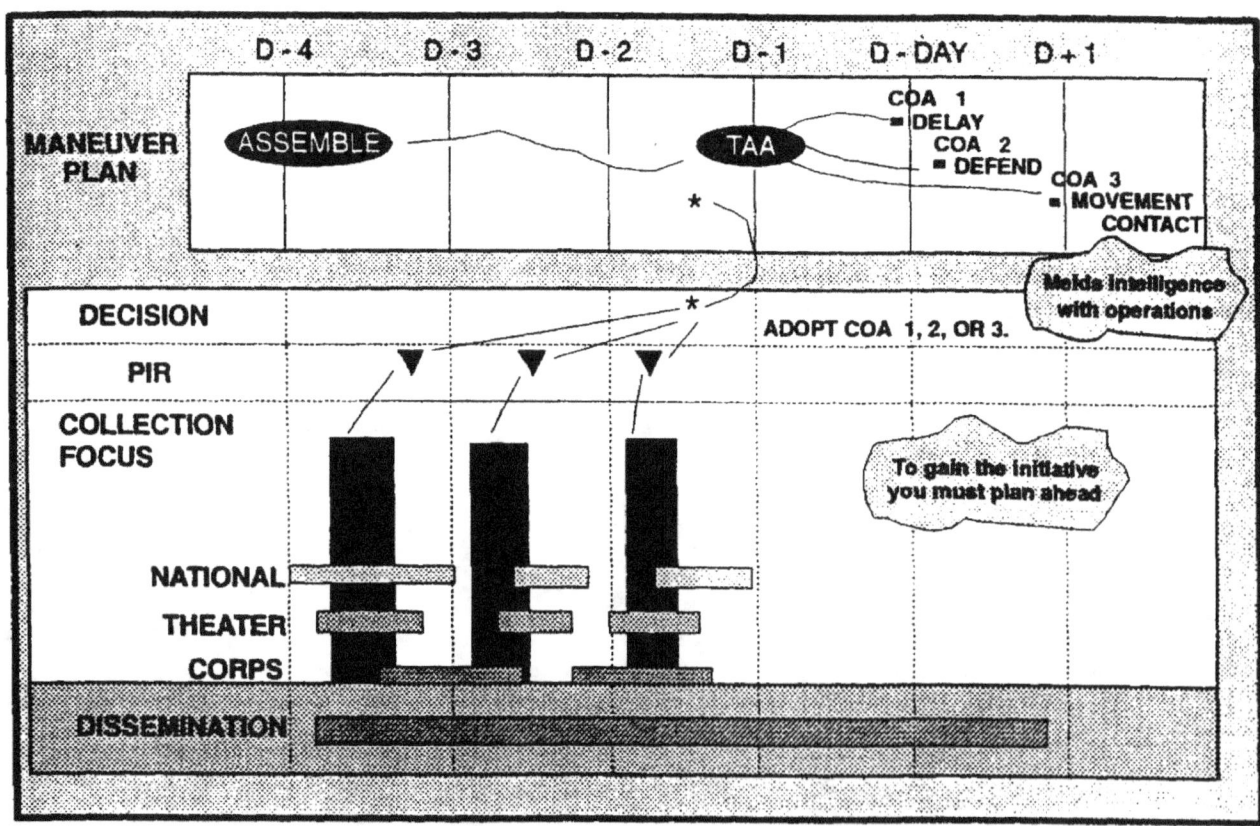

Figure 1-4. Intelligence synchronization.

94

Split-based Operations

Split-based operations are an integral part of IEW support to force projection operations. In split-based operations, the commander deploys small, flexible, tailored IEW organizations with access to intelligence databases and systems outside the area of operations (AO), particularly national systems. Split basing takes advantage of direct broadcast technology from collection platforms and assured intelligence communications to provide commanders with continuous, relevant, and timely IEW support during all stages of force projection operations. See Figure 1-5.

Organizations like the Deployable Intelligence Support Element (DISE) support split-based operations by bringing together communications capability, automated intelligence fusion systems, and broadcast down links in a scalable package able to deploy with the entry force. It is not a specific piece of equipment or a particular configuration of equipment. It is a flexible organization able to support any type of ground force commander whether from Army, Joint, or combined forces. The DISE provides the commander with a link from his forward-deployed force to an intelligence support base located in CONUS or other locations outside the AO.

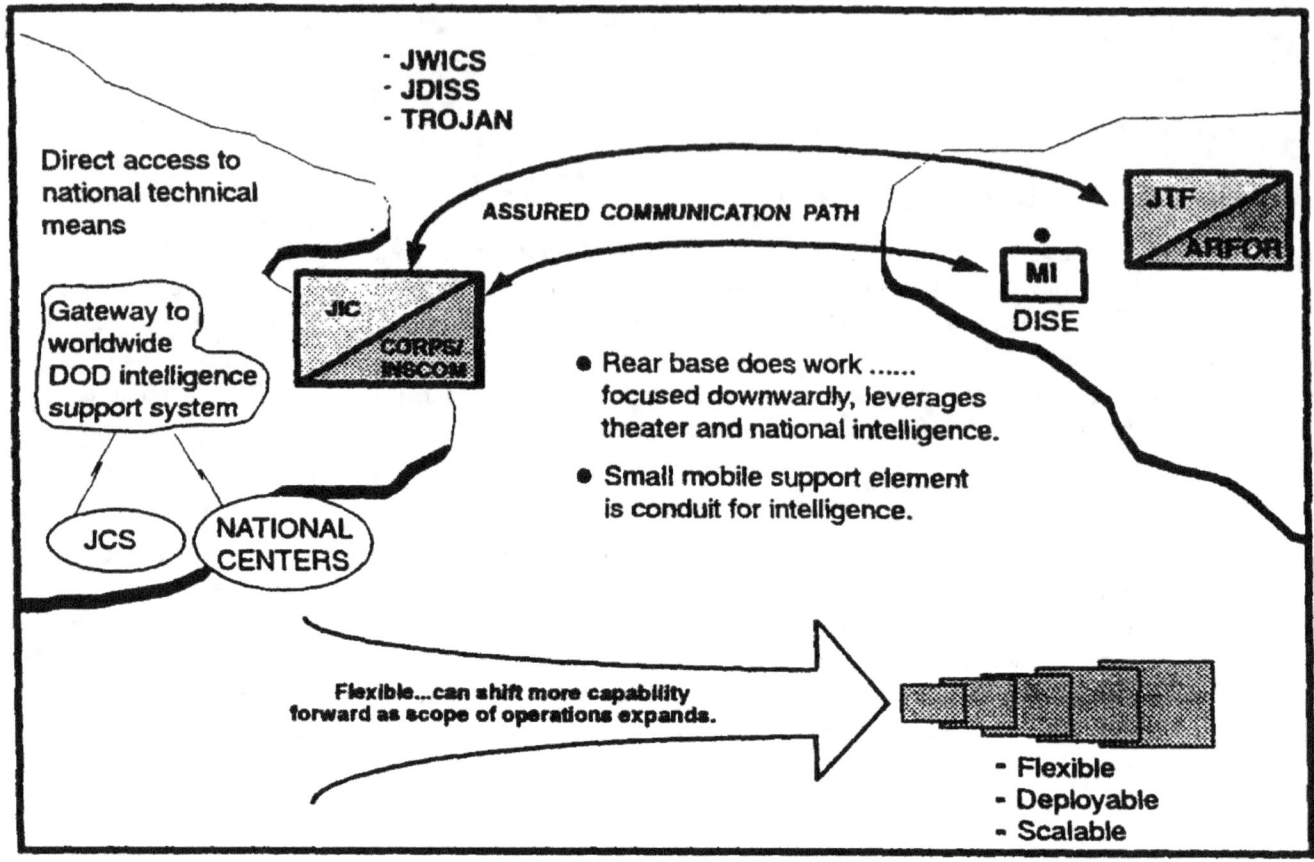

Figure 1-5. Split-based operations.

Tactical Tailoring:

In force projection operations, the commander tactically tailors IEW support for each contingency. Commanders should attempt to maintain unit integrity and established command relationships to the extent possible; however, deployment of a more traditional unit such as a divisional MI battalion Tables of Organization and Equipment (TOE) may not be the best organization for the mission. Tailoring allows the commander to build a more efficient, mission specific force by assessing IEW mission requirements. This includes determining the capabilities of remotely based and joint intelligence collection assets to support the mission.

- Identifying the composition of the IEW force based on mission, enemy, troops, terrain and weather, and time available (METT-T); determining communications and processing requirements; and planning the deployment sequence of IEW assets based on mission, strategic lift resources, and host nation support.

- Developing scalable IEW support packages like the DISE with communications, processing, and down link assets for top priority contingency missions. Employment of these packages should be practiced often to refine force researching and tailoring procedures, load plans, communications connectivity, and support relationships.

  Tailoring the Intelligence BOS to ensure it provides the commander with accurate and responsive intelligence. The intelligence system should cover the entire width and depth of the battle space and area of interest (AI) throughout the duration of the operation, at the resolution required by commanders at each echelon.

- Deploying early, an IEW package that is portable, logistically sustainable, and sufficient to conduct operations for the short-term. Sufficiency in the short-term includes being prepared to provide immediate IEW support for combat operations and force protection.

- Integrating IEW assets into the deployment flow early. Depending on the availability of information and threat capabilities, commanders must phase in intelligence personnel and equipment that offers redundancy and that serve as the cornerstone for assets that arrive in the theater later. These initial "building blocks" are critical to early success and follow-on capabilities. Follow-on IEW forces should enhance the capabilities of in-theater assets and satisfy the commander's long-term concerns.

- Maintaining habitual peacetime IEW support relationships and accesses between the forward deployed intelligence element and its higher echelon intelligence organization. This allows forward-deployed assets to pull from their "normal" intelligence sources between the predeployment and operations stages of force projection. This reduces the possibility of intelligence shortfalls, which could arise from reliance on evolving intelligence organizations. For example, a CONUS-based corps may commit a maneuver brigade as part of a forward-deployed joint task force (JTF). The deployed brigade could continue to receive support through a DISE from the CONUS-based analysis and control element (ACE) of its parent division in addition to support from the JTF Joint Intelligence Center (JIC).

- Maximizing intelligence support from the host nation by establishing, if possible, liaison with host nation intelligence organizations in peacetime. Figure 1-6 provides a sketch of some IEW tactical tailoring considerations.

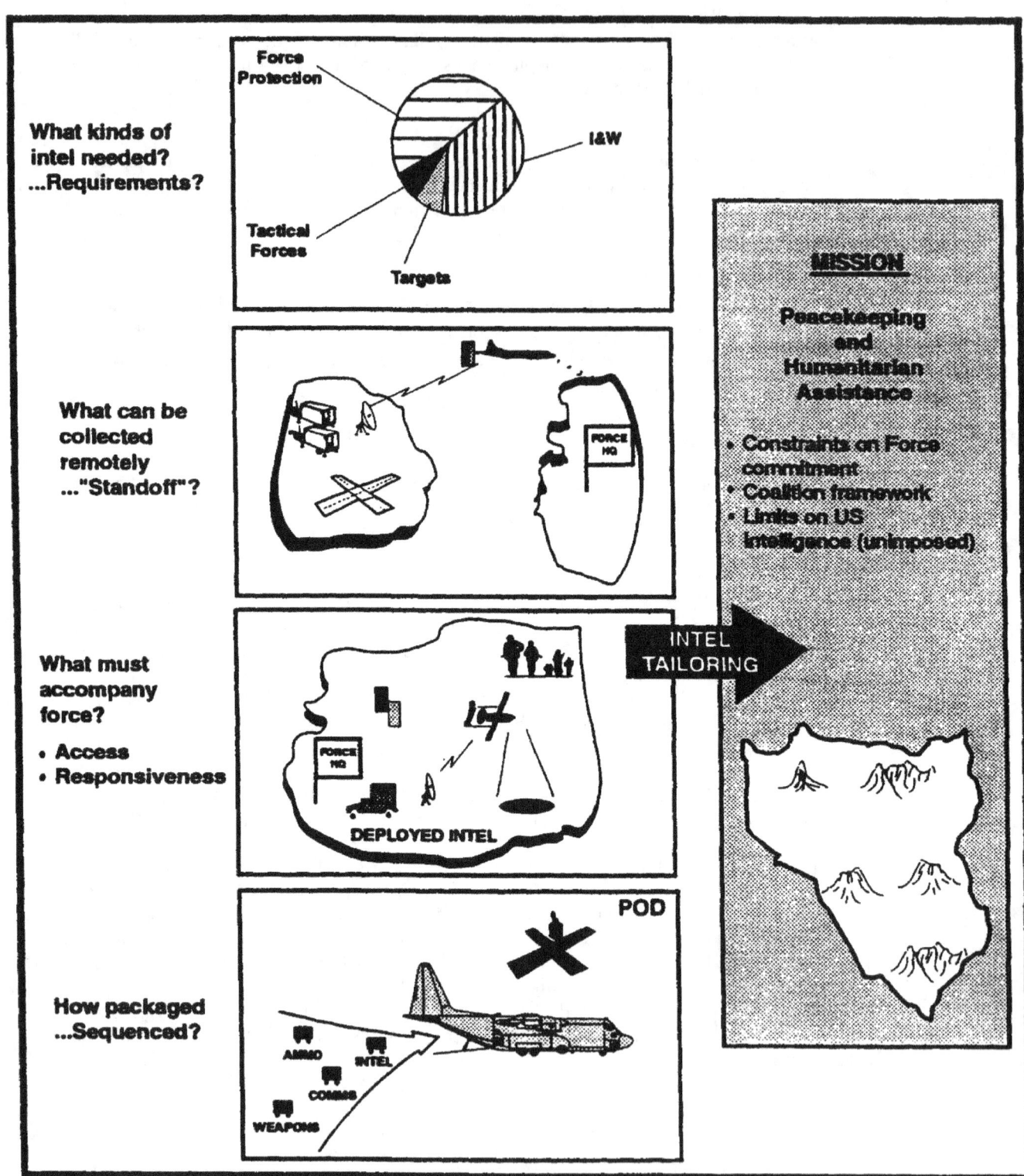

Figure 1-6. Considerations for intelligence task organization.

98

Broadcast Dissemination:

Broadcast dissemination of intelligence and targeting information is an important element in providing commanders at multiple echelons with a common intelligence picture of the battlefield. Broadcasting facilitates the direct or skip echelon "push" of information down to commanders in the field. Use of broadcast technology also reduces the number of collection sensors, processors, and personnel needed to support these operations. More importantly, broadcasting intelligence and targeting information directly to multiple terminals eliminates bottlenecks inherent in point-to-point communications and provides all echelons common sources from which to "pull" information. Some of the products available through broadcast systems are TENCAP imagery and targeting information, Joint STARS radar imagery, Unmaned Aerial Vehicle (UAV) video and Army GUARDRAIL signals intelligence (SIGINT) reports. Host terminals, when tied to broadcast terminals, are capable of providing filtered, processed, and tailored intelligence to satisfy specific intelligence and targeting requirements. See Figure 1-7.

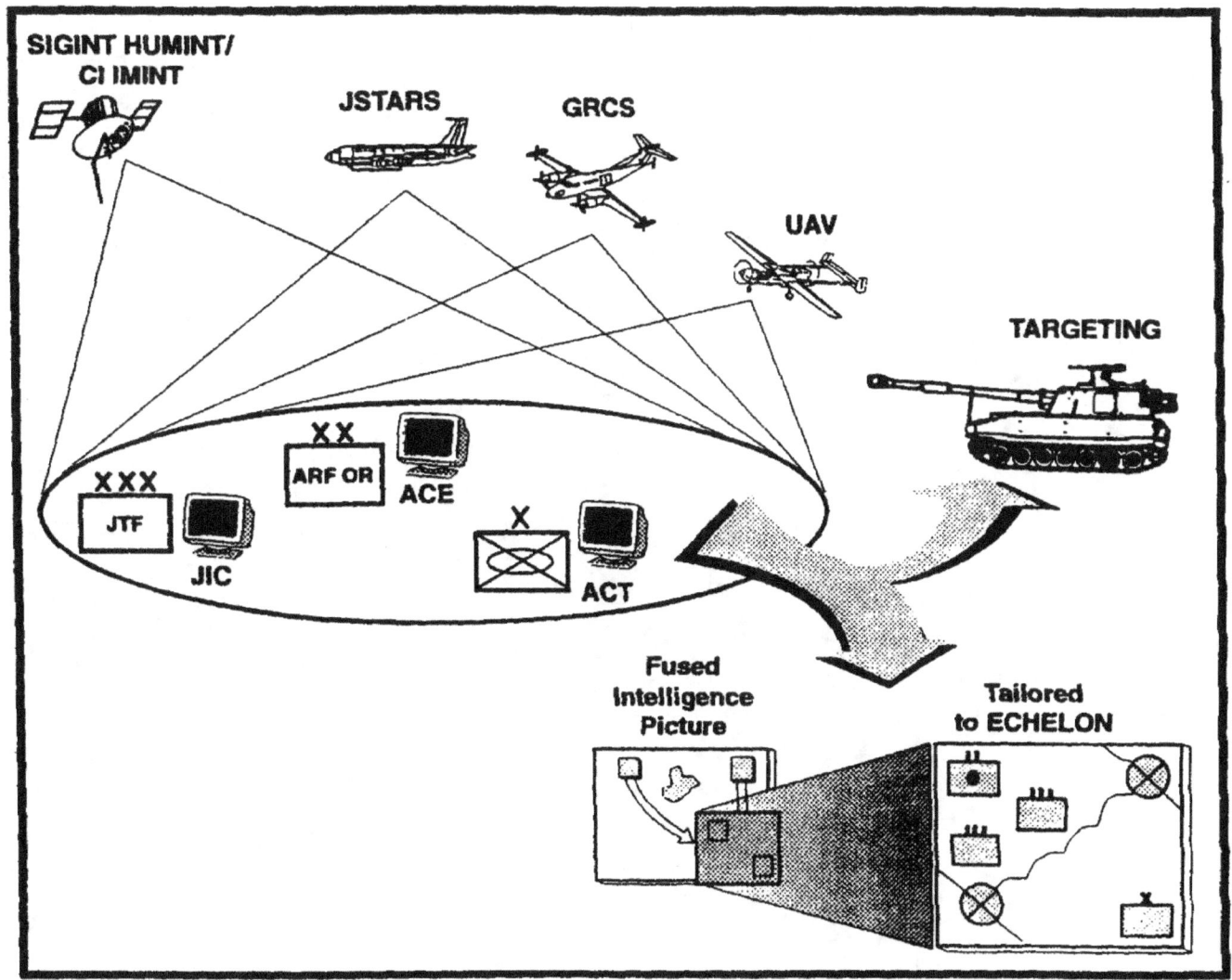

Figure 1-7. Broadcast intelligence and targeting data dissemination.

The ACE is the commander's primary organization for pulling information from broadcast systems and fusing it into tailored intelligence and targeting information. Through its capability to rapidly pull, process, and disseminate intelligence, the AC E- provides the commander with the means to focus and synchronize the intelligence system with his intent and concept of operation. In addition, the ACEs at brigade, division, corps, and theater form a seamless bridge linking the tactical commander with higher echelon organizations where intelligence databases and knowledge reside.

INTELLIGENCE BATTLEFIELD OPERATING SYSTEM

Intelligence supports the Army as a whole through the Intelligence BOS. The Intelligence BOS is a flexible and tailorable architecture of procedures, personnel, organizations, and equipment that responds to the intelligence needs of commanders at all echelons. These structures include intelligence organizations, systems and procedures for collecting, processing, analyzing, and delivering intelligence to decision-makers that need it. Effective communications connectivity and automation are essential components of this architecture.

Since no echelon has all the organic intelligence capabilities it needs to fully support the commander, IEW assets must be employed to support the needs of all echelons. This support is comprehensive and reaches across the range of military operations and levels of intelligence, see figure (2-1). It is the collective entity the force commander uses to produce the intelligence he needs to win on the battlefield. The Intelligence BOS is built upon the premise that the whole is greater than the sum of its parts. It is a combination of space, airborne, and ground-based systems providing the most comprehensive intelligence possible. The Intelligence BOS is always engaged in supporting the commander in war and SASO.

During force projection operations, MI uses Intelligence BOS procedures and architecture, established during peacetime, to ensure that the force commander is supported with accurate and responsive intelligence from predeployment through redeployment.

PRIMARY FEATURES OF THE INTELLIGENCE BOS

There are seven primary features of the Intelligence BOS. Each is described below.

Always Engaged:

The Intelligence BOS is always engaged. Through continuous peacetime intelligence operations, commanders ensure collection, processing, analysis, and dissemination infrastructure is in place and prepared to provide intelligence support throughout the range of military operations. Early intelligence preparation is critical to the commander's decision making and planning process for force projection operations. The commander and G2 (S2) must assess each contingency to determine intelligence requirements and

develop a plan for filling intelligence voids. This primary feature is tempered, however, by the imperative to prioritize efforts and prepare thoroughly for top priority contingency areas.

Downwardly Focused:

Commanders and MI organizations must focus intelligence downwardly to the commander on the ground. Intelligence should get to the subordinate commander, when requested, in a usable format, and focused on his echelon and battle space. Commanders and MI leaders at higher echelons should anticipate the intelligence needs of lower echelons, and "push" tailored intelligence support down to them. Staffs at each echelon should produce intelligence reports (INTREPs) and other products tailored to the needs of their subordinate units. To the extent possible, INTREPs and intelligence summaries (INTSUMs) should be in graphic format with enough text to reduce confusion. Higher echelons must also facilitate the "pull" of intelligence from their databases for both bulk-data requests and specific queries. The lowest echelons should be able to "skip" echelons to access the databases they require to support the commander.

Simultaneously Supported:

Advances in dissemination capabilities allow the Intelligence BOS to provide commanders at multiple echelons with a common picture of the battlefield derived from national, joint, and Army collection assets. In addition, the connectivity available through the Intelligence BOS architecture enables commanders to directly access and "pull" critical intelligence products from different echelons. Thus, while the IEW assets of a corps are focused on the corps commander's PIR, the corps' collection assets and intelligence products are also available and simultaneously supporting the needs of higher and lower echelon commanders.

Coverage Enhanced:

The capabilities and technologies embedded in MI systems enhance the commander's ability to see the width and depth of the battlefield at a higher, more consistent degree of resolution than ever. As a result, commanders have at their disposal more near real time (NRT) and real-time information with targeting accuracy. This enables G2s (S2s) to quickly gather and synthesize information. They can then present the intelligence so that the commander and his staff can quickly assimilate it. Intelligence organizations at each echelon facilitate the synthesis of information through complementing collection, processing, and balanced all-source reporting. For more information on IEW systems, refer to FM 34-8 and FM 34-10-2.

Skip Echelon Flexibility:

The flexibility of the Intelligence BOS supports skip echelon "push" of critical perishable intelligence from national, joint, and theater organizations to the tactical commander. At the same time, a tactical unit is capable of conducting skip echelon "pull" of information from theater, joint, and national data bases to answer the commander's intelligence requirements. The commanders and the intelligence organizations at each echelon determine the extent of skip echelon support. It is the responsibility of organizations conducting skip echelon activities to provide intermediate echelons with the same information. The utility of skip echelon intelligence support is most evident when preparing for and during force projection operations.

Organizations Redesigned:

MI organizations are, or will be, redesigned to take advantage of technology and incorporate lessons learned in order to better serve the needs of commanders. From theater MI brigade to direct support MI company, commanders are provided with a balanced, scalable, and flexible force, which can be tailored to meet any contingency. In cases such as the ACE, assets have been consolidated to permit more effective control and efficient use of limited resources. Organizations like the Corps Military Intelligence Support Element (CMISE), ACE, and DISE were developed to facilitate the "pull" of intelligence for all commanders. Underpinning these structural changes is the manning of MI organizations from battalion to national level with soldiers trained to deal effectively with new technology and concepts.

Disciplined Operations:

The following laws, regulations, and policies ensure disciplined operations support commanders:

- AR 381-10 ensures that intelligence activities will not violate the right to privacy of US citizens.

- United States Signal Intelligence Directives (USSIDs) are the policies and procedures that provide the authority for production and dissemination of SIGINT. USSIDs establish uniform techniques, standards, and support mechanisms for collecting, processing, and reporting SIGINT-derived information.

- Status of Forces Agreements (SOFAs), Rules of Engagement (ROE), international laws, and other documents ensure those intelligence activities does not exacerbate the political situation, which the intelligence operation supports.

- Doctrinal principles and Tactics, Techniques, and Procedures (TTPs) ensure that intelligence activities maximize support to the commander and eliminate nonessential operations.

LIMITATIONS OF THE INTELLIGENCE BOS

The Intelligence BOS is a seamless, unified system that anticipates and satisfies intelligence needs. Commanders ensure its proper employment by clearly articulating intent, decisively designating PIR, and boldly prioritizing the types of targets they want engaged to the entire Intelligence BOS. Commanders must, however, understand the limitations of the Intelligence BOS and not place unrealistic expectations on the system. Major limitations are discussed in the following paragraphs.

- Intelligence reduces uncertainty on the battlefield, but it cannot eliminate it entirely. The commander will always have to accept some risk.

- The Intelligence BOS is comprised of finite resources and capabilities. The density of MI soldiers and IEW systems within a unit is limited. Once lost to action or accident, these soldiers and systems cannot easily be replaced. The loss of qualified language-trained soldiers, and in particular soldiers trained in low-density languages, could adversely affect the ability of a MI unit to accomplish its mission. In addition, IEW systems operate within limited technical parameters and are designed to exploit a specific threat system or type of system.

- The Intelligence BOS cannot effectively and efficiently provide IEW support without adequate communications equipment, capacity, and connectivity. Commanders and G2s (S2s) must ensure communications support to intelligence is given appropriate priority during planning and execution of operations.

- Commanders and G2s (S2s) cannot expect everything needed will be automatically "pushed" to them from higher levels. The "push" of products from higher echelons does not relieve subordinate staffs from conducting detailed analysis and focusing the efforts of higher headquarters (HQ). Nor can they expect products "pushed" to them will always be at the level of detail they require. Commanders and G2s (S2s) must focus higher echelons by clearly articulating and actively pursuing intelligence requirements.

TRAINING THE INTELLIGENCE BOS

Training the Intelligence BOS means training commanders, MI leaders, MI soldiers, and organizations to use it correctly. Commanders must understand the capabilities of the Intelligence BOS and be trained to drive and integrate the system with their operations. MI leaders must understand the tactics of their supported command and learn to synchronize IEW operations with the commander's concept of operation.

MI soldiers must master the technical, tactical, and leadership skills required to employ and maintain sophisticated intelligence systems on the battlefield. Organizations and crew-served systems must be trained to function as a team and integrate their efforts within the Intelligence BOS and with other BOSs. The responsibility for training the Intelligence BOS rests with commanders and intelligence leaders. Commanders are ultimately responsible for the overall training proficiency of their units; however, the G2 (S2) and other intelligence leaders share in that responsibility. The G2 (S2) must assist the commander in developing and integrating realistic intelligence activity into the training of combat, combat support (CS), and combat service support (CSS) units. Realistic training fosters awareness of the capabilities and limitations of the Intelligence BOS in non-MI units while honing the skills of MI soldiers and organizations. Intelligence training should be derived from the organization's Mission Essential Task List (METL), battle tasks, and operation plan (OPLAN) requirements. To the extent possible, intelligence training should be cued to enhance and refine real-world intelligence operations of the organization. Force projection operations, in particular, require realistic and battle focused training of MI personnel and organizations to ensure intelligence readiness.

Training the Total Force in the Intelligence BOS requires embedding realistic intelligence activities into unit training and that conducted in the Combat Training Center programs. Whenever possible, commanders should expand the scope of training at these centers or home stations by linking field training exercises with computer simulations play at other locations. Combat information and intelligence should be incorporated into programs of system trainers and computerized battle simulations to provide realism to crew and staff training.

Intelligence Training Principles:

The following intelligence training principles assist the commander in training his unit:

Execute Real-World Operations. Real-world intelligence operations use all aspects of the Intelligence BOS from the commander developing his PIR to disseminating graphic intelligence products to subordinate commanders. Using the intelligence system in peacetime trains personnel to plan, collect, process, analyze, synthesize, report, and evaluate intelligence. It supports contingency planning and ensures the procedures and connectivity required for force projection operations is valid and available to the commander.

Integrate Intelligence. Integrate intelligence into training and field training exercises (FTX). Use the intelligence cycle and decision making process to train commanders and G2s (S2s) how to interact and develop plans that synchronize IEW support with the commander's operation. The G2 (S2) should always support this effort with appropriate intelligence products and integrate the Intelligence BOS with other battlefield systems.

Understand the Battlefield. Teach the G2 (S2) and MI unit personnel about friendly tactics and operations. Have the G2 (S2) staff participate in or observe training events of combat, CS, and CSS units. The performance of intelligence analysts and collectors at all levels is directly proportional to their understanding of battlefield dynamics.

Apply Standards. Apply standards to IEW training. Standards provide commanders a means of measuring intelligence readiness and equipping subordinates with clearly defined training objectives. TCs 34-10-20, 34-10-20-1, and 34-10-20-2 contains standards which commanders can use to develop a mission essential task list (METL), plan and execute training, and assess performance. By applying these standards with established doctrine and TTP, commanders can ensure commonality of operations between their units and contribute to the effectiveness of the Intelligence BOS.

Maintain Proficiency. Establish consistent approaches to collective and individual training. Collective training should be conducted at a baseline proficiency level consistent with unit readiness standards. Individual training, particularly language training, should be creative and challenge soldiers to go beyond Army standards. The Readiness Training (REDTRAIN) program is one means of maintaining both individual and unit proficiency. Through live environment training, REDTRAIN allows units to employ their soldiers and equipment against potential wartime or SASO targets. Other REDTRAIN opportunities allow soldiers to improve their military occupational specialty (MOS) skills and language proficiency through attendance at specialized technical and language courses.

LESSON 1

PRACTICE EXERCISE

The following items will test your grasp of the material covered in this lesson. There is only one correct answer for each item. When you have completed the exercise, check your answers with the answer key that follows. If you answer any items incorrectly, study again that part of the lesson, which contains the portion involved.

1.   What is done with IEW assets to meet the requirements of the mission and deployment Sequence?

   A.   Directing

   B.   Tailoring

   C.   Synchronizing

   D.   Tasking

2.   Successful force projection IEW support is based on which of the following?

   A.   Split Based Ops

   B.   Push Intel

   C.   Prioritized Intel

   D.   Targeting Requirements

3.   Intelligence synchronization ensures that MI unit commanders have what?

    A. Collection

    B. Requirements

    C. Guidance

    D. Execution

LESSON 1

PRACTICE EXERCISE

ANSWER KEY AND FEEDBACK

ITEM	CORRECT ANSWER AND FEEDBACK
1.	B. Tailoring (page 1-2, para 2)
2.	A. Split-Based Ops (page 14, para 1)
3.	C. Guidance (page 1-5, para 1)

LESSON 2

FUNDAMENTALS OF IEW OPERATIONS

CRITICAL TASKS: 301-372-2014

301-372-2015

301-372-2406

301-372-2602

OVERVIEW

LESSON DESCRIPTION:

In this lesson you will learn the basic concept of IEW operations.

TERMINAL LEARNING OBJECTIVE:

TASKS: Conduct IEW operations using these fundamentals and guidelines.

CONDITIONS: You will be given narrative information and illustrations from FM 34-1, and FM 34-2.

STANDARDS: Identify the fundamental information needed for conducting IEW operations.

REFERENCES: The material contained in this lesson was derived from the following publications:

     FM 6-20-10   FM 34-25-1

     FM 24-33   FM 34-25-2

FM 34-1

FM 34-2

FM 34-5(S)

FM 34-8

FM 34-10-1

FM 34-40(S)

FM 34-54

FM 34-60

FM 34-130

FM 101-5

INTRODUCTION

Throughout history, military leaders have recognized the importance of intelligence. IEW operations are the commander's keys to victory in wand success in SASO. Commanders use IEW to focus the combat power at their disposal to win decisively. Commanders also use IEW to protect and conserve combat power and resources during operations.

The Intelligence BOS described in Lesson 1 is a powerful tool. However, the commander, G2 (S2), MI unit commanders, and other leaders must work hard to exploit the full capabilities of the Intelligence BOS. IEW operations describe the execution of tasks related to the functions of intelligence and EW. This chapter describes the fundamentals of IEW operations.

TOTAL FORCE EFFORT

IEW operations are a total force effort. IEW supports all soldiers from the commander to the individual soldier in combat, CS, and CSS units. All soldiers must appreciate the importance of intelligence and the role IEW plays in-

- Applying and sustaining combat power.

- Contributing to the effectiveness of combined arms operations.

- Understanding the battlefield framework.

- Facilitating quick and accurate decision making during combat operations.

- Seeing, targeting, and simultaneously attacking the enemy throughout the depth of the battlefield.

- Conserving fighting potential of the force.

- Supporting other combat functions (maneuver, fire support, air defense, mobility and survivability, logistics, and battle command).

MI soldiers and organizations specialize in conducting IEW operations in support of the mission and in concert with the commander's intent. While MI units provide dedicated IEW support, all units, by virtue of their mission and AOs, have implied information collecting and reporting tasks. The G2 (S2) must know the intelligence collection and production capabilities of all units in the combat force and at higher echelons to optimize the use of intelligence assets at their disposal.

LEVELS OF INTELLIGENCE

The levels of intelligence correspond to the established levels of war: **strategic, operational,** and **tactical.** Like the levels of war, the levels of intelligence serve as a framework in which commanders and MI personnel visualize the logical flow of operations, allocation of resources, and assignment of tasks. The levels of intelligence are not tied to specific echelons but rather to the intended outcome of the operations, which they support. As illustrated in Figure 2-1, echelons and levels of intelligence vary; the relationship is based upon the political and military objectives of the operation and the commander's needs.

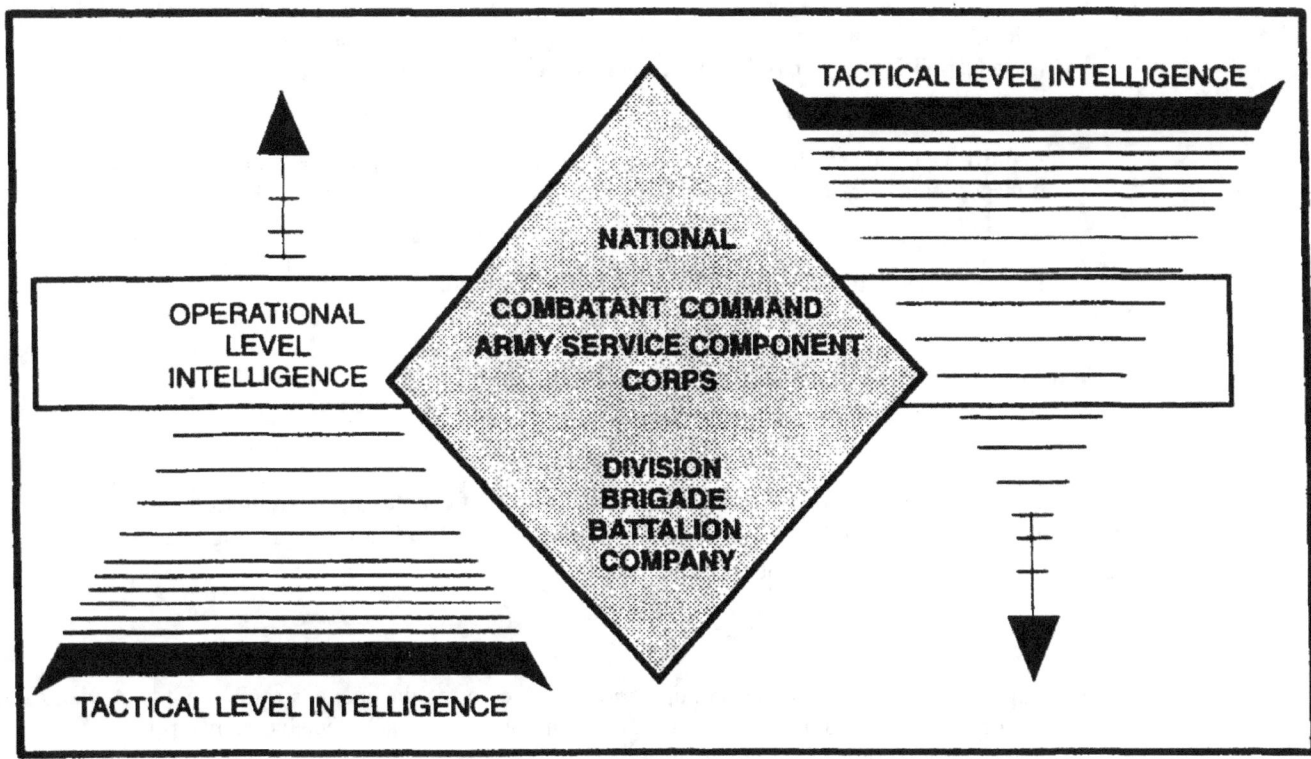

Figure 2-1. Levels of intelligence.

The commander on the pound, regardless of echelon, is provided a mixture of support from each level of intelligence. Strategic intelligence provides information on the host nation's political climate; operational intelligence identifies key objectives for the campaign; and tactical intelligence shows where the enemy can be decisively engaged. Advances in technology and the requirements of the modem battlefield also make the demarcation between strategic, operational, and tactical intelligence resources indistinguishable.

113

Collection assets, which normally support strategic intelligence, can and often are tasked to support operational and tactical intelligence requirements. This blending of levels and resources is a characteristic of intelligence in the post-Cold War era, a characteristic that the Intelligence BOS exploits.

Strategic Intelligence

Strategic intelligence supports the formation of strategy, policy, and military plans and operations at the national and theater levels. Strategic intelligence -

- Concentrates on the national political, economic, and military considerations of states or nations.
- It identifies the support for governments, the ability of states or nations to mobilize for war, the national political objectives, and the personalities of national leaders.

- Identifies a nation's ability to support US Forces and operations (for example, ports and the transportation infrastructure).

- Predicts other nations' responses to US Theater operations.

Operational Intelligence:

Operational intelligence supports the planning and execution of campaigns and major operations, and reflects the nature of the theater of war itself. Intelligence at this level serves as a bridge between strategic and tactical. Operational intelligence -

- Supports friendly campaigns and operations by predicting the enemy's campaign plans, identifying their military centers of gravity, lines of communication (LOC), decisive points, pivots of maneuver, and other components necessary for campaign design.

- Focuses primarily on the intelligence needs of commanders from theater through corps and task force.

Tactical Intelligence:

Tactical intelligence supports the execution of battles and engagements. It provides the tactical commander with the intelligence he needs to employ combat elements against enemy forces and achieve the objectives of the operational commander. Tactical intelligence is distinguished from other levels by its perishability and ability to immediately influence the outcome of the tactical commander's mission. Tactical intelligence normally supports operations by echelons corps and below (ECB) units.

INTELLIGENCE DISCIPLINES AND FUNCTIONS

To dearly describe MI, the various intelligence areas are divided into four intelligence disciplines: human intelligence (HUMINT), imagery intelligence (IMINT), measurement and signature intelligence (MASINT), and SIGINT. The two multidiscipline intelligence functions are: CI and technical intelligence (TECHINT). Personnel who specialize in one of the areas of intelligence operations perform these disciplines and functions. To be effective and minimize threat deception, every intelligence operation must attempt to use all disciplines. The disciplines themselves must complement and cue each other for maximum effectiveness. Rarely will separate disciplines produce a comprehensive picture of the threat. Instead, each discipline will produce bits and pieces of information which analysts will synthesize to create a total picture.

Human Intelligence:

HUMTINT is the oldest of the intelligence disciplines. HUMINT is particularly important in force protection during SASO. Although HUMINT can be a sole collection discipline, it is normally employed to confirm, refute, or augment intelligence derived through other disciplines. HUMINT is less restricted by weather or the cooperation of the enemy than technical means and does not require fire, maneuver, or communications to collect. HUMINT is restricted by access to targets and timeliness and, by its nature, can be risky to the safety of the collectors. HUMINT collection is well suited to the initial detection of emerging threats if placement and access are established early. The success of HUMINT in areas not previously targeted will be marginal in the early phases of a conflict or SASO. Its effectiveness improves as HUMINT refocuses its efforts on the AO.

Interrogation and document exploitation are examples of HUMINT operations. HUMINT collection may also be conducted by long-range surveillance units (LRSU), scouts, and patrols. Examples of other sources of HUMINT are pilot debriefings, refugees, and defectors. Furthermore, special operations forces (SOF) operating in hostile, denied, or politically sensitive areas provide a unique HUMINT source. For more information on HUMINT, refer to FM 34-5(S) and FM 34-52.

Imagery Intelligence:

IMINT is the product of imagery analysis. Imagery is derived from, but is not limited to, radar, infrared, optical, and electro-optical sensors. IMINT and imagery systems increase the commander's ability to quickly and clearly understand his battle space and AI. IMINT is an important source of intelligence for intelligence preparation of the battlefield (IPB), targeting, terrain and environmental analysis, and battle damage assessment (BDA). IMINT is often the primary source of intelligence for the physical damage assessment portion of BDA. IMINT is subject to some limitations. Because most imagery requires ground processing and analysis, IMINT may be unable to respond to time-sensitive requirements. Adverse weather and the vulnerability of the platform may also hamper imagery collection. As with other intelligence sources, IMINT is subject to threat attempts at deception. IMINT is most effective when used to cue other collection systems or to verify information provided by other sources. Systems that provide IMINT include the U2R Advanced Synthetic Aperture Radar System (ASARS), Joint surveillance target attack radar systems (J-STARS), unmanned aerial vehicle (UAV), and TENCAP systems. For more information on IMINT, refer to FM 34-25-1, FM 34-25-2; and TC 34-55.

Measurement and Signature Intelligence:

MASINT uses information gathered by technical instruments such as radar, lasers, passive electro-optical sensors, radiation detectors, seismic, and other sensors to measure objects or events to identify them by their signatures. MASINT is critical for updating data on smart munitions. As future adversaries develop new technologies to evade some of the SIGINT and IMINT collection systems, MASINT will be used as another means of sensing the enemy. MASINT exploits other information that is not gained through SIGINT, IMINT, or HUMINT. The Remotely Monitored Battlefield Sensor System (REMBASS) is an example of a MASINT collector. For more information on REMBASS, refer to FM 34-10-1.

Signals Intelligence:

SIGINT results from collecting, locating, processing, analyzing, and reporting intercepted communications and noncommunications (for example, radar) emitters. SIGINT provides the commander with valuable, often near real time (NRT) intelligence and targeting information on enemy intentions, readiness status, and dispositions by intercepting and locating enemy command, maneuver, fire support, reconnaissance, air defense, and logistics emitters. SIGINT operations require efficient collection management and synchronization to effectively overcome and exploit enemy efforts to protect his critical communications and weapons systems through emissions control, communications operating procedures, encryption, and deception. SIGINT is subdivided into: communications intelligence (COMINT); electronic intelligence (ELINT); and foreign instrumentation signals intelligence (FISINT).

Examples of SIGINT ground-based intercept and direction finding (DF) systems are the AN/PRD-12, the AN/TRQ-32A (V) 2 (TEAMMATE), and the AIWRQ-I 52 (TRACKWOLF) systems. The GUARDRAIL Common Sensor (GRCS) is an example of an airborne intercept and DF system for both communications and noncommunications emitters. The AN/FSQ-144V (TROJAN) is the Army's remote collection system supporting in-garrison collection by tactical MI units.

Counterintelligence:

The essence of the Army's CI mission is to support force protection. By its nature, CI is a multidiscipline (counter-HUMINT, counter-IMINT, and counter-SIGINT) function designed to defeat or degrade threat intelligence and targeting capabilities. Multidiscipline counterintelligence (MDCI) is an integral and equal part of IEW. MDCI operations support force protection through support to operations security (OPSEC), deception, and rear area operations across the range of military operations.

Examples of MDCI support to operations security (OPSEC) range from evaluating components of a unique signature for a particular unit's tactical command post (CP) to strategic level MDCI support to special access programs.

MDCI personnel advise deception planners on the vulnerabilities of threat foreign intelligence services (FISs) and associated battlefield collection systems to various friendly deception capabilities and techniques. This input is important because a deception plan cannot succeed if the enemy has no means to collect the details of the deception story. The MDCI estimate provides significant input to the deception estimate.

MDCI personnel support rear area operations through collection, analysis, and reporting of threats to the rear area. They work with military police, Civil Affairs (CA), and psychological operations (PSYOP) elements to provide intelligence support to rear area security. They assist combat, CS, and CSS staffs in developing the MDCI estimate of the rear area threat for integration into OPLANs and operation orders (OPORDs). Under the direction of the G2 (S2), MDCI personnel support the Rear Area Operations Center (RAOC) commander by assessing rear base vulnerabilities and recommending countermeasures. MDCI personnel also provide the RAOC commander with indications and warnings (I&W) on rear area threats and assist with the countermeasures to such threats. For more information on MDCI functions and activities, refer to FM 34-5(S) and FM 34-60.

Technical Intelligence (TECHINT):

TECHINT is a multidiscipline function, which supports commanders by either identifying or countering an enemy's momentary technological advantage, or by maintaining a friendly technological advantage. Collecting, analyzing, and processing information in foreign technological developments obtain TECHINT. It also results from studying the performance of foreign material and its operational capabilities. The two parts of TECHINT, battlefield TECHINT and scientific and technical intelligence (S&TI), support commanders at all levels.

- Battlefield TECHINT provides operational and tactical commanders with immediate and usable intelligence on the capabilities and limitations of captured threat equipment. Battlefield

117

TECHINT also results in the identification and evacuation of critical items of threat materiel requiring detailed S&TI analysis.

- S&TI provide detailed analysis on the technical characteristics of foreign systems and materiel. This results in the development of battlefield countermeasures to threat systems. S&TI also provide information on foreign developments in applied research, which support Army Force Modernization.
- Battlefield TECHINT frequently starts with one conscientious soldier who finds something new on the battlefield and takes proper steps to report it. The information or item is exploited at succeeding higher levels until a countermeasure is produced to neutralize the technological advantage or exploit the vulnerability. While a single weapon or technology seldom means the difference between final victory and defeat, it can give one side a battlefield advantage.

-

- A mutually dependent relationship that exists between the support the commander gets from the TECHINT system and the support the TECHINT system gets from the commander. Operational and tactical commanders provide the raw material analysts need to identify, capture, protect, and evacuate enemy equipment, documents, and other items. Commanders further ensure the success of the process by demanding TECHINT support for the tactical effort to defeat the enemy. The analysts then take the raw material and produce the countermeasures commanders need to overcome an enemy's technological advantage. For more information on TECHINT, refer to FM 34-54.

-

- **CHARACTERISTICS OF EFFECTIVE INTELLIGENCE**

-

- The effectiveness of intelligence is measured against the following standards:

-

- **Timely**:

- Intelligence must be provided early enough to support planning, influence decisions and execution of operations, and prevent surprise from enemy action. It must flow continuously to the commander before, during and after an operation. Regardless of distance and time, intelligence organizations, databases, and products must be available to develop estimates, make decisions, and plan operations.

-

- **Relevant**:

- Intelligence must support the commander's concept of operation and the unit's mission. It must be tailored to the capabilities of the unit and intelligence priorities of the commander. Intelligence must be in usable format, which meets the specific needs of the requestor and explains its own significance.

-

- **Accurate**:

Intelligence must give the commander a balanced, complete, and objective picture of the enemy and the operational environment. It should support and satisfy the priorities of the commander. To the extent possible, intelligence should correctly identify threat intentions, capabilities, limitations, and dispositions. It should be derived from multiple sources and disciplines to minimize the possibility of deception or misinterpretation. Alternative or contradictory assessments should be presented, when necessary, to ensure balance and bias-free intelligence.

Predictive:

Intelligence should tell the commander what the enemy is doing, can do, and his most likely course of action (COA). It should anticipate the intelligence needs of the commander.

PRIMARY INTELLIGENCE TASKS

MI accomplishes its mission through six primary tasks, which generate intelligence synchronized to support the commander's mission and intelligence requirements. The derived products assist the commander in focusing and protecting his combat power. Figure 2-2 illustrates how the six intelligence tasks aid the commander in decision making. The six tasks can be thought of as the METL for intelligence. As such, these tasks serve as a framework for intelligence training. The six intelligence tasks-

- Provide I&W.

- Perform IPB.

- Perform situation development.

- Perform target development and support to targeting.

- Support force protection.

- Perform BDA.

119

INTELLIGENCE TASKS	COMMANDER's FOCUS	COMMANDER's DECISION
I&W	ORIENT ON CONTINGENCIES	Increase intelligence readiness? Implement OPLAN?
IPB	PLAN A MISSION	Which COA will I implement? Where is my main effort?
SITUATION DEVELOPMENT	EXECUTE AND MANAGE A PLAN	Are these enemy actions expected? Is a FRAGO required now?
TARGET DEVELOPMENT AND SUPPORT TO TARGETING	DESTROY/SUPPRESS/ NEUTRALIZE TARGETS	Does destruction of this target accomplish my objective? When do I execute this fire mission?
FORCE PROTECTION	SECURE THE FORCE	Is my intent obvious to the enemy? Will I launch a preemptive strike?
BDA	REALLOCATE INTELLIGENCE AND ATTACK ASSETS	Is my fire and maneuve effective? Do I refire the same targets?

Figure 2-2 The G2 (2) tailors intelligence to the commander's needs.

Indications and Warnings:

The commander uses I&W for early warning to prevent surprise through anticipation and reduce the risk from enemy actions that are counter to planning assumptions. This enables him to quickly reorient the force to unexpected contingencies and shape the battlefield by manipulating enemy activities. I&W help a commander decide whether to maintain or increase unit readiness levels if hostilities are likely. In force projection operations, I&W provide the commander time to plan and surge the intelligence effort for the impending operation. Detection of developments which initiate force projection operations requires that intelligence readiness be developed and maintained through pre-crisis intelligence operations.

The commander and 02 (S2) integrate intelligence requirements to support I&W into the total unit collection plan. Collection plans and supporting SORs are developed during the decision making process. The G2 (S2) develops reporting procedures (for example, "FLASH" designation) in support of I&W requirements to ensure the commander can implement the appropriate OPLAN in a timely manner.

During war and SASO, the G2 (S2) identifies those actions by threat and potential threat groups that would change the basic nature of the operations. Examples of such activities include-

- First use of weapons of mass destruction (nuclear, biological, and chemical [NBC] weapons).

- First violation of international treaties.

- Introduction of weapons to counter a specific friendly advantage or strength.

- Unexpected commitment of threat forces into the battle space.

- Unexpected changes in the threat's intent, will, or targets.

- Changes in the population's support to friendly operations.

In all cases, I&W alerts the unit commander to move the unit from its current mission to a contingency, branch, or sequel operation.

Intelligence Preparation of the Battlefield:

The commander uses IPB to understand the battlefield and the options it resents to friendly and threat forces. IPB is a systematic, continuous process of analyzing the threat and environment in a specific geographic area. The process consists of four steps: defining the battlefield environment, describing the battlefield effects, evaluating the threat, and determining threat COAs. By applying the IPB process, the commander gains the information necessary to selectively apply and maximize his combat power at critical points in time and space on the battlefield.

The commander focuses the G2 (S2) effort and the PB process by clearly defining his PIR. The G2 (S2) then uses the PB process to continually assess threats to, and opportunities for, the friendly force. This assessment helps the commander initiate OPLANs, branches, and sequels. The PB process and access to the intelligence system also allows logistics planners to develop the logistics preparation of the theater plan and other support plans.

Using the PB process, the G2 (S2) predicts threat COAs and identifies the events that will enable them to confirm or deny each threat COA. The commander and staff use the results to wargame threat COAs against friendly actions, evaluate future threat actions, and perform situation and target development. This generates refined intelligence requirements, which the G2 (S2) staff includes in the intelligence synchronization matrix as well as the decision support template

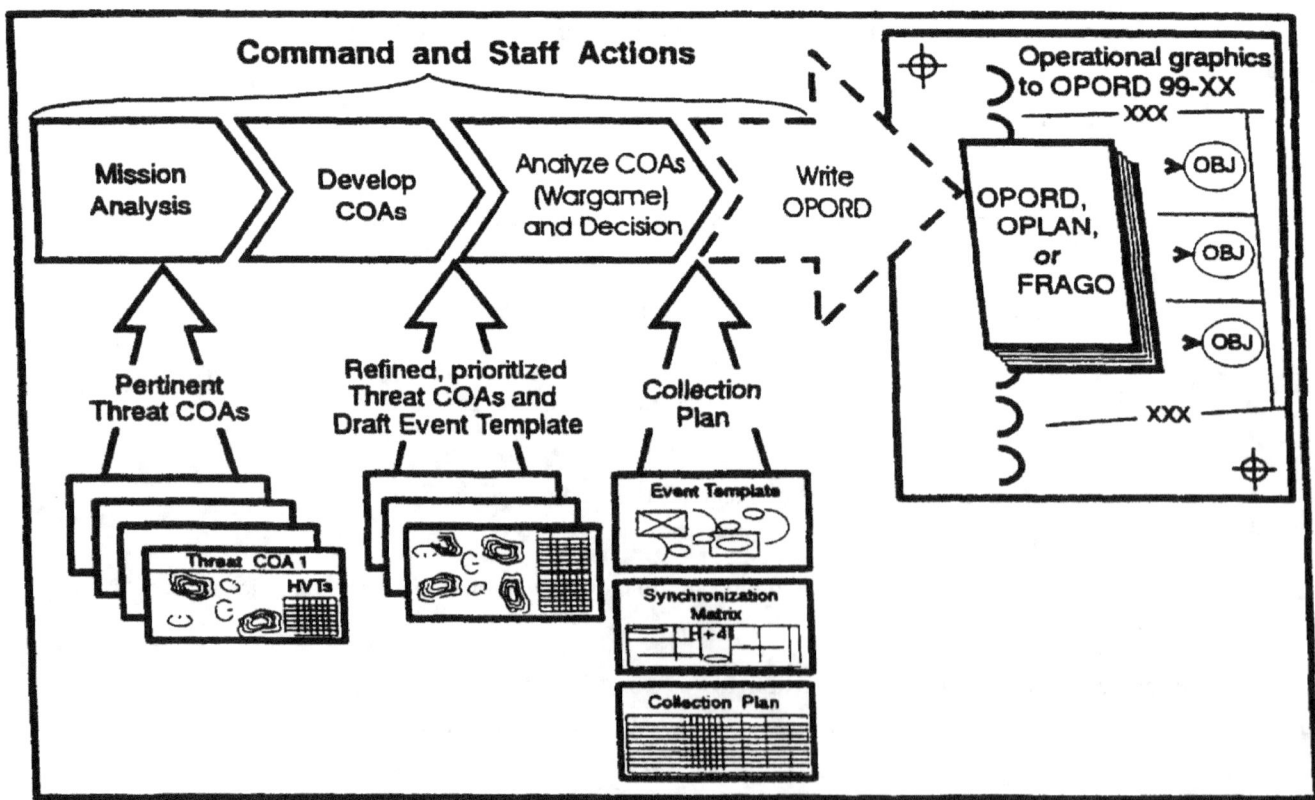

Figure 2-3. The G2 (S2) must support the decision makin process with specific products.

(DST) produced by the G3 (S3). These products support the commander and staff in decision making by developing specific unit OPLANs or OPORDs. As shown in Figure 2-3, the G2 (S2) must have some basic IPB products ready before the staff begins each step of the staff planning process. For more information on IPB, refer to FM 34-130.

Situation Development

The commander uses situation development to help understand the battlefield, thereby reducing risk and uncertainty while executing his plan. Situation development provides an estimate of the enemy's combat effectiveness. Based on the results of continuous IPB, it confirms or denies enemy COAs and explains what the enemy is doing in relation to the friendly force commander's intent. Situation development helps the commander in his decisions to execute branches and sequels as the operation develops.

In situation development, the G2 (S2) and collection managers use the DST, collection plan, intelligence synchronization matrix, and SOR. The G2 (S2) uses these tools to state types of information needed, the degree of specificity, and the latest time information is of value (LTIOV). These products synchronize intelligence requirements to the decisions that the commander and staff expect to make during the upcoming operation. See Figure 24.

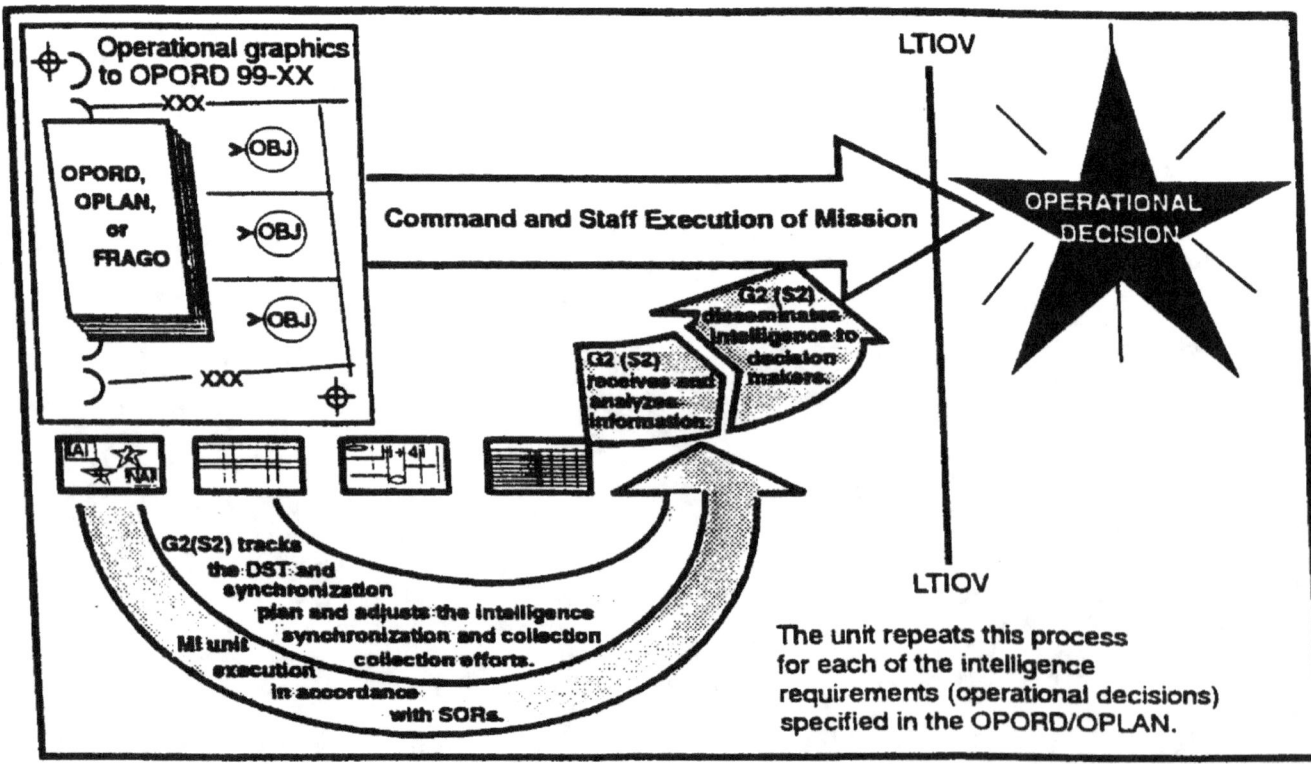

Figure 2-4. The G2(S2) must synchronize intelligence requirement.

As the battle, operation, or campaign progresses, the G2 (S2) uses the intelligence synchronization matrix and DST to anticipate which decisions the commander and staff will soon make. The G2 (S2) and collection managers implement the intelligence synchronization and collection plan by issuing SORs to intelligence BOS units, including non-MI units. SORs explicitly state the information required, where to focus collection, the LTIOV, and where to report the information. The G2 (S2) must anticipate future COAs to allow time for MI assets to be tasked and repositioned. The G2 (S2) monitors and, when required, redirects intelligence operations to deliver the intelligence required for each decision in a timely manner.

Situation development is especially demanding for MI units. As an asset manager, the MI commander must anticipate and wargame the collection positions for each of his IEW systems throughout the operation. Based upon the results of this wargaming, the MI unit commander may prompt the supported unit's staff to reconsider select elements of its plan.

Target Development and Support to Targeting:

The commander uses intelligence in target development to effectively employ nonlethal electronic attack (EA) and lethal fires. Target development provides targets and targeting for attack by fire, maneuver, and electromagnetic means. Our ability to broadcast target information to multiple echelons in NRT makes the "detect" function of targeting almost instantaneous. This demands that the "decide" phase of targeting be accomplished in detail as an integral part of the commander's concept of operation.

Intelligence support to target development provides targets and targeting to unit attack systems and collection assets for exploitation. The G2 (S2) uses the same techniques as described in the IPB and Situation Development sections above. Additionally, during wargaming, the G2 (S2) participates in the targeting process led by the fire support officer (FSO). During the "decide" function of the targeting process, the G2 (S2) will identify the high-value targets (HVTs) which are critical to the enemy commander's COA. Through wargaming, the targeting team or board reduces this set of targets to the high-payoff targets (HPTs). HPTs are HVTs, which must be acquired, tracked, and successfully attacked in order for the commander's mission to succeed. The G2 (S2) advises the commander on the viability of collection against each HPT.

As required, the G2 (S2) establishes procedures for the direct sensor to shooter" dissemination of targeting information from collection assets to the fire support element (FSE) and targeting cell. Direct dissemination enables the FSE and targeting cell to rapidly pass identified HPTs and other targets directly to the FSE of the supporting unit or, if authorized by the commander, to the firing unit. The G3 (S3) and FSO must identify the requirements for direct dissemination during the "decide" phase of the targeting process. The G2 (S2) and FSO must also establish controls in the "detect" phase to revalidate planned targets. The G2 (S2) must incorporate these requirements into the SOR and establish a system to track the status of each request. These procedures require considerable coordination between the commander, G3 (S3), G2 (S2), electronic warfare officer (EWO), FSO, field artillery intelligence officer, MI unit, and firing unit to be effectively executed. Additionally, targeting information relating to deep attack must be disseminated to elements such as the Deep Operations Coordination Cell (DOCC). The analysis and control element (ACE) is a crucial interface with the DOCC for intelligence support to the deep battle.

Commanders, G3s (S3s), G2s (S2s), and fire support personnel must realize that risks are inherent when acting upon NRT targeting information, particularly in an automated environment. Criteria should be established for using and confirming NRT targeting information to reduce the possibility of engaging the wrong enemy target or, worse, friendly forces. In addition, automation in the targeting process should not replace the human check and balance system needed to reduce the possibility of fratricide. For more information on the targeting process and intelligence, refer to FM 6-20-10.

Force Protection

The commander uses the Intelligence BOS to support force protection. Intelligence operations- MDC1 operations in particular-identify, locate, and target an enemy's ability to target and affect friendly forces, facilities, and operations. Intelligence support to force protection must-

- Identify and counter enemy intelligence collection capabilities.

- Assess, through MDCI, friendly vulnerabilities and the threat's ability to exploit those vulnerabilities.

- Identify the enemy's perception of friendly centers of gravity and how he will attack or influence them.

- Identify potential countermeasures to deny enemy access to friendly critical areas.

- Conduct threat and risk assessment.

With this intelligence, the commander decides which countermeasures must be used to shield his intentions, present false images to the enemy commander, and protect his force, Commanders and staffs use force protection intelligence to-

- Enable the commander to plan for passive and active OPSEC, counterreconnaissance, deception, and other security measures.

126

- Plan health service support, logistics operations, and troop safety measures.

- Reduce the probability of fratricide by accurately locating enemy forces through timely PB and situation development.

- Contribute to threat avoidance once the risk is identified.

Force protection prompts the commander and staff to develop countermeasures against the threat's best opportunities. These are usually in the form of preventive measures (for example, levels of readiness) and reactionary measures (for example, quick reaction forces). The preventive measures do not require support by a new intelligence requirement, but the reactionary measures might. The G2 (S2) also establishes appropriate reporting procedures (for example, FLASH precedence reporting) for force protection intelligence similar to those used for reporting I&W intelligence. Additionally, the G2 (S2) should periodically prompt a review of friendly vulnerabilities and the threat's ability for exploitation. Users of force protection intelligence support vary widely across the battlefield. For example -

- Commanders and G3s (S3s) need to know the effectiveness of deception operations.

- G2 (S2) and G3 (S3) staffs use it to plan aggressive force protection measures such as deception and counterreconnaissance, intelligence, surveillance, and target acquisition (C-RISTA).

- OPSEC and deception managers need to know where enemy intelligence assets are focused.

- Leaders of all units need to know which OPSEC countermeasures are effective and necessary, and which measures can be eliminated.

- Headquarters commandants, Level II response forces, and rear area commanders need to know the likelihood of Levels I and II threats to the rear area so they will know which security measures are necessary and which are unnecessary. For more information on threat levels, refer to FM 34-52.

- CA and PSYOP personnel use force protection intelligence to ensure that their activities support deception and CI operations.

Battle Damage Assessment

Intelligence supports the assess phase of the targeting process through the BDA process. The commander uses BDA to determine if his operational and targeting actions have met his conditions for initiating subsequent COAs or beginning the next phase of an operation. If the desired operational conditions have not been met, BDA gives the commander the information necessary to decide *if*, *when* and *how* the targets should be reengaged. It also estimates the enemy's remaining military capabilities and potential at different points throughout the mission or operation.

BDA is the timely and accurate estimate of damage resulting from the application of military force, either lethal or nonlethal, against an objective or target. BDA includes physical and functional damage assessments as well as target system assessment. The most accurate BDA is derived from multiple sources and the results of all-source analysis. Although producing BDA is primarily an intelligence responsibility, it requires extensive coordination with operational elements to be effective. It also requires that common procedures and methodology be established which synchronize and integrate Army BDA with those at joint and national levels.

The commander, supported by the G2 (S2), must decide what critical areas require BDA to determine if the targeting effect for operational success has been achieved. These areas form the commander's BDA-related PIR and must be prioritized against his other PIR developed during the targeting process. The G2 (S2) integrates the commander's BDA-related PIR into the intelligence collection plan and target engagement windows. Since allocating collection resources for acquiring and tracking damage could divert IEW assets from other missions, BDA-related PIR should only address the commander's most critical requirements. The G2 (S2) ensures intelligence collected on BDA-related PIR is integrated into the targeting process, specifically the G3 (S3) combat assessment.

BDA is a complex and dynamic process, which seldom falls out of routine intelligence collection. Commanders and staffs must conduct front-end analysis and establish criteria to identify the precise operational and targeting effect required to support specific decisions. Success in the BDA process and the combat assessment function of the targeting process are achieved when the commander has the information necessary to quickly decide -

- When to proceed with his original concept of operations and schedule of fires.

- When to restrike a target to ensure the desired effect is accomplished.

- When to execute a branch to the operation because the desired effect cannot be achieved with constrained resources.

THE INTELLIGENCE CYCLE

Intelligence operations follow a five-step process known as the intelligence cycle. The intelligence cycle is focused on the commander's mission and concept of operation. The overarching principle of the cycle is intelligence synchronization. Each step within the cycle must be synchronized with the commander's decision making and operational requirements to successfully influence the outcome of the operation. See Figure 2-5.

Plan and Direct:

IPB is the primary intelligence task, which helps the G2 (S2) focus and direct this step and the remaining steps of the intelligence cycle. Planning and directing involves task organizing MI assets; identifying personnel, logistics, and communications requirements, identifying, prioritizing, and validating intelligence requirements, developing a collection plan and synchronization matrix, issuing SORs for collection and production, and monitoring the availability of collection information.

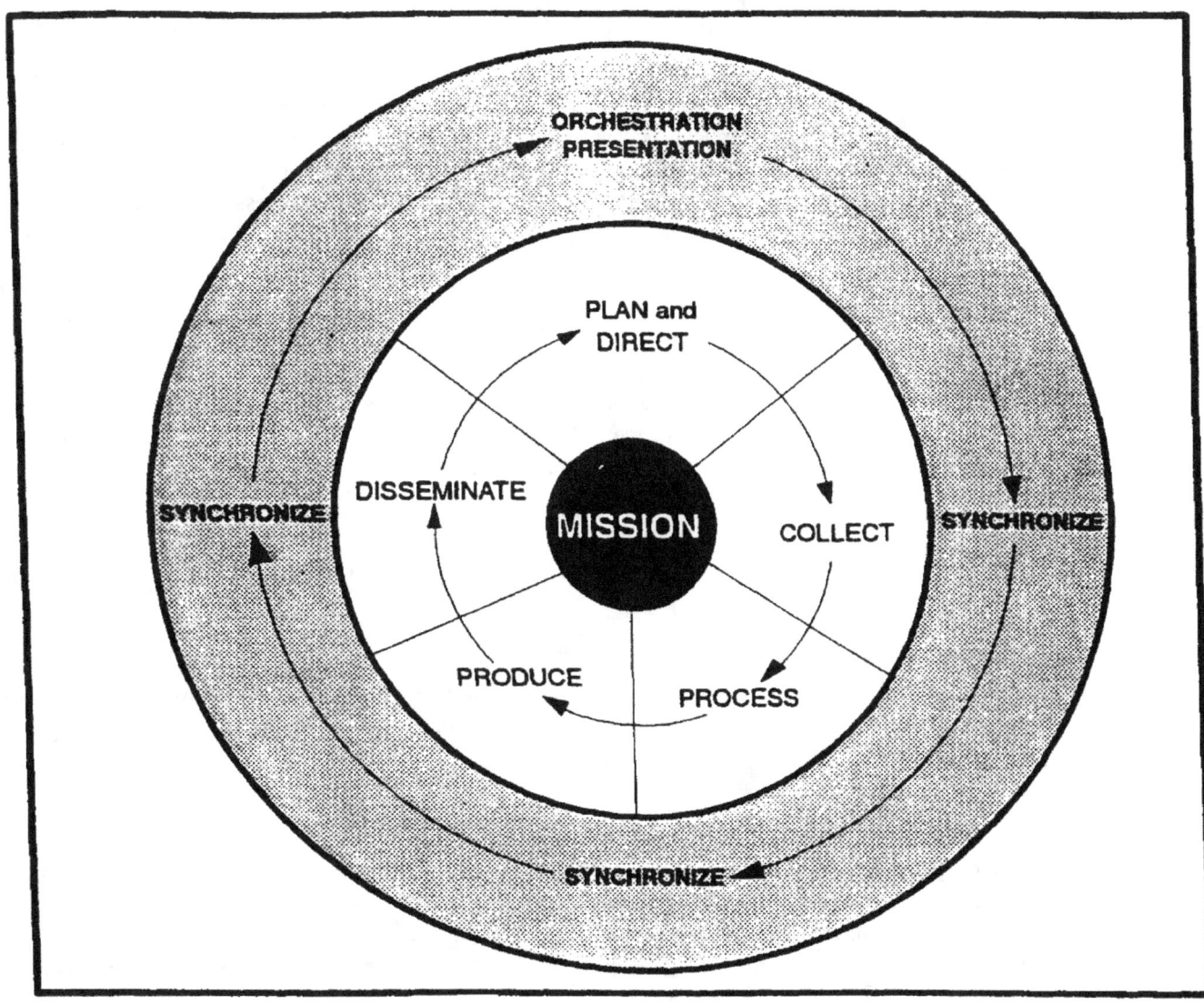

Figure 2-5. The intelligence cycle.

Collect:

Collecting is acquiring information and providing this information to the processing and production elements. It includes the maneuver and positioning of intelligence assets to locations favorable to satisfying collection objectives.

Process:

Processing is the conversion of collected information into a suitable form that can be readily used to produce intelligence. Processing includes data from conversion, photographic development, and transcription and translation of foreign language material. As with collection management, processing must be prioritized and synchronized with the commander's PIR. Effective processing management ensures that critical information is extracted and processed ahead of information of lesser immediate value.

Produce:

Producing involves the integration, evaluation, analysis, and synthesis of information from single or multiple sources into intelligence. At the tactical level, time constraints and demands of the battle tend to make the processing and producing steps indistinguishable.

Disseminate:

Disseminating intelligence is the timely conveyance of intelligence to users in a usable form. The diversity of forms and means requires interoperability among command, control, communications, and intelligence (C^3I) systems.

The intelligence cycle is a continuous process in which steps are executed concurrently, though not always sequentially. For example, while new information is being collected to satisfy one set of requirements, the G2 (S2) plans and redirects efforts to meet new demands while intelligence produced from previously collected information is disseminated. One or several iterations of the intelligence cycle may be conducted depending on the time constraints of the mission.

COMMANDERS INTELLIGENCE REQUIRMENTS

The commander directs the intelligence effort by selecting and prioritizing intelligence requirements. They support the commander in conducting and planning operations. The information the commander needs to visualize the outcome of current operations is called the commander's critical information requirements (CCIRs). CCIRs include information on both friendly and threat forces. The threat information portion of the CCIR is the commander's PIR. In designating PMR, the commander establishes-

- **What** he wants (intelligence required).

- **Why** he wants it (dependent decision).

- **When** he wants it (LTIOV).

- **How** he wants it (format, method of delivery).

The commander uses the decision making process to define PIR, select friendly COAs, and refine intelligence requirements. The decision making process includes mission analysis; developing COAs; analyzing and comparing COAs; decision making; and execution. The staff assists commander in developing intelligence requirements and will generate additional ones in support of the concept of operation and targeting as needed. Each requirement supports a decision expected to occur during the execution of the selected COA. The commander and staff establish these requirements to fill the gaps and voids in the unit's common understanding of the battlefield as shown in Figure 2-6. For more information on PIR development, refer to FM 34-2, Appendix B, and FM 34-8, Appendix A.

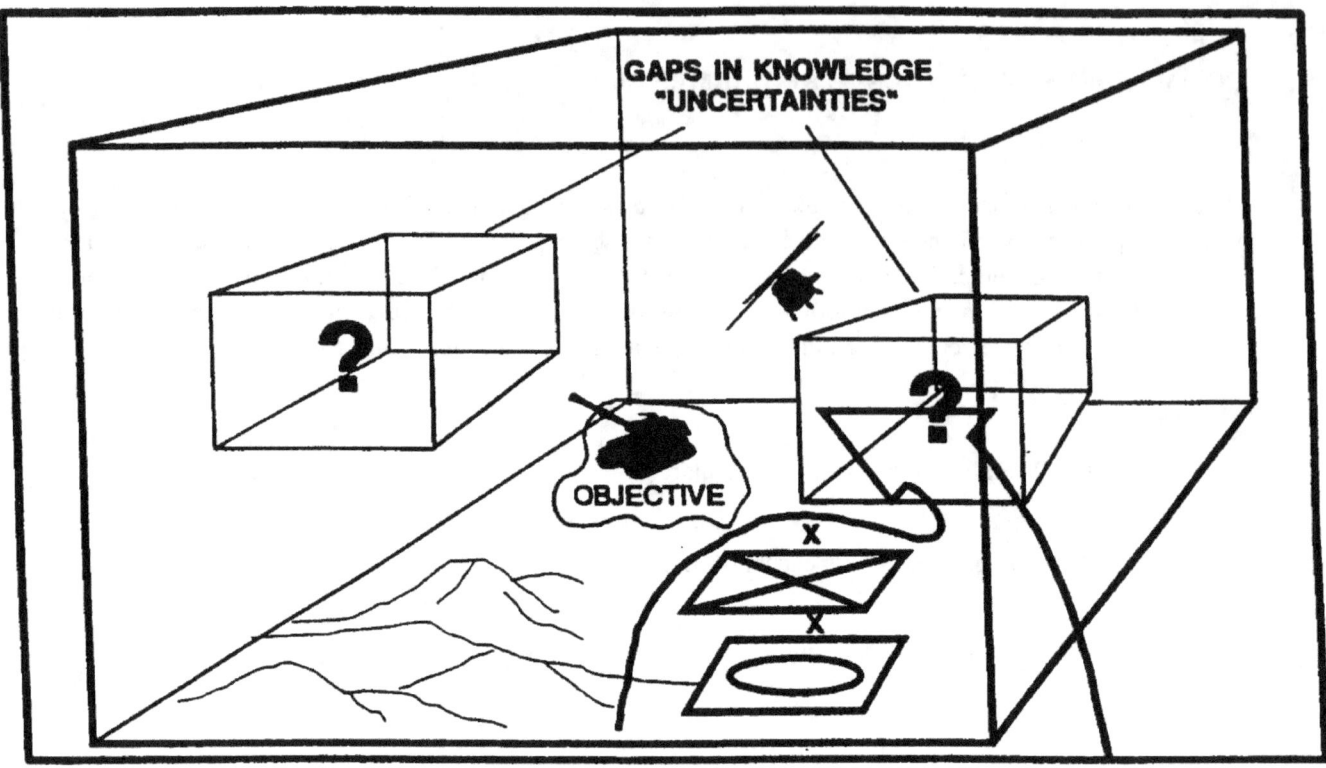

Figure 2-6. The common understanding of the battlefield.

Mission Analysis:

The commander uses IPB products to assess the facts about the battle space and to understand how friendly and threat forces will interact on the battlefield. Mission analysis, supported by IPB, identifies gaps in the command's knowledge of threat forces, the operational environment, and its effects on potential COAs. During mission analysis, the commander identifies his CCIR which provide the G2 (S2) with initial PIR.

Develop Courses of Action:

The commander and staff develop friendly COAs based on facts and assumptions identified during mission analysis. The G2 (S2) ensures that realistic expectations of the intelligence BOS are considered when developing friendly COAs and that most likely enemy COAs are accurately presented.

Analyze and Compare Courses of Action:

132

Using wargaming, the commander and staff" fight" the set of threat COAs against each potential friendly COA. This enables them to assess when and where they might require intelligence about the threat or events at key areas. These key areas become named areas of interest (NAIs). When, as a result of wargaming, the commander determines he must make a decision based on activity at an NAI, that NAI becomes a decision point (DP) or creates a DP related to that NAI. The information needed by the commander to make that decision becomes an intelligence requirement.

Among the tools the staff uses to record the results of wargaming are the DST and BOS synchronization plan. The DST normally depicts DP and time phase lines (TPLs) associated with an event or decision as well as the commander's options. The synchronization plan supports the DST. It depicts NAIs and DPs, the LTIOV, the commander's options for each BOS, and TPLs associated with a DP and the commander's options.

The G2 (S2) incorporates NAIs, decision points, and HPTs identified during the wargame into a prioritized list of intelligence requirements. He develops and evaluates collection strategies for each intelligence requirement and ensures that intelligence collection is capable of supporting the friendly COA.

Decision Making:

The commander, with staff recommendations, decides upon a COA and issues implementing orders. He approves the intelligence requirements associated with that COA and designates the most important as PIR.

The commander prioritizes the complete set of intelligence requirements which includes his-

- Own command.

- Subordinate commands and adjacent units in the form of specific requests for intelligence.

- Higher command in the form of specific requests for intelligence.

PIRs are the key intelligence requirements, listed in priority order, which the unit must answer or satisfy to achieve mission success. PIRs support the planned operation and associated branches and sequels. The commander's PIRs drive the intelligence cycle.

Execution:

The G2 (S2) synchronizes the intelligence operation with the combat operation to ensure the Intelligence BOS provides the required intelligence when needed. He identifies the indicators and specific information requirements (SIR) necessary to satisfy each PIR. The G2 (S2) will allocate most of his efforts to those requirements designated as PIR, and develops a collection plan and synchronization matrix.

This collection plan includes direction to organic assets and coordination with higher echelons for collection requirements beyond the organic capabilities of the unit. The collection management and synchronization process orchestrates, prioritizes, and focuses the Intelligence BOS. The plan includes the collection, processing, and dissemination required to support each intelligence requirement. The intelligence synchronization matrix ensures intelligence collection, analysis, and dissemination are in concert with the commander's operation. Synchronization ensures the commander receives the intelligence he needs, in the form in which he can use it, and in time to influence his decision making.

As the commander executes his selected COA, the G2 (S2) and collection managers monitor the execution of the collection plan. They use the intelligence synchronization matrix to ensure -

- Collection assets are focused on the proper PIR at each stage of the operation.

- Intelligence, required to support the commander's decisions, is delivered on time.

As information arrives, the G2 (S2) uses various techniques to keep track of the degree to which PIR are satisfied. Understand that 100 percent satisfaction rarely occurs. Using the intelligence cycle, the commander and G2 (S2) continually prioritize the set of requirements and reassess the designation of PIR as the operation progresses.

For more information on the decision making process, collection management, and intelligence synchronization, refer to FM 34-2 and FM 101-5.

ELECTRONIC WARFARE

EW is an essential component of command and control warfare (C^2W). As part of C^2W, EW is used in conjunction with MDCI to protect friendly command and control (C^2) while attacking the enemy's C^2 structure. Effective use of EW as a decisive element of combat power requires coordination and integration of EW operations with the commander's scheme of maneuver and fire support plan. The integrated use of

EW throughout the battlefield supports the synergy needed to locate, identify, damage, and destroy enemy forces and their C structure.

ELECTRONIC WARFARE COMPONENTS

EW is an overarching term that includes three major components: electronic attack (EA), electronic warfare support (ES), and electronic protection (EP). The overlapping ovals in Figure 2-7 illustrate that some EW actions are both offensive and protective and may use ES in their execution. Other EW functions, such as the use of wartime reserve modes (WARM), can fall under either EA or EP. The actions listed under each of the major components are illustrative, not all-inclusive.

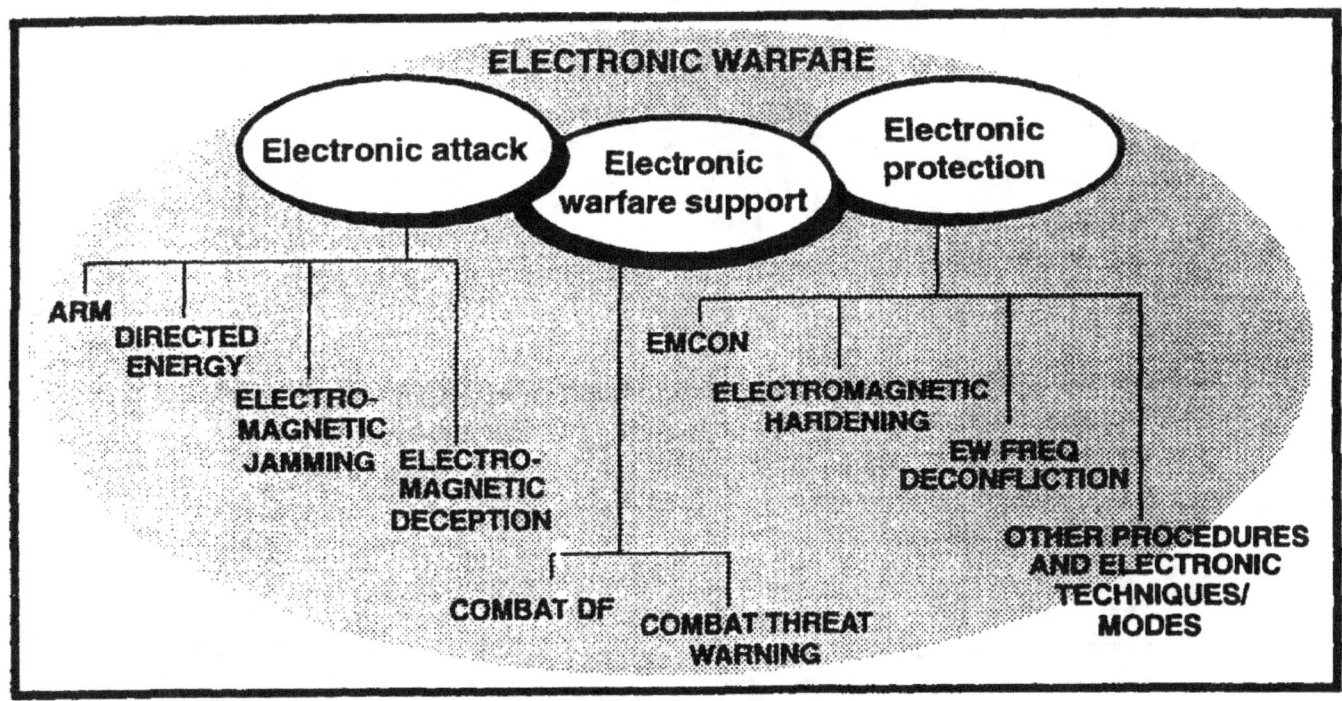

Figure 2-7. The scope of electronic warfare.

Electronic Attack

EA uses lethal (directed energy) and nonlethal (jamming) electromagnetic energy to disrupt, damage, destroy, and kill enemy forces. MI units use nonlethal EA to jam enemy C^2 and targeting systems. It can also support psychological and deception operations. Jamming degrades or denies the enemy effective use of his C^2 and targeting systems. Electronic deception causes an enemy to misinterpret what is received by his electronic systems. For more information on Electronic Attack, refer to FMs 24-33, 34-40(S), 34-40-7, and FM 34-1.

Electronic Warfare Support

ES gathers information by intercepting, locating, and exploiting enemy communications (radios) and noncommunications emitters (radar). ES gives the commander timely information upon which he can base his immediate decisions. Intelligence obtained through ES supports all-source analysis, EA, and EP. As one source of combat information, ES focuses on the commander's immediate needs for identifying the enemy's intent and obtaining targeting information.

Electronic Protection:

EP protects personnel, facilities, or equipment from the effects of friendly or enemy EW, which degrades or destroys friendly communications and noncommunications capabilities. Good electromagnetic emanation practices are the key to a successful defense against the enemy's attempt to destroy or disrupt our communications and noncommunications systems. Proper management of electromagnetic emanations makes the use of our communications equipment appear to be without pattern; as a result, it is difficult for the enemy to target and is consistent with good EP practices. For more information on Electronic Protection, refer to FM 24-33 and FM 34-40(S).

Army EW operations are developed and integrated as part of the commander's overall concept of operations. The execution of EW operations occurs across all BOSs and units. EW often provides commanders with substantial capabilities to electronically influence and control the battlefield.

LESSON 2

PRACTICE EXERCISE

The following items will test your grasp of the material covered in this lesson. There is only one correct answer for each item. When you have completed the exercise, check your answers with the answers with the answer key that follows. If you answer any items incorrectly, study again that part of the lesson which contains the portion involved.

1. Which intelligence discipline is responsible for the physical damage assessment portion of BDA?

    A. IMINT

    B. MASINT

    C. HUMINT

    D. CI

2. The effectiveness of intelligence is measured against what four standards?

    A. Accurate, equipment, relevant, timely

    B. Accurate, predictive, relevant, timely

    C. Mission, terrain, timely, troops

    D. Equipment, mission, observation, timely

3.   What do commanders use to define their PIRs?

   A.   Decision making process

   B.   Intelligence preparation of the battlefield process

   C.   Synchronization process

   D.   Targeting process

LESSON 2

PRACTICE EXERCISE

ANSWER KEY AND FEEDBACK

<u>ITEM</u>		<u>CORRECT ANSWER AND FEEDBACK</u>	
1.	A	IMINT	(page 2-5, para 3)
2.	B.	accurate, predictive, relevant, timely	(page 2-8, and 2-9)
3.	A.	Decision Making Process	(page 2-19, para 5)

LESSON 3

FORCE PROJECTION OPERATION

CRITICAL TASKS: 301-372-2001

301-372-2003

301-372-3001

301-372-3003

OVERVIEW

LESSON DESCRIPTION:

In this lesson you will be given information on why successful IEW support during force projection relies on continuous peacetime information collection and intelligence and intelligence production.

TERMINAL LEARNING OBJECTIVE:

TASKS: Anticipate, consider, and evaluate all potential threats to a force as a whole throughout force projection operations.

CONDITIONS: You will be given narrative information and illustrations from FM 34-1.

STANDARDS: Identify the eight stages of force projection operations.

REFERENCES: The material contained in this lesson was derived from the following publications:

FM 34-1

INTRODUCTION

Currently the Army relies largely on a CONUS-based force with a relatively small forward presence that can rapidly project combat power anywhere in the world. IEW provides the commander with the intelligence he needs to successfully plan and execute force projection operations. IEW support to force projection operations rests on the understanding of five principles: the Commander drives intelligence, intelligence synchronization, split-based operations, tactical tailoring, and broadcast dissemination. These principles, executed in joint, combined, or interagency environments, are critical to successful force projection operations.

PEACE TIME IEW OPERATIONS

Successful IEW support during force projection operations relies on continuous peacetime information collection and intelligence production. Peacetime IEW operations support contingency planning and develop baseline knowledge of multiple potential threats and operational environments. They engage and challenge the Intelligence BOS to respond effectively to the commanders' contingency planning intelligence requirements. During peacetime, commanders conduct critical examinations of M force structures, operations, and training. These examinations ultimately lead to a mission-ready IEW force that supports the needs of the commander, and meets the key force projection imperatives of flexibility, scalability, and tailorability.

Peacetime IEW operations are particularly important to corps and division commanders. In force projection operations, the Army force (ARFOR) in the joint force will be drawn largely from CONUS-based corps and divisions. In addition, a corps or division commander could also be appointed the ARFOR or Joint Task Force (JTF) commander. Corps and division commanders must, therefore, be prepared not only to provide the ARFOR to the JTF but also to assume the duties of the ARFOR or JTF commander. Both responsibilities require the commander to place additional emphasis on intelligence readiness. The corps and division commanders need intelligence to support contingency-based training and planning. They need the broad understanding of the operational environment of the contingency area that comes from continuous interaction with higher echelon and joint intelligence organizations. Commanders must focus and drive the intelligence system daily to ensure this support is available and that their forces and staffs are ready to conduct force projection operations.

IEW AND THE STAGES OF FORCE PROJECTION

IEW supports the eight stages of force projection operations.

- Mobilization.

- Predeployment activity.

- Deployment

- Entry operations.

- Operations.
- War termination and post-conflict operations.

- Redeployment and reconstitution.

- Demobilization.

These stages are not necessarily distinct or sequential and therefore present the commander with planning and execution challenges. Intelligence personnel and organizations must be prepared to assist the commander in overcoming these challenges.

IEW operations must anticipate, identify, consider, and evaluate all potential threats to the force as a whole throughout force projection operations. This is especially critical during the deployment and entry operations stages of force projection. During these stages, US Forces are particularly vulnerable to threat actions. Intelligence personnel must, therefore, emphasize the delivery of I&W products that indicate a basic change to the nature of US operations in theater.

Mobilization:

Mobilization is the process by which the Armed Forces or part of them are brought to a state of readiness for war or other national emergency. The Army Mobilization and Operations Planning and Execution System (AMOPES) and FM 100-17 provide guidance for mobilization of assets for contingencies and large protracted conflicts or wars. To prepare for and execute mobilization, commanders and G2s (S2s) should consider the following:

- In peacetime, Active Component (AC) and Reserve Components (RC) units plan, train, and prepare to accomplish mobilization and deployment tasks. MI units establish habitual training relationships with their supported AC and RC units as well as higher echelon intelligence organizations as identified in existing OPLANs

- Force requirements are identified in OPLANs and concept plans. Reserve augmentation programs organize and integrate AC and RC MI units to meet the requirements in these plans. Individual manpower requirements for military, civilian, and contractor personnel are also identified.

- Selected RC MI units and individuals are alerted then proceed to designated mobilization stations.
- At higher echelons, mobilization prompts MI units that are consolidated for training to detach their assets to deploying forces.

- Mobilization stations and parent units will begin providing current intelligence to their RC units as mobilization begins.

Predeployment Activity:

Predeployment activity provides the foundation for subsequent force projection operations. During this stage, commanders ensure AC and RC MI organizations are trained and equipped to conduct IEW operations. Commanders integrate mobilization and deployment tasks into unit METL and training. Commanders also emphasize and integrate critical aspects of force projection into battle tasks and planning.

In planning force projection operations, the commander establishes intelligence requirements that direct peacetime intelligence operations supporting contingency planning. Key contingency planning ingredients are to stay out front in intelligence planning by developing broad baseline knowledge on contingency areas, and to understand how to get intelligence support. As OPLANs are activated, the commander focuses on intelligence to support specific mission decisions and planning requirements. In addition, the commander begins planning for the crossover point in intelligence when tactical IEW assets within the AO replace initial reliance on higher echelon intelligence. See Figure 3-1.

The G2 (S2) supports peacetime contingency planning with IPB products and databases on likely contingency areas. The OPLAN identifies the IEW requirements supporting that plan, to include-

- Identification of MI units providing IEW support, both in and outside the AO.

- Command and support relationships of collection assets (agencies and systems) at each echelon.

- Report and request procedures not covered in unit tactical standing operating procedures.

  Sequence of deployment of MI personnel and equipment. Early deployment of key MI personnel and equipment is essential for force protection and combat readiness. Composition of initial and follow-on deploying IEW assets is influenced by METT-T, availability of communications, availability of lift, and ability of the national collection system to support the operation.

- Communications architecture supporting both intelligence staffs and collection assets. Signal commands must be involved communications planning.

- Friendly vulnerabilities to hostile intelligence threats and plans for conducting OPSEC, deception, and other force protection measures. MDCI personnel must begin this type of planning as early as possible to ensure adequate force protection of deploying and initial entry forces.

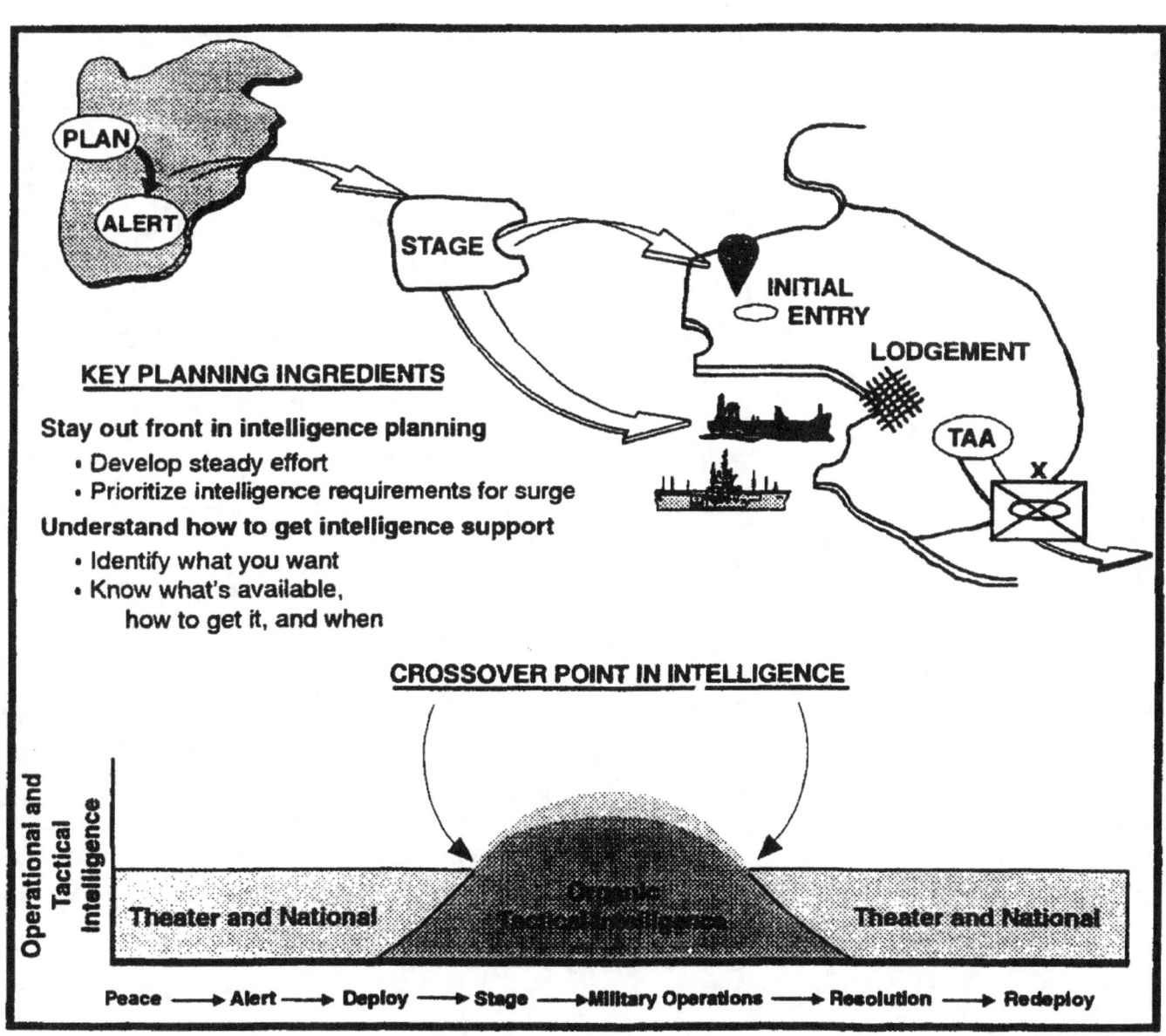

Figure 3-1. Force projection intelligence planning.

The OPLAN also establishes collection strategies and plans that will activate upon alert notification. For smooth transition from predeployment to entry, intelligence staffs must coordinate collection and communications plans before the crisis occurs.

The G2 (S2) and MI units must continually monitor and update their OPLANs to reflect the evolving situation, especially during crisis situations. National intelligence activities monitor regional threats throughout the world and can answer some intelligence requirements supporting the development of OPLANs. The commander and G2 (S2) must be proactive in focusing national and theater intelligence on emerging requirements.

Upon alert notification, intelligence staffs update estimates and IPB products needed to support command decisions on force composition, deployment priorities and sequence, and the AO. At the strategic level, planners use the updated IPB products to assist in developing the logistics preparation of the theater plan that attempts to minimize requirements for strategic lift and maximize the in-theater support capabilities. MI organizations at all echelons reassess their collection requirements immediately after alert notification. Collection managers begin verifying planning assumptions within the OPLANs. MDCI and other IEW personnel provide force protection support to optimize OPSEC and antiterrorism measures.

Throughout the predeployment and deployment stages, intelligence activities provide deploying forces with the most recent intelligence on the AO. G2 (S2) and MI units also update technical databases and situation graphics.

Deployment:

Success in force projection operations hinge on the capability of airlift and sealift assets to move forces to the AO, as well as the timely deployment of air and seaport transportation, terminal, and deployment control units. The size and composition of forces requiring lift are based on METT-T, the availability of pre-positioned assets, the capabilities of host nation support, and the forward-presence of US Forces. Force or tactical tailoring is the process used to determine what is the correct mix and sequence of deploying units.

One of the first tailored IEW assets to deploy with the force G2 (S2) is the deployable intelligence support element (DISE). The DISE is the initial forward intelligence support team of split-based operations. The mission of the DISE is to provide the deployed commander accurate, detailed, continuous, and timely intelligence in support of the rapid introduction of US Forces. Depending on the size and mission of the deployed force, the DISE may be the only MI asset actually deployed in country to support the G2 (S2). In large operations, the DISE may deploy with and support the early entry force G2 (S2) until the complete processing capability of the unit's ACE arrives. Once the ACE is in place, the DISE rejoins the ACE, moves forward to support the tactical command post, or moves to wherever its capabilities may be required. The two types of tailorable DISE configurations are the Mini-DISE (man portable packages), and DISE (vehicular). Together, these DISE configurations provide the commander with a robust intelligence capability in support of a deploying force. Figure 3-2 provides an example of two possible initial entry packages.

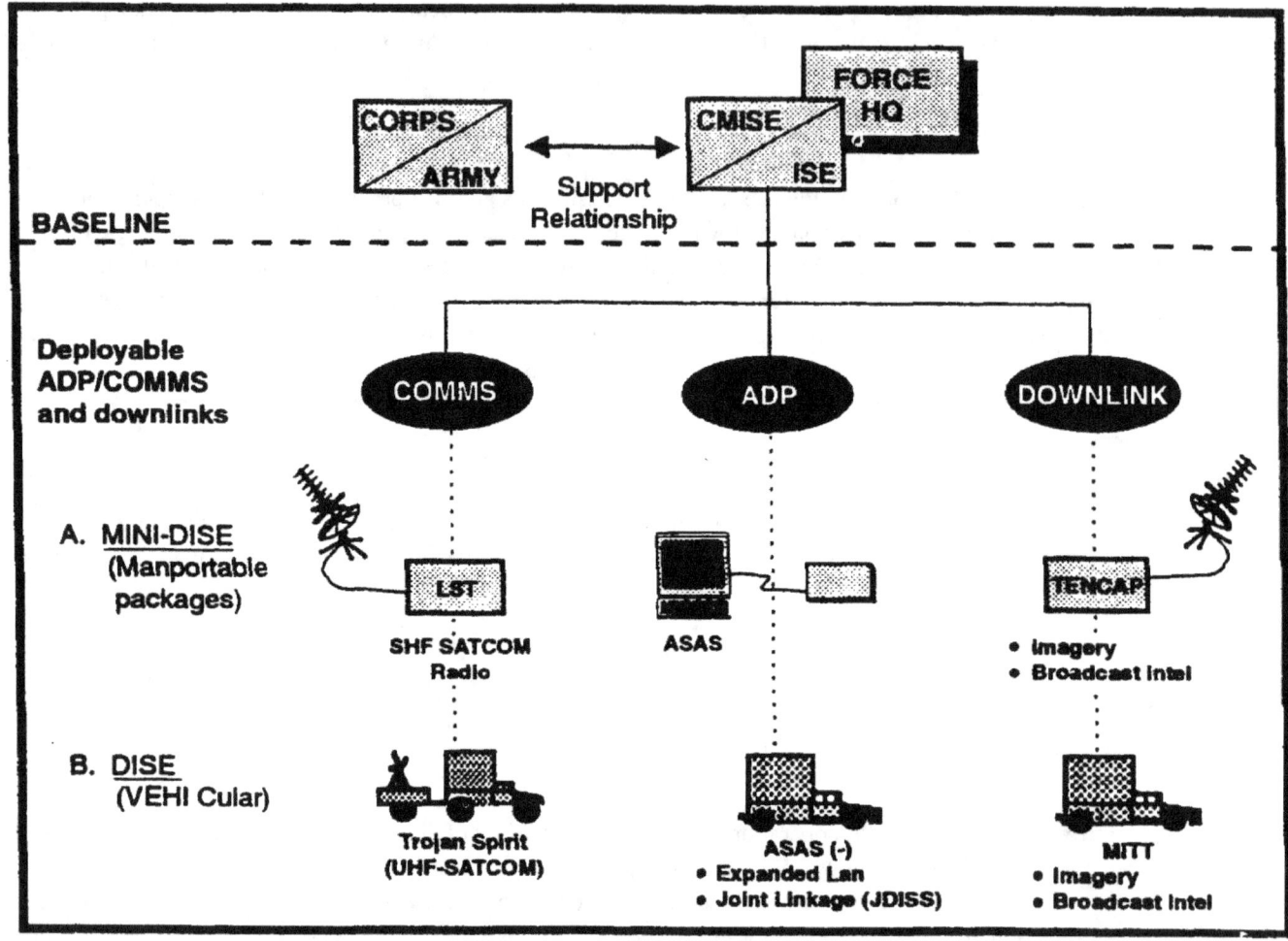

Figure 3-2. Example of initial entry packages for force projection operations.

During deployment, intelligence organizations in the rear such as the CMISE and the ACE of the theater MI brigade take advantage of modem satellite communications (SATCOM), broadcast technology, and

automatic data processing (ADP) systems to provide graphic and textual intelligence updates to the forces enroute. Enroute updates help eliminate information voids and allow the commander to adjust OPORDs prior to arrival in theater.

Intelligence units extend established networks to connect intelligence staffs and collection assets at various stages of the deployment flow. Where necessary, new communications paths are established to meet unique demands of the mission. The theater ACE and the CMISE play a critical role in making communications paths, networks, and intelligence databases available to deploying forces.

Space-based systems play an important part in supporting IEW during the deployment and the subsequent stages of force projection operations by-

- Providing communications links between forces enroute and in the CONUS.

- Providing I&W information from national intelligence systems and organizations.

- Permitting MI collection assets to accurately determine their position through the Global Positioning System (GPS).

- Providing timely and accurate weather information to all commanders through the Integrated Meteorological System (IMETS).

Entry Operations:

Force protection and situation development dominate IEW activities in this stage. Intelligence staffs attempt to identify all threats to arriving forces and assist the commander in developing force protection measures.

During initial entry operations, echelons above corps (EAC) organizations provide major intelligence support. This support includes providing access to departmental and joint intelligence and deploying scalable EAC intelligence assets. The entire effort focuses downwardly to provide tailored support to deploying and deployed echelons in response to their commanders' PIR and IR.

Collection and processing capabilities are enhanced as IEW assets build up in the deployment area. Particular attention is given to the buildup of the in-theater capability required to conduct sustained IEW operations. As the buildup continues, intelligence staffs strive to reduce total dependence on extended split-based "top-driven" intelligence from outside the AO. As organic IEW sets flow into the theater, intelligence staffs begin to rely on them for tactical intelligence although national and theater organization remain a source of tactical and operational intelligence. Figure 3-3 illustrates IEW tactical tailoring and imperatives.

149

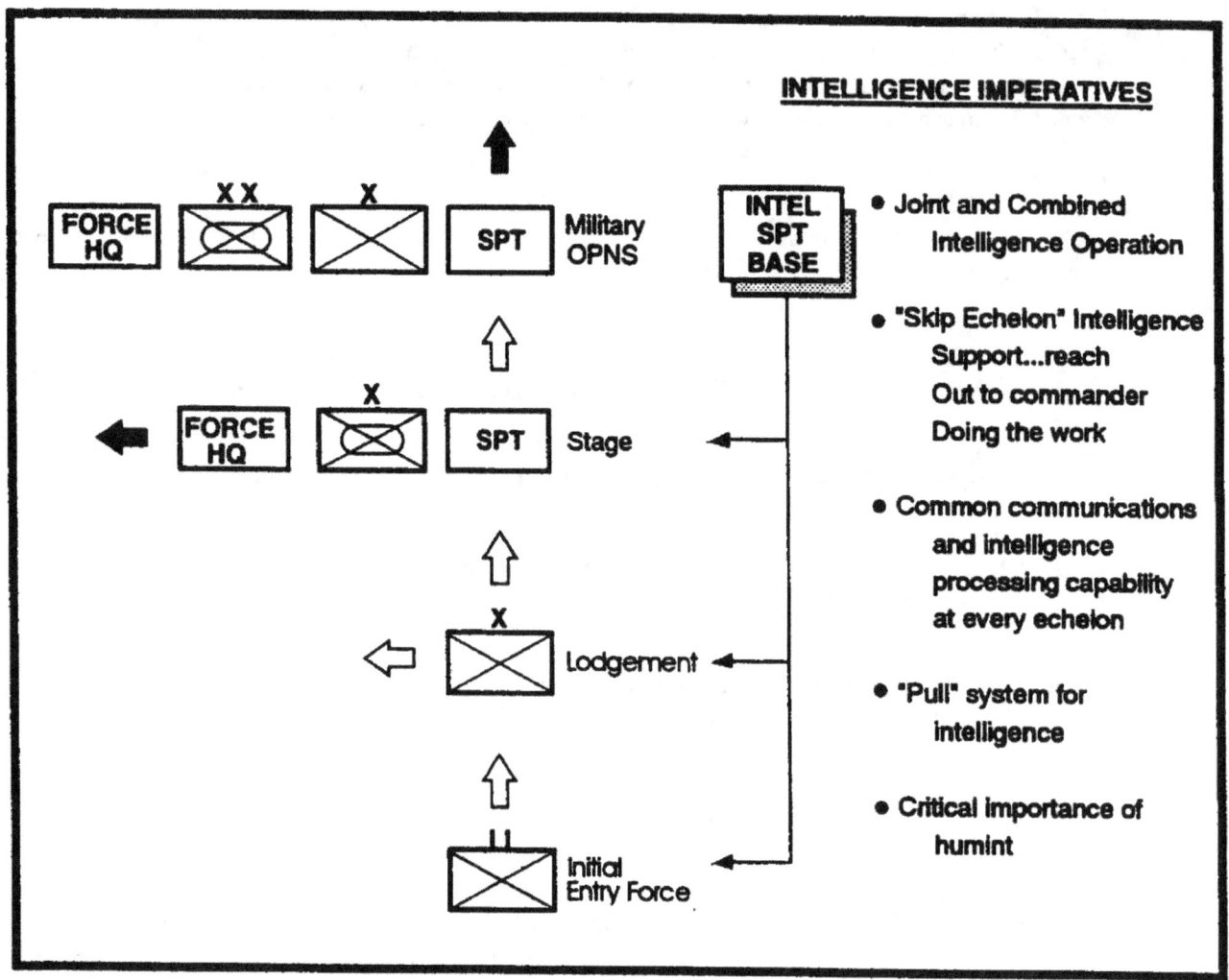

Figure 3-3. Force projection tactical tailoring.

Intelligence staffs provide the commander support in planning the composition and deployment of follow-on combat, CS, and CSS units. As ARFOR enter the theater of operations, the JTF J2 implements, and where necessary, modifies the theater intelligence architecture planned during predeployment.

Deploying intelligence assets establish liaison with staffs and units already present in the AO. Liaison personnel and basic communications should be in place prior to the scheduled arrival of parent commands. MI units establish intelligence communications networks to support combat commanders.

Coordinating staffs at all levels establish reporting and request procedures to ensure the timely receipt of intelligence.

CONUS and other secure intelligence support bases outside the AO continue to support deployed units. In a mature theater, as systems such as Joint STARS begin operating, units equipped with the Joint STARS ground station module (GSM) or the common ground station (CGS) will be able to receive downlink data in NRT tailored to each unit's area of operation.

Systems capable of rapid receipt and processing of intelligence from national systems and high capacity, long-haul communications systems are critical to the success of split-based support of a force projection operation. These systems can provide a continuous flow of intelligence, including annotated imagery products, to satisfy many operational needs. Examples of these type systems are the Imagery Processing and Dissemination System (IPDS), the Electronic Processing and Dissemination System (EPDS), TROJAN SPIRIT, and SUCCESS radio.

Intelligence staffs help plan friendly deception, deep attack, and other operations that create conditions for decisive operations. They also adjust collection activities to look deeper into the battle space as combat strength builds and begin to concentrate on situation and target development.

Operations:

With sufficient combat power and resources in place, the commander shifts his focus from IEW support for deployment to support required for sustained operations. At the beginning of the operations stage, intelligence reaches the crossover point where tactical intelligence becomes the commander's primary source of support, replacing top-driven national and theater intelligence. The commander uses both tactical and operational intelligence to decisively engage and defeat the enemy in combat operations. In SASO, the commander may use all levels of intelligence to accomplish his mission.

During operations, intelligence staffs and units support the development and execution of plans by identifying threat centers of gravity and decisive points on the battlefield. The G2 (S2) ensures the collection management and synchronization processes focus on the commander's PIR. MI units continually evolve their concepts of employment to reflect changes in the operation.

Figure 3-4 provides an example of IEW support during this stage of force projection operations.

War Termination and Postconflict Operations:

Upon cessation of hostilities or truce, deployed forces enter a new stage of force projection operations. Postconflict operations focus on restoring order, reestablishing host nation infrastructure, preparing for redeployment of forces, and planning residual presence of US Forces. While postconflict operations strive to transition from war to peace, there remains a possibility of resurgent hostilities by individuals and forces. As during deployment, this stage and the next will place renewed emphasis on force protection.

During this stage, commanders redirect their PIR and IR to support units conducting restoration operations. These might include-

- Engineer units conducting mine clearing or infrastructure reconstruction operations.

- Medical and logistics units providing humanitarian relief.

- Military police units providing law and order assistance.

Collection management continues to support the commander's PIR. The nature of the PIR shifts from assessing threat forces to assessing political, economic, and other conditions that affect force protection and the desired end state.

Redeployment and Reconstitution:

As combat power and resources decrease in the AO, force protection and I&W become the focus of the commander's intelligence requirements. This in turn drives the selection of those MI units that must remain deployed and those which may redeploy.

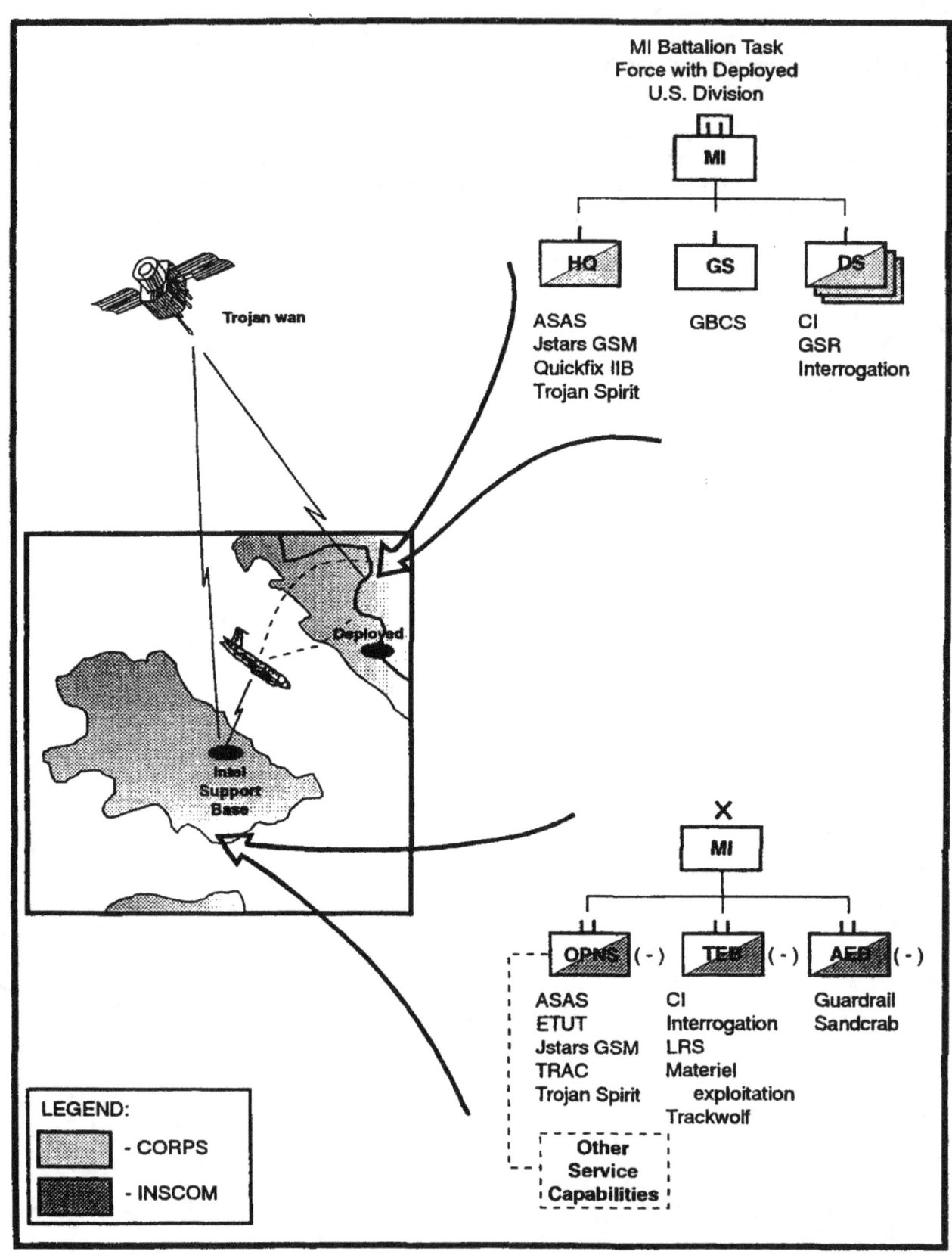

Figure 3-4. Example of IEW support to lore projection operations.

Demobilization:

Demobilization is the stage where MI individuals and units return to premobilization posture or predeployment activities. MI units resume contingency-oriented peacetime IEW operations. RC MI units deactivates and return to peacetime activities.

LESSON 3

PRACTICE EXERCISE

The following items will test your grasp of the material covered in this lesson. There is only one correct answer for each item. When you have completed the exercise, check your answers with the answers with the answer key that follows. If you answer any items incorrectly, study again that part of the lesson, which contains the portion involved.

1. Where are force requirements identified?

    A. Directing

    B. Tailoring

    C. Synchronizing

    D. Tasking

2. Who supports peacetime contingency planning with databases on likely contingency areas?

    A. S-3

    B. Commander

    C. G-3

    D. G-2

3.   Who adjusts collection activities to look deeper into the battle space as combat strength builds and begins to concentrate on situation and target development?

   A.   Commander

   B.   S-3, G-3

   C.   FSO

   D.   S-2, G-2

LESSON 3

PRACTICE EXERCISE

ANSWER KEY AND FEEDBACK

<u>ITEM</u>	<u>CORRECT ANSWER AND FEEDBACK</u>		
1.	B.	TAILORING	(page 3-6, par 5)
2.	D.	G-2	(page34, para3)
3.	D.	S-2, G-2	(page 3-10, para 6)

LESSON 4

COMBAT OPERATIONS

CRITICAL TASK: 301-372-3007

OVERVIEW

LESSON DESCRIPTION:

In this lesson you will be given information on how IEW supports Army combat operations.

TERMINAL LEARNING OBJECTIVE:

TASKS: Anticipate the battle, understand the battlefield framework, and influence the outcome of the battle using IEW support.

CONDITIONS: You will be given narrative information and illustrations from FM 34-1.

STANDARDS: Identify the ways that combat operations are supported by IEW and how each application is tailored to the commander's requirements.

REFERENCES: The material contained in this lesson was derived from the following publications:

FM 3-100	FM 34-37	FM 90-6
FM 31-70	FM 34-40 (s)	FM 90-10
FM 31-71	FM 34-80	FM 100-5
FM 34-1	FM 34-81	FM 100-10

FM 34-10	FM 90-3	FM 101-5
FM 34-25	FM 90-5	

INTRODUCTION

IEW supports Army combat operations in war, conflict, and, when necessary SASO. Combat operations may involve heavy, light, or special operations forces. They may be large-scale during war or small-scale in SASO. Commanders may conduct combat operations anywhere in their AO as part of close, deep, or rear operations. MI units and resources support the commander in executing offensive, defensive, and retrograde operations.

IEW SUPPORTS COMMANDERS

Commanders use IEW support to anticipate the battle, understand the battlefield framework, and influence the outcome of operations. IEW enables commanders to focus and protect their combat power and resources. All commanders use IEW to support force protection. And, while IEW support is required for every situation, each application will be tailored to the commander's requirements at each echelon and operation.

Combat Commanders use IEW to plan and execute operations. These operations may be combat operations during war or SASO. Intelligence helps the combat commander understand the AO, visualize his battle space, and construct the battlefield framework. Intelligence shows where the commander can apply combat power to exploit threat vulnerabilities or capitalize on opportunities with minimum risk.

Combat Support Commanders use IEW to plan, execute, and protect support operations. For example, before establishing a communications site, a signal unit requires specific information on the capabilities of the enemy to intercept, locate, identify, and target friendly communications sites. The signal unit uses MDCI to assess vulnerabilities and plan force protection measures. During operations, the unit uses EP to counter enemy $C^2 W$.

Combat Service Support Commanders use IEW to identify the vulnerabilities of CSS sites and operations to enemy action, both in the forward and rear areas. In addition, CSS commanders use intelligence to anticipate friendly logistic requirements and locate routes and positions for logistic operations. As an example, indicators of an enemy attack might cue the use of rear area security forces or the forward positioning of medical evacuation assets.

Melding MI "electronic cavalry" with traditional reconnaissance enhances understanding and building the battlefield framework. By melding the "top down" intelligence of MI with the "bottom up" combat information gathered by cavalry and other combat arms reconnaissance assets, the G2 (S2) can give commanders the information they need to visualize their battle space. Split-based operations further improve the commander's ability to understand and direct the battle by allowing them to receive reconnaissance and downwardly focused intelligence support during the battle while on the move. The linking of MI electronic cavalry with traditional reconnaissance, the ability to conduct split-based operations, and the availability of downwardly focused intelligence provide commanders the tools they need to win decisively on the battlefield. See Figure 4-1.

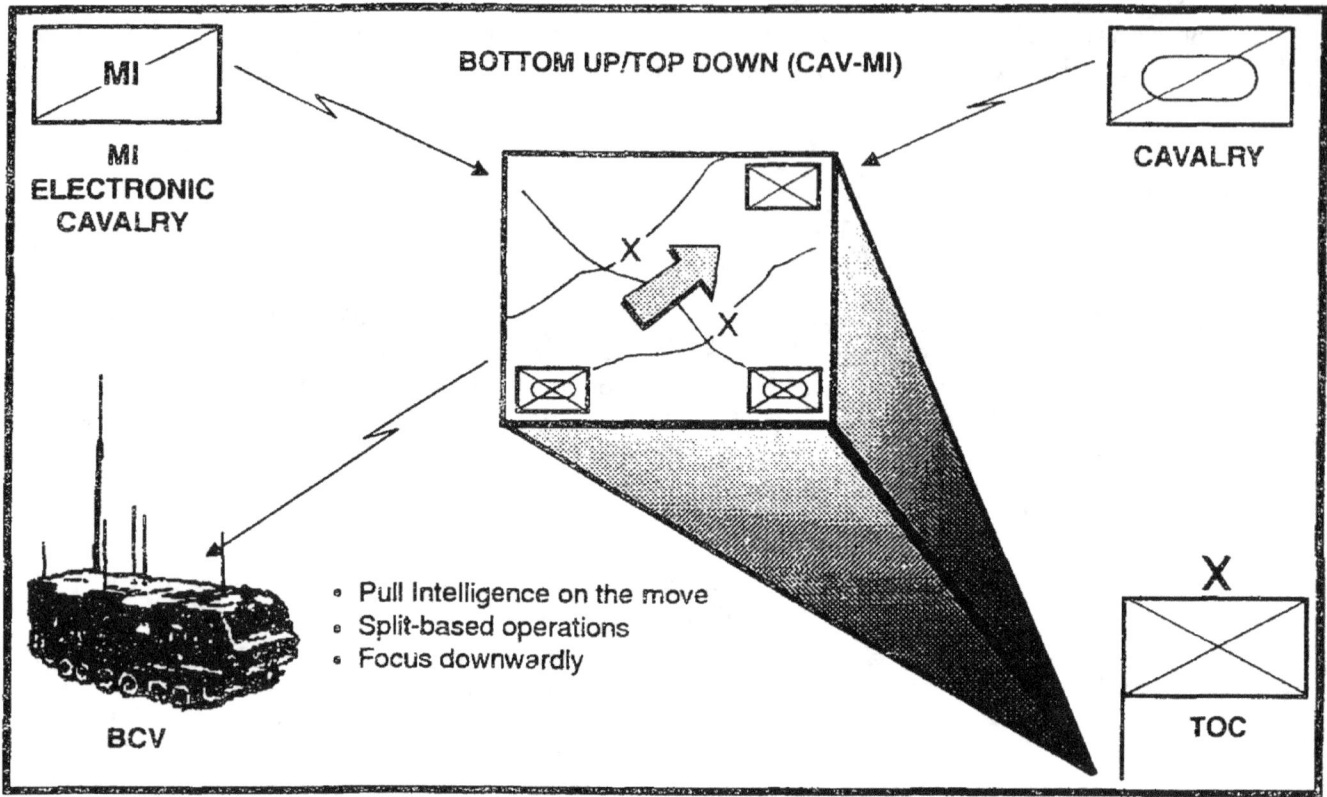

Figure 4-1. Melding electronic cavalry and traditional reconnaissance.

COMMANDER'S INTELLIGENCE TEAM

The G2 (S2) and MI commanders are a team whose mission is to provide IEW support to the commander. As a team, they are responsible to the commander for planning and directing the intelligence activities of the command. Together they develop standards for IEW training and operations.

The G2 (S2) is the commander's senior intelligence officer and primary staff officer for intelligence a Army service component-level through battalion. The G2 (S2) directs and supervises the commander's intelligence and CI operations. He ensures the commander is supported with timely intelligence, targets, and BDA. The G2 (S2) ensures that the intelligence needs of all staff elements are addressed and supported. He coordinates the employment of IEW assets with the G3 (S3) and the FSO to ensure full integration of EW with the Fire Support BOS. He prepares and issues SORs to supporting MI units. The G2 (S2) maintains close and continuous contact with JEW elements at higher echelons to ensure his commander's critical IEW needs are understood and acted upon. The G2 (S2) supervises the intelligence training of the unit and his staff.

The MI commander executes IEW operations using his organic and attached assets. He is responsible for providing the commander with a trained and mission-ready EW force. He develops MI leaders capable of leading small teams in SASO, and companies or battalions in war. In war and SASO, the MI commander is responsible for the C^2, maneuver, sustainment, and protection of his MI unit. The MI commander ensures his unit executes the G2 (S2) intelligence SOR and G3 (S3) EW SOR in concert with the concept of operation. The MI commander anticipates the IEW operational requirements of future operations.

RANGE OF MILITARY OPERATIONS

IEW supports commanders across the range of military operations. Military operations are categorized as peacetime, conflict, and war.

PEACETIME:

During the first environment, peacetime, the Army serves as a deterrent to war and helps keep tensions between nations below the threshold of conflict. Examples of peacetime operations are disaster relief and nation assistance.

CONFLICT:

Confrontation and hostilities short of war characterize the second environment, conflict. Examples of conflict are peacekeeping, noncombatant evacuation operations (NEO), counterinsurgency, and support to insurgency.

The Army classifies its activities during peacetime and conflict as SASO. In addition to traditional intelligence, these operations require intelligence that identifies political, social, economic, and demographic issues. These needs might be as diverse as the identification of weather conditions that might interfere with disaster relief operations, or locating drug processing centers as part of counter-drug operations.

War:

The third environment, that of war, is a state of armed conflict, which involves large-scale combat operations against a state or nation. Wars may be limited or general in scope. Operation Just Cause is an example of a limited war. A general war is one in which major powers mobilize all national resources in a struggle for survival or dominance. World War II is an example of a general war. War requires multidisciplined intelligence, which gives the commander the information necessary to successfully plan and execute military operations.

IEW AND THE TENENTS OF ARMY OPERATIONS

The following describe IEW and the tenets of Army operations:

Initiative:

Initiative sets or changes the terms of battle by action and implies an offensive spirit in conduct of all operations. The commander uses the intelligence system to gain advance warning and to anticipate probable enemy COAs. With foreknowledge of the enemy's intent, the commander can act or react faster than the enemy, avoid or neutralize enemy strength, strike at enemy weaknesses, and take maximum advantage of opportunities.

Agility:

Agility enables the commander to act or react faster than the enemy and is a prerequisite for seizing and holding the initiative. The commander uses the intelligence system to see and understand the entire battlefield, predict enemy COAs and vulnerabilities, and anticipate changes in the operational environment. With this intelligence, the commander can quickly recognize decisive points, anticipate the enemy COA, and rapidly adjust his plan to exploit opportunities or enemy vulnerabilities.

Depth:

Depth is the extension of operations in time, space, resources, and purpose. The commander uses the intelligence system to see the battlefield in depth, anticipate situations, and plan future COAs. Armed with intelligence, the commander conducts or influences operations, which attack the enemy simultaneously throughout the depth of the battlefield, and forces the enemy to fight on the commander's terms. With knowledge of the enemy's disposition, movement, and intent, the commander safeguards his freedom of action by protecting his forces and resources needed for sustained operations from enemy action.

Synchronization:

Synchronization is arranging activities in time and space to mass at the decisive point. The commander integrates the activities of the Intelligence BOS with other BOSs to gin overwhelming combat power at decisive times and places. Intelligence predicts where and when those decisive points will occur. It provides commanders what they want (intelligence and targets), when they want it (in time to influence the operation), in the format they requested (immediately usable), and in concert with their concept of operations.

Versatility:

Versatility enables units to meet diverse mission requirements. The commander employs the intelligence system to acquire intelligence about potential enemy forces and operational environments. With this intelligence, the commander can rapidly and effectively shift his focus, tailor his forces, and move from mission to mission across the full range of military operations.

BATTLEFIELD FRAMEWORK

Commanders build the battlefield framework by establishing relationships between the AO, the battle space, and the battlefield organization. This section addresses each of these parts as they relate to IEW.

Area of Operations:

Commanders allocate AOs to subordinate units based on METT-T and the unit's capability. The G2 (S2) assists the commander in allocating areas by providing him with the best intelligence on possible AOs. He advises the commander on the availability of information on the AO, the ability of the IEW system to cover those areas, and the support needed from other parts of the intelligence system. The G2 (S2) also coordinates with the G3 (S3) on deploying organic and supporting MI units within the AO.

By knowing the AO, commanders at every level can anticipate developments, prepare options, and exploit battlefield opportunities. They can attack or defend over advantageous terrain, seize key terrain, and exploit weaknesses in the enemy's use of terrain.

Battle Space:

The commander's battle space extends beyond the boundaries of the AO. The dimensions and content of the commander's battle space change as the operation progresses. Within the battle space, the commander must understand the physical environment in which his forces will operate; employ available resources to their fullest capability; and integrate joint or combined assets, which can be used to engage the enemy. The commander must also have an appreciation for the ability of enemy forces within and outside his battle space to jeopardize his operations. Understanding the battle space allows the commander to plan, organize, and synchronize his operations and successfully protect his force while dominating the enemy within the battle space.

Area of Interest:

In the context of IEW operations, the AI is the AO, the battle space, and the regions beyond the battle space. IEW operations directed at the AI attempt to identity enemy forces or other potentially hostile forces outside the battle space, which could jeopardize current or future operations. In force projection operations, the AI could include areas through which US Forces must transit to reach the AO. Coverage of the AI would probably exceed the capabilities of organic IEW assets; therefore, the G2 (S2) must plan support from higher echelons and national intelligence activities to cover the AI.

Battlefield Organization:

Three closely related sets of activities (deep, dose, and rear area) characterize operations within the AO. IEW supports these activities simultaneously in the following manner:

Deep Operations. IEW supports deep operations by-

- Dedicating adequate acquisition systems to effectively support targeting deep attack and BDA.

- Planning EW support, especially requirements for joint EW support.

- Identifying uncommitted enemy reserve forces.

- Conducting MDCI operations to prevent the enemy from gaining knowledge of deep OPLANs and preparations

- Identifying enemy logistics assets, support infrastructure, and critical nodes.

- Supporting suppression of enemy air defenses (SEAD).

Close Operations. IEW supports dose operations by-

- Providing tactical intelligence on the disposition, strength, weaknesses, composition, and intent of the enemy in contact.

- Conducting multidiscipline operations that support targeting and BDA.

- Conducting EA that disrupts or denies the enemy's effective use of C^2 and fire support communications.

- Providing predictive intelligence, which includes identifying probable COAs for uncommitted enemy forces.

- Supporting SEAD.

Rear Area Operations. IEW supports rear area operations by-

- Assisting in identifying, analyzing, and early warning of potential threats to the friendly rear area.

- Identifying terrain which supports friendly rear area operations.

- Using OPSEC and EP to protect C^2 centers and systems.

OFFENSIVE OPERATIONS

The main purpose of offensive operations is to defeat, destroy, or neutralize the enemy force. Successful offensive actions take the fight to the enemy in such a way as to achieve decisive victory at the least cost. Offensive operations at all levels require effective IEW support to help the commander avoid the enemy's main strength, and to deceive and surprise the enemy. IEW helps the commander decide when and where to concentrate sufficient combat power to overwhelm the enemy. At the tactical level, effective reconnaissance and counterreconnaissance are essential for the commander to preclude surprise from the enemy, maintain the initiative on the battlefield, and win the battle. Commanders at all levels synchronize intelligence and fires with their combat and CS systems to maximize their ability to see and strike the enemy simultaneously throughout the AO. IEW fundamentals apply to each basic form of offense.

Movement to Contact:

Movement to contact operations are conducted to develop the situation and to establish or regain contact. A movement to contact may take one of several forms: approach march, search and attack, reconnaissance in force, and meeting engagement. The extent and form of the operation depends on whether threat forces were previously in contact. Establishing and maintaining contact with the enemy is a central tenet of a movement to contact operation. The role of JEW in these operations is to ensure commanders have the intelligence they need to conduct mobile, force-oriented battles with minimum risk of surprise. For IEW operations, this means providing commanders with the enemy's locations, activities, and probable intentions with sufficient time to influence friendly operations. Traditional reconnaissance and security operations are a vital factor in finding and physically fixing the enemy. By effectively combining traditional reconnaissance and security operations with systems like the UAV and Joint STARS, IEW operations ensure commanders have the knowledge they need to execute movement to contact.

Attack:

The purpose of the attack is to defeat, destroy, or neutralize the enemy. The attack usually follows a movement to contact but is also used after defensive operations, exploitations, and pursuits. The commander must decide when to begin and end an attack based on its contribution to meeting his objectives. *Successful attacks* are preceded by *successful* re*connaissance*. IEW operations help the commander identify the conditions needed to begin, conduct, and terminate an attack regardless of the type of attack.

Exploitation:

Exploitation is the extension of destruction of the defending force by maintaining offensive pressure. Such actions may include seizing objectives deep in the enemy rear, cutting LOC, isolating and destroying enemy units, and disrupting enemy C^2. Aggressive exploitation of enemy vulnerabilities can disintegrate and demoralize the enemy to the point where his only options are to surrender or withdraw. Commanders must be able to quickly recognize fleeting opportunities for exploitation or pursuit. Ml of the attacking commander's information resources must immediately report indications of enemy vulnerabilities resulting from the initial attack. Increased enemy prisoners of war (EPWs), disintegration of enemy units after initial contact, disorganized defense, and capture or absence of enemy leaders are all indications of friendly opportunities to transition to exploitation.

IEW assets support the commander's decision to exploit by identifying exposed flanks or any weakness in the enemy's defense. They determine the enemy's intentions to defend in place, to delay, or to withdraw to other defensive positions. IEW resources confirm destruction of enemy fighting and support capabilities. They identify and locate vulnerable targets in the enemy rear area, such as communications, supply, and maintenance centers. They also track enemy forces, which could counter exploitation forces.

Pursuit:

The pursuit is an operation against a retreating force and follows attack or exploitation. When the enemy can no longer resist and decides to withdraw, the commander may elect to pursue and destroy the enemy force. Although the commander may not always be able to anticipate pursuit, he should always include withdrawal and retreat among enemy COAs considered in planning and wargaming.

Any of the commander's information resources can provide indications that the enemy force is abandoning its position and equipment, and retreating. The commander needs this information as fast as possible to transition from attack or exploitation to pursuit.

IEW assets continually report the enemy's location, direction, and rate of movement. They locate and track HPTs and report targeting data to FSEs. If the enemy force reconstitutes its defense, IEW resources report the time, place, and type of defense. They report any attempt to counterattack, outflank, or cut off friendly forces, which have driven deep into enemy territory.

DEFENSIVE OPERATIONS

The immediate purpose of defensive operations is to defeat an enemy attack. Since only offensive operations can destroy the enemy and win the battle, the ultimate purpose of defensive operations is to create the opportunity to shift to the offense. In the defense, commanders may use any combination of combat operations at different times and places on the battlefield to defeat the enemy. Commanders defend to buy time, hold key terrain, hold the enemy in one place while attacking in another, or destroy enemy combat power while reinforcing friendly forces. IEW fundamentals apply to both primary forms of defensive operations and to defense in depth.

Mobile Defense:

A mobile defense employs a combination of fire and maneuver, offense, defense, and delay to destroy the enemy and defeat his attack. Commanders employing a mobile defense attempt to get the most from terrain and obstacles while employing fire and maneuver to take the initiative from the attacking enemy. IEW supports the commander in gaining the initiative by identifying key terrain and potential enemy avenues of approach, tracking the enemy throughout his attack, supporting the targeting of the enemy's critical nodes and fire support assets, and aiding in the neutralization of enemy's reconnaissance through deception and EW. Most importantly, intelligence helps the commander identify the place and time when the enemy is most vulnerable to a decisive counterattack by the friendly mobile striking force. IEW should determine the enemy's strength, intent, main avenue of approach, and location of his follow-on forces. The defending commander can then decide where to arrange his forces in an economy of force role to defend, yet still shape the battlefield. This will afford him the time necessary to commit the striking force precisely.

Area Defense:

An area defense focuses on denying the enemy access to designated terrain for a specified period of time, rather than on the outright destruction of the enemy. The commander conducts area defense by using a series of mutually supported positions in depth. IEW support in area defense identifies, locates, and tracks the enemy's main attack and provides the commander time to allocate sufficient combat power to strengthen the defense at the point of the enemy's main effort. Intelligence should also identify where and when the commander can most decisively counterattack the enemy's main effort or exploit enemy vulnerabilities.

Defense in Depth: In the defense as well as in the offense, operations in depth are the basis for success. Simultaneous application of combat power throughout the depth of the battle space defeats the enemy rapidly with minimum friendly casualties. Commanders conducting combat operations in depth require IEW support for deep, close, and rear operations.

Deep Operations. MI units provide early warning of enemy approach. They find, track, and target enemy forces enabling the commander to attack them effectively at long range. Corps and division aerial resources, LRSUs, theater, other services, and national systems provide information needed for deep operations. The primary tasks of deep IEW are to identify the enemy's main effort and support target development. Deep collection operations locate such HPTs as enemy second and follow-on echelons, critical C^2 nodes, reconnaissance elements, FSEs, and logistics trains.

Close Operations: Close operations are the activities of the main and supporting efforts in the defensive area to slow, canalize, and defeat the enemy's major units. The success of close operations depends on aggressive maneuver and counterattack as well as successful defense of key positions. As the enemy attack begins, the commander's first concerns are to identify the enemy's committed units and direction of attack, and gain time to react. The first sources of this information will be reconnaissance and security forces, MI units, SOF, and air elements conducting deep operations. Commanders rely heavily on combat information for immediate reports of enemy activities and vulnerabilities. Combat information from units in contact supports friendly fire and maneuver to attack exposed HPTs and vulnerable enemy units.

IEW resources concentrate on tracking enemy units, providing early warning of threats against exposed flanks, gaps in defensive positions, or any attempt to outmaneuver the defending force. IEW identifies and targets HPTs, supports OPSEC and deception, and conducts EA coordinated with planned fire and maneuver.

Close IEW strives to identify the enemy's intentions and main effort as early as possible to support the commander's battle planning. The commander ensures that the G2 (S2) collection strategy supports the PIR and IR developed for the operation.

Rear Operations: Rear operations sustain friendly, close, and deep combat operations. Successful defense in friendly rear areas prevents disruption of C^2, fire support, logistics, and movement of reserves. The threat to rear operations includes all enemy deep battle forces: conventional ground, air, and missile forces, unconventional forces, enemy agents, and sympathizers.

The keys to rear area defense are sound planning, early waning, continuous OPSEC, and immediate deployment of sufficient forces and resources to counter any threat.

171

Detection of the enemy is the responsibility of every soldier in the command and all intelligence collectors at every echelon. The operations and intelligence section of the RAOC coordinates intelligence preparation for rear operations. The RAOC recommends intelligence requirements to the G2 (S2) for consolidation into the unit's PIR and IR. The RAOC also requests intelligence collection, MDCI, and CA support for rear operations. MDCI personnel and interrogators provide HUMINT to identify and help neutralize enemy agents, sympathizers, and unconventional forces in the rear area.

Other IEW assets may, on order, redirect their efforts from deep and close operations to support combat operations against a rear area threat from conventional forces. The corps depends on EAC and national systems for early warning and intelligence on threats from beyond the corps' AO, such as an attack by enemy airborne forces.

RETROGRADE OPERATIONS

Retrograde operations are maneuvers to the rear or away from the enemy. The purpose of a retrograde operation is to improve the situation for the friendly force, draw the enemy into an unfavorable position, regain the initiative, and defeat the enemy. Units conducting retrograde operations conceal the movement of the main force and avoid decisive engagements. IEW supports all retrograde operations by tracking the disposition of the enemy force and denying the enemy intelligence on movement of the friendly force. Retrograde operations are more effective when deception and OPSEC confuse the enemy about the true disposition of the friendly force. There are three types of retrograde operations-delays, withdrawals, and retirements.

Delays. In delays, the commander yields ground to gain time, retain freedom of action, and inflict the greatest possible damage on the enemy. IEW support concentrates on measures that obscure the size and intent of the delaying force and create the element of surprise. Each time the enemy commander is engaged by the delaying force, he must be convinced through the application of combat power, deception, and OPSEC that he has engaged the main force. This causes the enemy commander to stop, deploy his forces, and prepare to attack or defend. The delaying force then disengages and withdraws to the next delay position.

Withdrawals. Commanders conduct withdrawals to avoid combat under undesirable conditions, preserve the force, adjust defensive positions, or relocate the entire force. In all withdrawals, the commander attempts to deceive the enemy. Some friendly elements remain in contact and simulate activity of the larger unit, including electronic activity, to mask the withdrawal from enemy intelligence. MDCI teams monitor the simulative deception based on OPSEC evaluation of normal friendly force signatures, patterns, and profiles.

Retirements. Retirements are rearward movements conducted by units not in contact with the enemy. The commander retires his force to shorten LOC, remove the force from the area of combat, or reposition the force to permit its use elsewhere. IEW support includes determining routes and favorable terrain for the retirement, identifying enemy forces, which could interdict the movement, and denying the enemy knowledge of the operation.

MILITARY INTELIGENCE UNITS

MI units are organized to support a wide range of possible missions. The doctrinal principles for the C^2 and employment of MI units are similar to those used by non-MI units (for example, field artillery [FA] or engineer units). FM 101-5 discusses the doctrinal principles and tactics, techniques, and procedures (TTPs) on how to command and control units. This section briefly discusses the C^2 and employment considerations of MI units.

Tailoring the Force:

When the commander receives a mission, he considers METT-T and the capability of his assets in tailoring the force to optimize IEW support. To ensure continuous and responsive IEW support, he establishes early the C^2 structure and means required to effectively C^2 IEW assets. The commander also-

- Designates the command relationship of subordinate units. (Options include assigned, attached, or operational control [OPCON].)

- Designates the support relationship of subordinate units. (Options include direct support [DS], general support [GS], reinforcing [R], and general support reinforcing [GS-R].) These are also called standard tactical missions.

An example of a support relationship is the DS MI company habitually associated with a maneuver brigade. The mission of the company commander is to support the maneuver brigade commander. However, the company commander retains the authority to organize his unit as he judges to accomplish the mission. At the same time, the MI battalion commander helps the company commander support the maneuver brigade commander (much like the division artillery [DIVARTY] commander helps the DS FA battalion commander support the maneuver commander). FM 101-5 contains additional information on command and support relationships.

Planning IEW Support:

When the MI commander receives a mission, he conducts the decision making process like any other unit commander. The SORs become the specified tasks that drive mission analysis. Implied tasks will include the maneuver and support of subordinate MI units so that they can accomplish the specified tasks.

The MI commander's concept of operation revolves around the organization, deployment, allocation, and employment of subordinate MI units necessary to accomplish the IEW requirements throughout the mission. To satisfy his collection or EW mission, he will forward deploy systems into air or groundspace owned by other units. This requires coordination with forward maneuver units.

Executing IEW Support:

During execution, the MI commander follows the supported commander's operation and attempts to anticipate IEW tasks required to sustain the operation or execute subsequent COAs. He ensures MI units in GS accomplish assigned tasks and continues to provide DS MI unit commanders with intelligence and logistics support. The following tasks assist the MI commander in successfully executing his unit's IEW mission:

- Track the battle. The MI unit continually monitors the progress of the supported unit and satisfaction of tasks directed in the SOR, the collection plan, and the intelligence synchronization matrix. This enables the MI commander to anticipate rapidly changing priorities and deadlines for IEW support.

- Know MI unit status. The MI commander must know the status of IEW personnel and systems at all times. He must ensure that collection managers also know the status of all collection assets under his control. Timely, accurate status reporting enables the commander and his staff to monitor the execution of collection plans and make adjustments, when necessary, to ensure synchronization with the operation.

- Coordinate employment of MI units. A maneuver unit generally owns the ground or airspace for each collection location. The MI commander coordinates movement and use of space to minimize the possibility of fratricide and risks from enemy action.

- Reference all reporting to original SOR. The MI unit annotates reporting with the SORs it supports.

Because of the dynamics of combat, the MI commander may frequently have to reposition and redirect the employment of his assets. Sometimes he must adjust forward asset locations to ensure protection by friendly maneuver forces. To sustain this protection, the MI unit commander must know when the

174

maneuver unit withdraws or moves forward and have a well-rehearsed plan to conduct a complementary move.

Survivability of IEW assets is essential in any type of operation. Consistent with security and communications requirements and mission responsiveness, IEW assets should disperse to the maximum extent possible and apply all possible OPSEC measures.

FMs 34-10, 34-25, 34-37, and 34-80 discuss TTPs for the organization of intelligence assets at brigade, division, corps, and theater.

Sustaining MI Units:

Sustaining MI units is similar to logistics required for other combat support units operating at the operational and tactical levels. However, MI units are distinctive in that they are equipped with some low-density and classified IEW systems requiring specialized maintenance and components. A sustainment challenge for MI unit commanders is to provide logistics support to subordinate units which are widely dispersed in the AO but are not attached to the maneuver unit in whose area they are operating. For example, some low-density IEW systems can only be serviced by contractors. To maintain these systems, MI unit commanders must establish some mixture of equipment evacuation and forward deployment of civilians.

Sustaining combat effectiveness of MI units requires commanders and staffs to follow the five logistic imperatives addressed in FM 100-5 and FM 100-10. These imperatives are discussed below:

Anticipate. Commanders and staffs must anticipate IEW logistics requirements before and during operations.

Integrate. Commanders and staffs must integrate IEW logistics requirements and support concepts into strategic, operational, and tactical plans.

Continuous. Through planning, commanders and staffs must ensure continuity of support during operations and reduce the possibility of diminished combat effectiveness through lapses in support, particularly IEW system maintenance.

Responsive. Commanders must be supported by a responsive logistics operation capable of reacting rapidly to unforeseen situations.

Improvise. Commanders and staffs must be able to improvise logistics solutions to unforeseen situations that mean the difference between success and failure of IEW support to the operation.

Currently, IEW equipment maintenance is performed within the four-tiered system-unit, DS, GS, and depot. Due to the transformation from a forward-deployed Army to a force projection Army, MI is moving towards the two-tiered system-field and sustainment with the rest of the Army. Unit and DS are under the field tier. The sustainment tier includes GS and higher. The goal is rapid repair as far forward as tactically feasible. Due to low-density and different generations of EW equipment in the field, the transition from four to two tiers will not occur at the same rate for each type of equipment.

Commanders and logistics personnel must contend with the following problems that in some ways, are peculiar to IEW equipment.

- Beyond the year 2010, MI will conduct operations using equipment that essentially covers three generations of technology. The IEW logistics manager must be able to support all of these equipment variants as they exist in the inventory. Failing this, certain items must be identified as nonsupportable and be removed from the inventory so that scarce resources will not be diverted to nonproductive ends.

- The small number of most IEW systems make their procurement, replacement, and repair expensive when compared to other items such as wheeled vehicles, where economies of scale can be realized. Consequently, JEW logistics planners must ensure that adequate funding exists to support and field equipment at all levels.

- Combined with low-density, the per unit cost to repair parts and components for IEW equipment is higher than the cost for items purchased in greater numbers, regardless of complexity. This lends urgency to the requirement to thoroughly manage both end items and support packages from strategic to tactical levels of logistics.

- For some IEW systems, technical competence to repair or replace may only exist at the original equipment manufacturer (OEM) level. As the levels of technology continue to rise, more IEW equipment will be nonrepairable or even non-diagnosable at the unit or perhaps anywhere below the OEM level. This will lead to throwaway equipment, direct exchange with the manufacturer, or salvaging by repairing parts from the repair prescribed load list (PLL).

- Adherence to normal Army logistics systems and procedures may not always be possible.

PROCESSING AND DISSEMINATING INTELLIGENCE

176

Commanders and G2s (S2s) must thoroughly plan the intelligence processing and dissemination structure required to support military operations. Communications

and ADP equipment connectivity, capacity, and redundancy must be in place at the beginning of each operation to ensure seamless multiecheloned intelligence support from national intelligence centers down to the combat commander in the field.

The intelligence networks, planned and used in peacetime, should be similar to, if not the same as, those used during military operations. Communications and ADP used by MI units to process and disseminate intelligence in garrison, should also be used by these units when they deploy. Once established in the AO, communications and ADP capabilities, connectivity's, and interfaces must remain flexible enough to adjust to changing operational requirements.

Processing and Disseminating Capabilities:

Systems such as the ASAS and TROJAN SPIRIT represent major leaps in MI's ability to process and disseminate intelligence. These and other systems like them provide the commander and G2 (S2) with the ability to-

- Receive and transmit digital imagery, templates, graphics, terrain products, and bulk databases.

- Conduct split-based operations simultaneously between CONUS, outside continental United States (OCONUS), and deployed forces.

- Access and pull intelligence from worldwide multiechelon data bases at national, theater, corps, and division from deployed MI units.

- Receive direct broadcast dissemination of intelligence and targeting data.

- Collate, analyze, and synthesize information into intelligence products tailored to the echelon.

Echelon Connectivity:

Connectivity for intelligence interfaces between echelons must be planned and maintained continuously to ensure the commander receives timely and responsive intelligence support throughout the operation. Critical intelligence products must be capable of uninterrupted flow from national to deployed units.

This connectivity is achieved by linking existing communications networks such as the Defense Secure Network 3 (DSNET3) with the organic and special purpose systems of the deployed force. Special purpose systems like TROJAN SPIRIT and TENCAP require early planning to ensure connectivity and access to national intelligence support networks and systems. Gateways and protocols for exchanging information between and among all intelligence systems must be planned early and exercised in garrison to ensure successful operations.

INSCOM plays a valuable role in providing connectivity and gaining access to national systems and organizations.

Automation in Analysis and Synthesis:

Intelligence and communications systems can easily overwhelm a CP with information. The G2 (S2) establishes electronic and human "pertinence filters" to weed out irrelevant information. He must also take advantage of the computers ability to establish a relational database of messages. This will enable analysts to access all information that falls within the specified location, time, and subject parameters. In collection management, relational databases and automated journals allow complete and thorough cross-indexing, solving many of the problems collection managers often experience in relating requirements to reports, and tracking dissemination. He must also plan and train for operations without computer support due to power or system failure.

ELECTRONIC WARFARE PLANNING

EW planning is crucial to the success of C^2W operations. The effectiveness of EW operations depends upon the degree to which they are integrated with the commander's scheme of fire and maneuver. Systematic planning and full understanding of employment factors are critical to achieving full integration.

Effective EA requires timely intelligence and must be synchronized with critical events. The desired result determines the method of EA. This is especially important since many IEW systems can identify targets to the accuracy required by lethal fire systems. The thought should be, "Why jam when I can kill?" If the decision is to use nonlethal EA, then use it to maximize enemy confusion and minimize the loss of continuity on ES exploitable targets. If lethal fire is used, then coordinate support actions with the appropriate staff personnel. Regardless of which type of EA is used, it must be part of a well-coordinated action.

The tools that allow for effective EA and EP are the EW estimate and the EW annex. The G3 staff and EWO prepares the estimate based on the commander's guidance. It is coordinated with the MDCI analysis

178

section, which has the responsibility for assessing enemy intelligence capabilities. The EW estimate is a logical presentation of enemy and friendly EW capabilities as they relate to a given mission. It includes EW options available to the commander and weighs the relative merits of each.

The EW annex contains the details of EW mission, concept and tasks to be performed by elements of the force. It describes how EW is used to support the operation. The G3, with input from the G2, EWO, and signal officer, prepares the EW annex in the 5-paragraph OPORD format. Amplifying details are covered in appendixes to the annex. For example, separate annexes for electronic deception, signal, and EP may exist. FM 34-40(S) provides samples of EW estimates and annexes.

The G3, G2, EWO, and FSO continually assess the effectiveness of EW operations. Assessment is crucial to the EW process. It identifies strength and weaknesses in current EW operations and provides a base of knowledge for planning and executing future operations. Assessment is conducted at each step of the EW process to ensure that EW operations are responsive to the commander's needs.

IEW SUPPORT IN SPECIAL ENVIRONMENTS

The following describe some operational and sustainment considerations of IEW operations in special environments:

Desert:

Desert operations involve rapid movement of troops, good observation, long fields of fire, mandatory use of deception, and a lack of what might normally be considered key terrain. Consider the following when planning IEW operations in a desert environment:

Operational. Desert expanses necessitate wide dispersal of MI units and IEW systems. The desert climate causes some degradation in amplitude modulation (AM) and frequency modulation (FM) radio communications due to thermal heating and dead spots. IMINT systems may be subject to heat-wave distortion. The collection capability of SIGINT systems may also be reduced by seasonal atmospheric conditions.

MI units must consider how to employ IEW assets during rapid movement of maneuver forces across desert terrain. Stopping and establishing a collection site may cause the MI unit to fall behind the supported unit and quickly place it out of range of the enemy targets. Staying with the maneuver force will prevent collection operations and limit access to high capacity intelligence communications systems. For

MI aviation assets, blowing sand and high winds may prevent or limit airborne collection operations, which could keep pace with rapidly moving forces.

Sustainment. Wind-blown dust and sand are responsible for increased wear and tear on equipment and, therefore, increasing maintenance and supply requirements. Operator maintenance of equipment is required continuously to keep sand and dust out of the equipment.

FM 90-3 contains additional information on desert operations.

Jungle:

Primarily climate and vegetation affect jungle operations. Both factors constrain IEW operations and sustainment capabilities. Consider the following when planning IEW operations in a jungle environment:

Operational. Ground mobility restrictions require that IEW systems be lighter, manportable, and rugged. The same restrictions can increase reliance on helicopters for transport and IEW operations. IMINT systems will be degraded by jungle terrain. The dense vegetation, cloud cover, and precipitation will conceal targets. Some radar systems may be unable to penetrate the jungle depending on the density of vegetation and type of system used.

Sustainment. Jungle operations require increased daily operator maintenance of equipment due to a high incidence of rust, corrosion, and fungus caused by high jungle moisture. Troop health hazards-including gastrointestinal disease, immersion foot, and fungus infection-are prevalent. Reliance on helicopter mobility for supplies is increased.

FM 90-5 contains additional information on jungle operations.

Mountain:

Mountain operations are characterized by reduced ranges for direct fire weapons, increased importance of indirect fire, canalized mobility along valley floors, decentralized combat, increased collection operations from heights dominating LOCs, and reduced C^2 capabilities. Consider the following when planning IEW operations in mountainous terrain.

Operational. Use IEW systems that are light, rugged, and portable to exploit the advantages of higher terrain. Irregular terrain patterns create dead space, which reduces the effectiveness of EW and degrades C^2. Use the mountain heights for observation posts to reduce the effect of terrain masking.

Sustainment The key to sustainment in mountain environments is training. The increased altitudes in mountain combat will affect a soldier's mental alertness, cause dehydration and sickness, and increase fear of heights.

FM 90-6 contains additional information on mountain operations.

Urban:

Shorter engagement ranges, structural obstructions to visual and electronic line of sight (LOS) characterize military operations in urban terrain, and the addition of a new vertical dimension provided by subterranean structures such as sewers and buildings. Consider the following when planning IEW operations in an urban environment:

Operational. The nature of urban combat may necessitate decentralized operations. MI units are normally placed in DS of, or attached to, maneuver units assigned urban operations. DF operations are impeded because signals reflect off structures. The urban environment restricts the effectiveness of AM and FM communications. Whenever possible, consider using wire and operational civilian telephone systems. Urban operation also increase the requirement for linguists in non-English speaking countries due to the increased interaction with the indigenous population.

Sustainment. There are no unique sustainment considerations for IEW equipment, supplies, and MI soldiers in an urban environment.

FM 90-10 contains additional information on urban operations.

Nuclear, Chemical, Biological:

The capability and willingness of a growing number of nations to employ NBC weapons makes it urgent that US Forces plan o fight in an NBC environment. US Forces cannot allow enemy surprise or first use of NBC weapons to decide the outcome of the conflict. The employment of these weapons drastically alters the traditional concept of fire and maneuver. Their use can rapidly and effectively decide the outcome of the battle.

Consider the following when planning IEW operations in an NBC environment:

Operational. MI operational objectives are to survive and continue IEW operations in an NBC environment. Achieving those objectives require that MI leaders and soldiers fully understand the NBC weapons and the vulnerabilities of IEW systems. It also requires those individual soldiers and teams are well trained and prepared to operate with minimal mission degradation. Prestrike actions include OPSEC measures, which help a unit avoid becoming a target.

Sustainment. When NBC weapons are used, catastrophic losses may occur in seconds or minutes. Regeneration of combat power must be initiated immediately. The commander will have an immediate need for intelligence on which to base tactical decisions and force reconstitution. With the havoc that can be created by NBC weapons, MI units must recover rapidly for their own survival as well as that of the combined arms team.

FM 3-100 contains additional information on nuclear, biological, chemical operations.

Cold Weather:

Winter conditions have a significant effect on IEW operations due to brittleness of antennas, ice and fog on optic sights, and ice loading on antennas and intake filters. Consider the following when planning IEW operations in a cold weather environment:

Operational. MI units operating in a cold weather environment should be afforded a higher than normal density of IEW systems due to severe terrain and climate conditions. Consider requirements for increased setup time to stabilize temperature and humidity so signal equipment will not fail.

Sustainment. Units preparing for cold weather operations require larger than normal PLLs and authorized stockage lists (ASLs). Higher PLL usage should be expected for hoses, lubricants, filters, spark plugs, and all types of seals. For soldiers, there is greater susceptibility for frostbite, trench foot, and the effects of vision whiteouts and high wind-chill factors.

FMs 31-70, 31-71, and 34-81 contain additional information on cold weather operations.

LESSON 4

PRACTICE EXERCISE

The following items will test your grasp of the material covered in this lesson. There is only one correct answer for each item. When you have completed the exercise, check your answers with the answers with the answer key that follows. If you answer any items incorrectly, study again that part of the lesson, which contains the portion involved.

1. Who uses IEW to plan and execute operations?

    A. Combat Service Support Commanders

    B. Combat Support Commanders

    C. Combat Commanders

    D. All the above

2. What farther improves the commander's ability to understand and direct the battle?

    A. Combat Operations

    B. Split-based Operations

    C. Conflict Operations

    D. Peacetime operations

3. Knowing what will let commanders at every level anticipate developments, prepare options, and exploit battlefield opportunities?

A. Battle space

B. Area of Operation

C. Area of Interest

D. Battlefield Organization

LESSON 4

PRACTICE EXERCISE

ANSWER KEY AND FEEDBACK

ITEM	CORRECT ANSWER AND FEEDBACK	
1.	C. Combat Commanders	(page 4-2, para 2)
2.	B. Split-Based Ops	(page 4-2, para 5)
3.	B. Area of Operation	(page 4-6, para 4

LESSON 5

JOINT, COMBINED AND INTERAGENCY OPERATIONS

CRITICAL TASK: 301-372-3006

OVERVIEW

LESSON DESCRIPTION:

In this lesson you will be given information on joint, combined, and interagency operations and how IEW supports them.

TERMINAL LEARNING OBJECTIVE:

TASKS: Identify the procedures of each of the operations and how they differ between them.

CONDITIONS: You will be given narrative information and illustrations from FM 34-1.

STANDARDS: Identify how IEW support is conducted and managed in these operations

REFERENCES: The material contained in this lesson was derived from the following publications:

FM 34-1

INTRODUCTION

The Army conducts operations in concert and cooperation with other services, allied or coalition forces, agencies of the US Government at all levels, nongovernment agencies, and international agencies. Uncertainty about potential threats to the US and the requirements of force projection make almost any combination possible. Joint and combined operations are the primary means of conducting force projection operations and warfighting. In SASO, Army operations will likely involve support to a civilian agency and some form of direction or control of the operation by that agency. The Intelligence BOS supports all such operations. Effective IEW in joint, combined, or interagency operations demands mutual intelligence support, sharing of IEW capabilities and assets, robust liaison, and agreement on policies and procedures among all participants.

JOINT OPERATIONS

Force projection is, by nature, a joint operation. In joint operations, Army MI units support the ARFOR and JTF commander. Army intelligence resources and capabilities are fully integrated and linked to the combatant command or JTF J2 and JIC. Within the joint intelligence organizations, Army MI personnel provide expertise on threat ground forces and the IEW needs of Army commanders.

Joint Intelligence Organizations:

Army IEW operations in joint operations focus on providing multidiscipline IEW support to the combatant command, the Army service component command and ARFOR, and the JTF. They build upon the foundation of joint intelligence developed during peacetime operations. Support to joint operations, therefore, should not require significant modification to the Intelligence BOS nor change the IEW principles of force projection. It does, however, demand greater awareness of the organizations, procedures, capabilities, and limitations of the Air Force, Navy, and Marine Corps IEW operations. And, for personnel working in a 2, JIC, or other joint intelligence organization, it means applying joint procedures and principles. The goal of Army IEW operations remains the same whether conducted in a joint or Army-only operational environment. That goal is a seamless system capable of meeting the IEW and targeting needs of the commander.

Joint intelligence organizations allow ARFOR commanders to build a continuous bridge from the deployed ARFOR to the JIC and beyond to national agencies. Figure 5-1 shows the joint intelligence architecture.

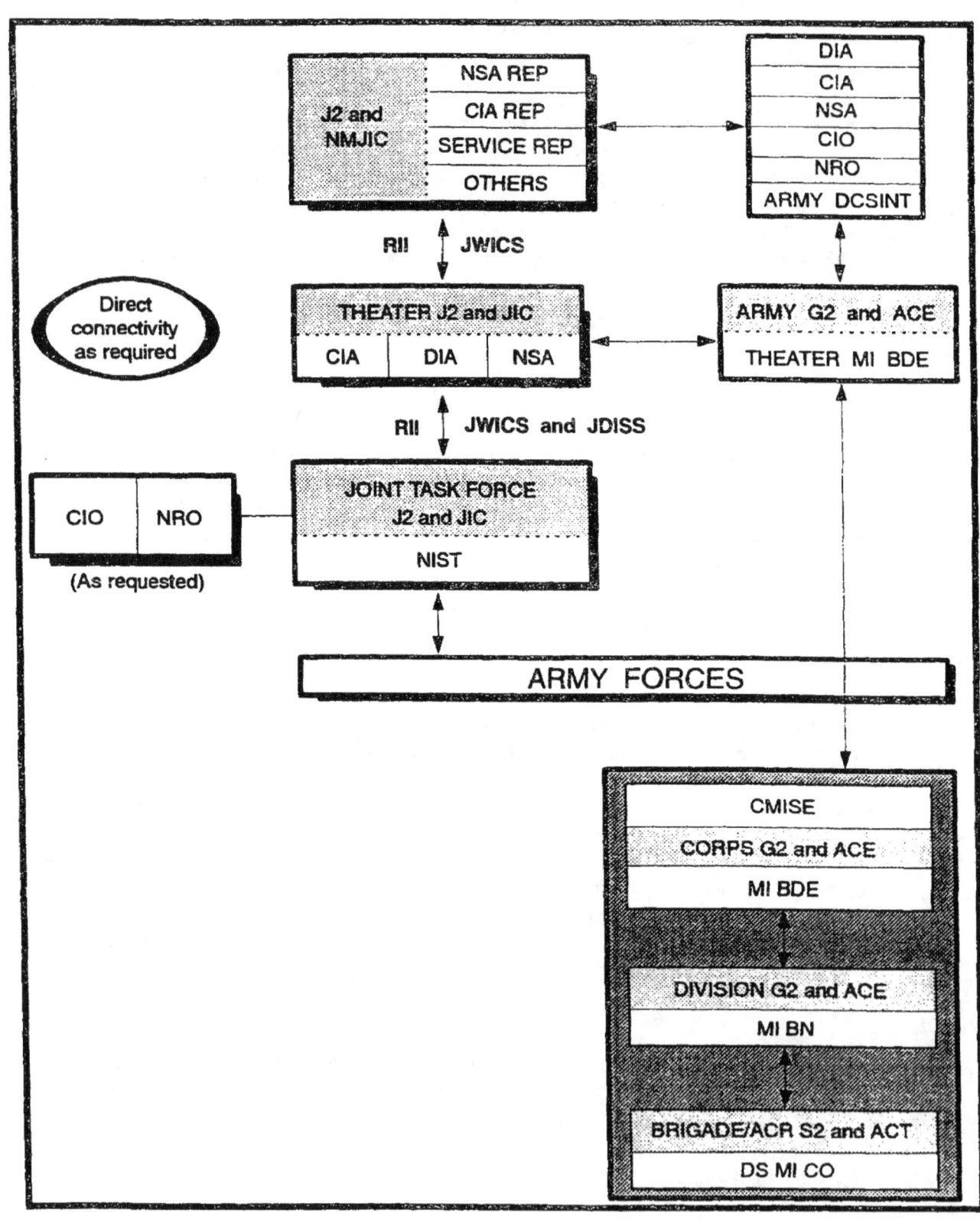

Figure 5-1. Formal joint intelligence architecture.

Described below are some of the intelligence relationships, which support joint intelligence operations.

National Security Council (NSC). The NSC advises the President and national leadership on integration of domestic, foreign, and military policies relating to national security. Statutory members of the NSC are the President, the Vice President, the Secretary of State, and the Secretary of Defense. The Director Central Intelligence and Chairman, Joint Chiefs of Staff (CJCS) participate as advisors. The NSC provides review of, guidance for, and direction to the conduct of all national foreign intelligence and CI activities.

Director, Central Intelligence (DCI). The DCI coordinates the efforts of the intelligence community at the national level. As the DCI and head of the Central Intelligence Agency (CIA), he is the primary advisor to the President and the NSC on national foreign intelligence matters. The DCI and the intelligence community staff provide guidance and direction to all intelligence agencies and organizations at the national and departmental level.

Joint Staff Director for Intelligence, J2 (Joint Staff J2). The Joint Staff J2 is the senior intelligence officer to the CJCS. As the Joint Staff J2, he provides intelligence support to the CJCS, Joint Chiefs of Staff (JCS), unified commands, and forces of joint combatant commands. He is responsible for day-to-day and joint staff functions including control of the National Military Joint Intelligence Center.

National Military Joint Intelligence Center (NMJIC). The NMJIC is the focal point for intelligence support to joint operations. The NMJIC is composed of representatives from the Defense Intelligence Agency (DIA), CIA, National Security Agency (NSA), Central Imagery Office (CIO), National Reconnaissance Office (NRO), and military services. It has access to all DIA resources and the agencies within the national intelligence community. As the top level of joint intelligence architecture, the NMJIC is the channel through which joint force commander's intelligence and CI needs are tasked to appropriate national agencies. The NMJIC coordinates direct connectivity as required between national intelligence activities and deployed forces. The NMJIC also coordinates deployment of National Intelligence Support Teams (NISTs) comprised of representatives from DIA, CIA, and NSA. These teams deploy with portable communications equipment and provide direct connectivity into the national intelligence community and the NMJIC. A NIST can deploy to any echelon to include deployed operational forces.

Deputy Chief of Staff, Intelligence (DCSINT). The DCSINT directs, coordinates, and develops policy for Army IEW and Army IEW supports to joint operations. He oversees numerous Army intelligence organizations at the national and departmental levels that support joint operations. The office of the DCSINT is the Army authority for intelligence operations, intelligence policy matters with national level agencies, and coordination with Joint Staff and other services as well as allied and foreign countries.

Theater J2. The theater or combatant command J2 assists the theater Commander in Chief (CINC) in developing strategy, planning theater campaigns, organizing the theater intelligence effort, and establishing command relationships for effective unified and joint operations. The J2 is responsible for determining the requirements and direction of the intelligence effort to support the commander's objectives. He assists the commander in ensuring that intelligence objectives are correct understood, prioritized, synchronized, and acted upon. The J2 is also responsible for employing joint force intelligence resources, identifying and integrating additional intelligence resources such as the JIC, and applying national intelligence capabilities. He works with other J2s and service G2s to develop complementary intelligence operations, which support the commander's requirements. He oversees the theater's CI operations and force protection effort. The theater J2 also-

- Recommends to the CINC the priorities for intelligence planning, products, and acquisition of intelligence resources.

- Establishes the intelligence architecture within which the component commands and other subordinate commands operate.

- Sets intelligence collection priorities through collection and production tasking and the allocation of intelligence resources and communications.

- Directs the activities of the J2 staff and the JIC.

- Serves as the focal point for receiving, validating, and issuing requests of national systems' support of theater, joint, and component intelligence requirements.

- Manages theater intelligence communications and processing systems, and ensures subordinate commands possess adequate intelligence communications and processing capabilities.

Functional and geographical combatant commands are uniquely organized for their particular missions and area of responsibility. US European Command and US Pacific Command are examples of theater or geographical combatant commands. US Special Operations Command is an example of a functional combatant command. The command's IEW structure is tailored to support these requirements. The intelligence assets available at each command include-

- Intelligence and CI.

- I&W.
- Special security office (SSO).

- Cryptologic support group (CSG).

- Liaison officers.

- Joint Interrogation Facility (IF), Joint Captured Materiel Exploitation Center (JCMEC), and Joint Document Exploitation Center (JDEC).

The J2 staff has intelligence experts from each of the command's subordinate service components. The staff provides the CINC and 12 with information on each component's intelligence capabilities, limitations, and requirements. The staff may include additional support elements from each subordinate command.

Theater JIC. The theater or combatant command NC is the principal element for ensuring effective intelligence support for combatant command CINC and theater forces. Not all CINCS have a AC assigned to their command, but are supported by a regional NC. The NC is an all-source center that produces intelligence to satisfy the requirements of the CINC and subordinate units. The HC also provides intelligence support to national and subordinate commands within the theater. The NC can expand or contract in size and scope of operations based on the requirements of the CINC and theater forces. The NC may also attach an intelligence support element (ISE) to supported commands within the theater. Combatant commanders, who have a NC, organize it in the manner best suited to satisfy their intelligence requirements. Normally the theater NC-

Coordinates the intelligence efforts of subordinate commands.

- Coordinates the theater collection plan and employment of theater organic sensors.

- Provides national and subordinate commands with a single, coordinated intelligence picture by fusing national and theater intelligence into all-source estimates and assessments.

- Develops and maintains databases which support planning, operations, and targeting.

- Provides IEW support to US military assistance advisory groups.

- Supports deep targeting.

- Validates BDA from higher, lower, and adjacent sources.

Joint Task Force J2. The JTF J2 is responsible for determining the requirements and direction of the intelligence effort to support the JTF commander's objectives. He assists the commander in ensuring that intelligence objectives are correct, understood, prioritized, synchronized, and acted upon. The J2 is also responsible for employing joint intelligence resources, identifying and integrating additional intelligence resources such as the JIC, and applying national intelligence capabilities. He works with subordinate service G2s (S2s) to develop complementary intelligence operations, which support the JTF commander's requirements.

Joint Task Force JIC. The JTF JIC is the primary J2 organization supporting the joint force commander and the ARFOR. The JIC facilitates efficient access to the entire Department of Defense (DOD) intelligence system. The composition and focus of each JIC varies according to the commander's needs but each possesses the capability to perform I&W, current intelligence, collection management, and dissemination. The BC is dynamic, flexible, and an expandable structure exemplified by the NMJC and theater JICs such as the Central Command (CENTCOM) i/C. Through the J/C, ARFORs coordinate support from Air Force, Navy, and Marine Corps, national, interagency, and combined or allied resources.

Theater Army G2. The theater Army G2 is responsible to the Army service component (ASC) commander for all Army intelligence activities within the ARFOR assigned to the unified or subunified command. He supports and receives guidance from the combatant command J2. The G2-

- Serves as the component focal point for ground force intelligence.

- Supervises all facets of the theater Army IEW operations, including collection management, and all-source production to satisfy the intelligence needs of the commander.

- Provides ISEs for liaison with Army, joint, combined, and allied military organizations and their associated intelligence organizations and services.

- Recommends standard tactical missions and command relationships of theater IEW assets supporting the ground forces of subordinate, joint, or combined commands or other IEW organizations in the theater.

- Exercises direct supervisory control of the ACE of the theater MI brigade.

Theater Military Intelligence Brigade. Each theater MI brigade is regionally and functionally tailored according to the requirements of the specific theater. The theater MI brigade provides multidiscipline IEW support normally to the Army G2; however, in certain theaters, the brigade provides echelon above division support to the theater under the direction of the J2 versus G2 and may be integrated into the J2's operations. The theater MI brigade may provide support to a JTF or to forward-deployed ECB forces. The theater MI brigade provides-

- Multidiscipline IEW support to ASC, JTF, and forward deployed ECB forces.

- Personnel for the CMISE which reinforce organic capabilities of the deployed corps. The combination of the theater JIC, CMISE, and theater MI brigade ACE, forms a continuous bridge from the corps to the JIC and beyond to national agencies.

- Support to the joint intelligence structure with ground component intelligence.

The theater MI brigade organic assets vary by theater. Its capabilities may include-

- Deployable high frequency, LOS intercept, DF, and jamming.

- Reinforcement to national sensor nodes in the theater to leverage strategic signals and IMINT collection and processing systems for the ASC and supported corps.

- MDCI.

- Interrogation, document exploitation, and other HUMINT collection.

- TECHINT collection and exploitation.

- MASINT collection, analysis, and reporting.

- Operational intelligence products for deployed forces such as graphic templates and annotated imagery.

- Access to weather information through the IMETS and the EAC Air Force weather team.

- Finished products pertaining to general MI, S&TI (to include support to reprogramming of smart weapons), and CI.

Theater Army ACE. The theater Army ACE supports the Army commander and subordinate ARFOR. It is directly supervised by the G2 and normally collocates with the G2 staff. In certain theaters, the ACE may be integrated into the J2 operations and serve as the nucleus for the JIC. The theater Army ACE is the focal point for planning, directing, and coordinating ground force IEW operations.

Theater SIGINT control and analysis resources are integrated with all-source analysis, production, and collection management within the ACE. The theater Army ACE-

- Performs collection management, all-source intelligence production, and intelligence and information dissemination.

- Supports national, joint, and combined commands with key intelligence products through the Intelligence BOS.

- Manages the exchange of intelligence, tasking, and requests among all Army IEW elements in the theater.

- Coordinates requests for IEW support between national-level agencies, sister services, allied forces, and ECB units. It supplements the organic collection capabilities of supported commands.

- Translates SORs into specific SIGINT collection requirements and tasks specific SIGINT assets.

- Coordinates directly with the Army technical control and analysis element (TCAE) which is collocated with NSA for access to national SIGINT databases.

- Is the point through which Army ECB MI units receive SIGINT information and technical support from national assets, other services, or allied SIGINT assets.

- Works and coordinates with the Regional SIGINT Operations Center to create and maintain threat databases.

Corps Military Intelligence Support Element. The CMISE provides the corps commander with an expanded and flexible intelligence capability. The CMISE is a direct support unit from the theater MI brigade tailored to meet the intelligence requirements of the supported corps. Its soldiers form a team of experts familiar with corps, theater, and national intelligence systems and structures. The CMISE fully integrates into the corps intelligence structure under the operational control of the corps G2.

The CMISE serves as a bridge between theater and national intelligence agencies and their tactical consumers at ECB. Within the theater, CMISE leverages the JIC to ensure it focuses on support to the corps during operations. It must work in cooperation with, and be complementary to, the JIC to fully exploit the capabilities of the intelligence system. The CMISE also provides the corps greater access to national intelligence structures through affiliation with the theater MI brigade and INSCOM. Figure 5-2 shows joint and services intelligence organizations accessible through the CMISE.

The CMISE can perform the following functions for the corps:

194

- Provides additional capability to do split-based operations. Members of the CMISE provide continuity during exercises or contingencies when they remain at home station, pull intelligence from higher echelons, and push finished intelligence to the corps.

- Provides an ISE with deployed elements of the corps to facilitate greater continuity and expanded links to higher echelons.

- Monitors other countries in the corps AI while the Ma brigade focuses on an exercise or contingency operation.

- Expands the number of regions or countries the corps can monitor and provides a strategic intelligence capability focused on the commander's requirements.

- Supports the corps at any point during an operation with versatility in intelligence support and access to higher echelon intelligence.

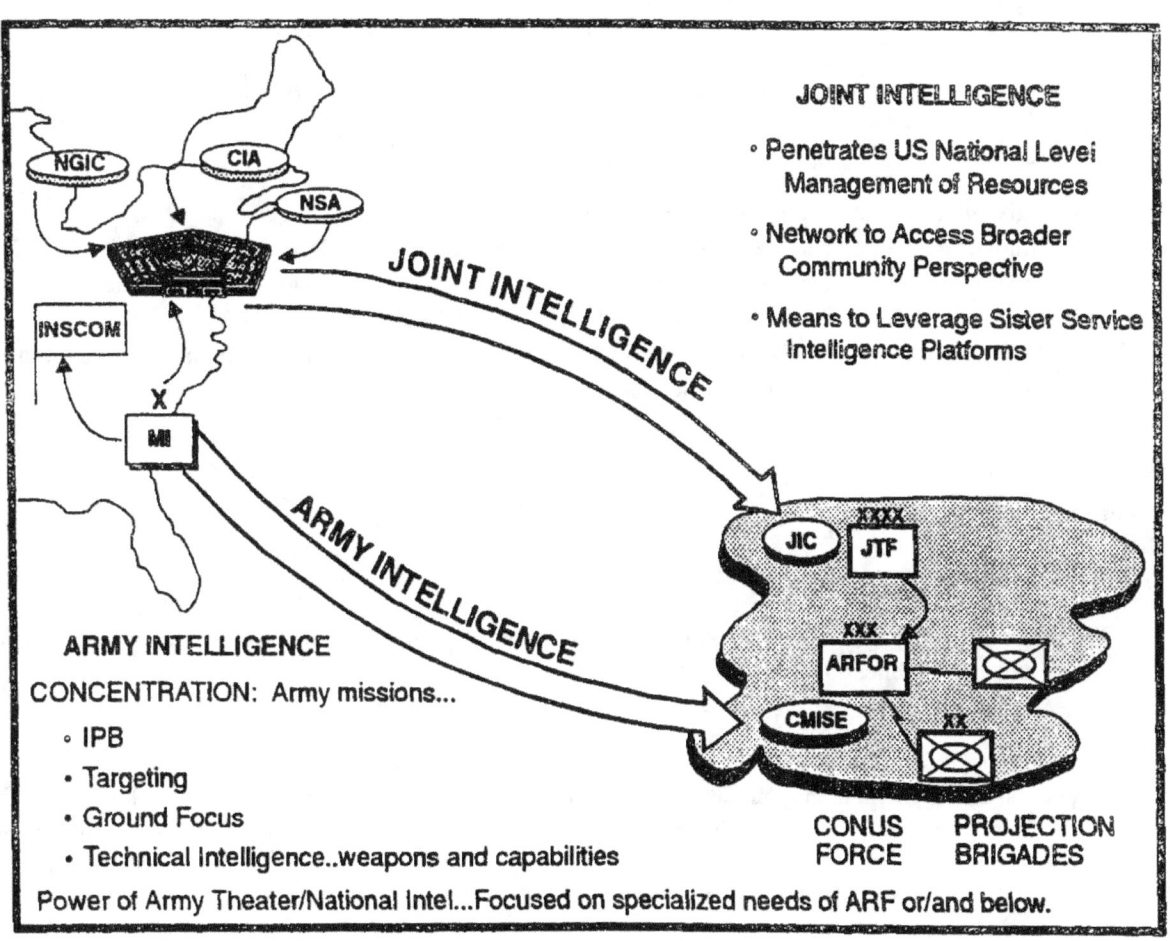

Figure 5-2. Joint and service intelligence organizations accessible through the CMISE.

Joint Intelligence Operations:

Key responsibilities of intelligence organizations in joint intelligence operations are to-

- Support unified JTF, and component commanders.

- Establish, if necessary, a JTF JIC to centrally manage the joint intelligence effort.

- Integrate intelligence received from component units with that provided by the joint, national, combined, and interagency resources to satisfy the needs of the joint commander.

- Coordinate component EW efforts to support the joint effort.

- Facilitate expedient and efficient access to the entire DOD intelligence structure in support of joint operations.

The combatant command and joint force commanders do not have organic collection assets. The CINC or JTF commander relies on national and subordinate commands for collection assets. These may include joint force collection assets, assets organic to the service component commands, SOF, or other subordinate commands within the theater. They may be Air Force, Navy, Marine Corps, or Army assets organic to NSCOM EAC brigades. The J2 must task collection assets through the component command, combined command, or other appropriate command channels.

Joint Intelligence Procedures:

When serving on a joint staff, Army intelligence personnel comply with joint doctrine, Joint Publication 2-series, and Joint Publication 3-0.

Collection management at the joint level differs slightly from Army doctrine. At the joint level, dissemination responsibility lies with the joint equivalent of the mission manager not the asset manager.

The joint staff ensures that component data bases and communications systems are interoperable.

Joint Publications 2-0, 2-01, and 2-02 contain more details on national intelligence agencies; the NMJIC and lower echelon JCs; joint TTPs for intelligence support to joint combined, and allied commands; and the communications and ADP systems which make that support possible.

COMBINED OPERATIONS

In combined operations, forces of two or more nations work to accomplish the mission. Combined organizations conduct IEW operations based on established international standards, such as the North Atlantic Treaty Organization (NATO) and STANAG 2936. Other coalitions and alliances must adjust the concept of IEW support to meet the common goal. Furthermore, most potential allies will not possess the range of US capabilities to collect and process intelligence. All personnel work to eliminate differences in culture, language, terminology, and operational concepts. See Joint Publication 2-0 for specific information on this subject.

Combined Intelligence Organizations:

Combined intelligence organizations vary according to the type of operation, commander's intelligence requirements, security concerns, and capabilities of each participant. The joint intelligence structure discussed earlier provides a framework for organizing the combined intelligence effort. However, the final combined intelligence structure should be one in which allied, coalition, and US commanders receive the information necessary to successfully conduct the operation.

Allied organizations like NATO are permanently organized with established relationships and procedures. The Army helps resource the permanent intelligence staff but may still augment that staff with an ISE.

Military operations with coalition partners take place under bilateral, multinational, or United Nations (UN) auspices. Military coalitions are temporary organizations that last only for the duration of a crisis or war. The coalition commander establishes organizations, relationships, and procedures for coalition units. The Army helps resource an ISE to coalition staffs from the theater MI brigade.

Combined Intelligence Operations:

Army staffs coordinate support from coalition and allied partner intelligence resources through the ISE of the combined staff. Coalition and allied partners provide translator and interpreter support to complement Army linguist capabilities.

Combined IEW operations are based on the following principles:

Adjust National Differences Among Nations. Effective combined operations require adjusting IEW operations to minimize differences in national concepts of IEW support. Routinely conducting combined exercise and intelligence operations are two ways of eliminating differences and improving intelligence readiness.

Unity of Effort Against Common Threat. The threat to one member of an alliance or coalition should be considered a threat to all.

Determining and Planning Intelligence. The combined command and national forces' intelligence requirements, production, and use should be agreed upon, planned, and exercised in advance.

Special Arrangements. Special arrangements should be made, when necessary, to accommodate national differences in culture, language, terms, doctrine, methods of operation, communications, and structures. An example would be the positioning of a Joint STARS downlink terminal with a non-US coalition command.

Full Exchange of Intelligence. Each nation should share intelligence, which supports military operations and attains alliance or coalition objectives. Every attempt should be made to ensure alliance and coalition commanders are provided the intelligence needed to protect their forces and achieve success. This may require gaining permission from national intelligence agencies for the declassification or sanitation of previously restricted intelligence. Once permission is gained, the exchange of intelligence must be monitored to ensure it complies with foreign disclosure policies and procedures.

Complementary Intelligence Operations. The strengths and weaknesses of each nation's IEW forces and operations should be evaluated to determine the best blend of capabilities available to accomplish the mission.

Combined Intelligence Centers. Where there is a combined command, there should also be a combined intelligence center. The center should consist of an intelligence staff composed of members from each nation and, in addition to conducting intelligence operations, be able to translate and disseminate products in various national languages of the command.

Liaison Exchange. The exchange of intelligence personnel between alliance or coalition partners bridges national differences and ensures access to intelligence resources of each nation.

Combined Intelligence Procedures:

Joint Publication 2-0 provides specifics for these procedures. In addition, the-

- Coalition commander determines standardized procedures for coalition forces.
- Combined staff ensures that allied and coalition forces use interoperable databases and communication systems.

- American, British, Canadian, and Australian (ABCA) forces have agreed to abide by Quadripartite Standardization Agreements (QSTAGs), which generally mirror Standardization Agreements (STANAGs). AR 34-1 contains further information on these agreements.

NATO Forces have agreed to abide by STANGs which--

- Ensure a five-step intelligence cycle (plan and direct, collect, process, produce, and disseminate).

- Standardize the intelligence estimate content and format.

- Establish intelligence reporting procedures and format of request for intelligence information (RU).

INTERAGENCY OPERATIONS

MI units routinely operate as part of an interagency team or receive support from nonmilitary intelligence agencies. Interagency operations occur between Army units and Federal, state and local agencies or international agencies. In a particular crisis or operation, the Army component may be under the direction of a US Government agency or other civilian agency. Interagency operations require a cooperative approach to the coordination, exchange, and integration of intelligence within the constraints of AR 381-10. MI units involved in this type of operation need to understand how the agency provides support to operators, planners, and policymakers to conduct successful operations. Joint Publication 2-01 contains more information on interagency operations.

Interagency Intelligence Organizations:

The organization varies depending upon the situation and the mission. Certain efforts such as counter-drug operations are well established. More often than not, the Army component staffs negotiate specific relationships with other US agencies during specific crises. Some agencies such as NSA and DIA have long established interagency relationships with the military.

Interagency Intelligence Operations:

Other US agencies can provide HUMINT, SIGINT, and IMINT support to Army units. Army intelligence should take advantage of this capability, whenever possible.

Interagency Intelligence Procedures:

Usually the Army component establishes new procedures for each operation involving another US agency. Some key procedural issues in interagency operations are releasability, write-in authority, and dissemination of intelligence.

Releasability. The Intelligence BOS supports all operations to the maximum extent possible. In interagency operations, maximum intelligence support requires that the tasked Army and US Government agencies or other civilian organizations have authority to exchange information and intelligence required to carry out their responsibilities. This two-way flow of information is part of a seamless Intelligence BOS architecture.

At a minimum, the Army component needs authority to release information, when necessary, to subordinate and adjacent units and to other services. Some types of information may require sanitization to protect sources and follow-on collection operations. Intelligence staffs must establish procedures for release of specific types of information between the Army and other agencies before the operation begins, if possible. Various US Government, DOD, and Army regulations (ARs) control releasability and specify procedures for release. ARs 380-5, 381-1, 381-10, and other 380- and 381 -series regulations contain further information.

Write-in Authority. Army intelligence elements at each echelon require the ability and the authority to write information into data bases, which they receive from higher echelons. National intelligence agencies, JCs, and theater ACEs maintain a wide variety of intelligence databases. Each echelon needs the capability for automated receipt. update, transfer, and return of databases between echelons.

One example is the DIA's military intelligence integrated data base system/integrated database (MIIDS/IDB). The ACE at corps, division, or separate brigade, or the intelligence element of an Army component in any interagency, joint, or combined operation. may need the capability to receive a portion of the MIIDS/IDB which focused on the requirements of that echelon or operation. They also need the write-in authority and automation to update the MHDS/IDB at their echelon, to manipulate the data, and to pass it back to DIA or transfer the database to subordinate or adjacent units. A two-way flow of data base information is part of the seamless intelligence architecture. It can help provide a common picture of the AO to commanders at all echelons and support distributive production of intelligence in the Intelligence BOS.

Dissemination. In interagency operations, Army commanders and civilian leaders require information and intelligence upon which to base decisions as urgently as in any other category of operations. Dissemination of intelligence must be as fast and direct as possible. US Government, DOD, and Army security requirements must be considered. Memorandums of Understanding or Letters of Agreement may be required. The Army and civilian agency intelligence staffs should complete negotiations and agreements on intelligence dissemination policies and procedures before the operation begins.

Exchange of intelligence liaison teams can greatly enhance the effectiveness of dissemination. The intelligence liaison officer can sanitize incoming information as it is received, and when necessary, interpret the information which nonmilitary staffs may not understand.

The Army and the government agency should use compatible communications and ADP systems. The commanders and leaders in an interagency operation must be able to receive information from anywhere in the intelligence system and also contribute information into the system.

LESSON 5

PRACTICE EXERCISE

The following items will test your grasp of the material covered in this lesson. There is only one correct answer for each item. When you have completed the exercise, check your answers with the answers with the answer key that follows. If you answer any items incorrectly, study again that part of the lesson, which contains the portion involved.

1. Which of the following does NCS provide?

    A. review

    B. guidance

    C. direction

    D. All the above

2. The CMISE provides expanded and flexible intelligence capabilities to who?

    A. Bn. Commanders

    B. Corps Commanders

    C. Bde. Commanders

    D. Div. Commanders

3.   Which of the following is a key procedural issue in interagency operations?

A. timeliness

B. write-out authority

C. releasability

D. organizational structure

LESSON 5

PRACTICE EXERCISE

ANSWER KEY AND FEEDBACK

ITEM	CORRECT ANSWER AND FEEDBACK	
1.	D.	(page 5-4, para 1)
2.	B.	(page 5-9, para 2)
3.	C.	(page 5-15, para 3/4)

LESSON 6

STABILLITY AND SUPPORT OPERATIONS, SPECIAL OPERATIONS AND

INFORMATION OPERATIONS

CRITICAL TASKS: 301-372-3006

301-372-3052

301-372-3600

OVERVIEW

LESSON DESCRIPTION:

In this you will be given information on SASO, Special operations, and Information operations and how IEW supports these operations.

TERMINAL LEARNING OBJECTIVE:

TASKS: Identify the doctrinal foundation for SASO, special operations, and information operations.

CONDITIONS: You will be given narrative information and illustrations from FM 34-1.

STANDARDS: Recognize the doctrine for each type of these operations.

REFERENCES: The material contained in this lesson was derived from the following publications.

FM-34-1

INTRODUCTION
205

US Army units conduct SASO, special operations and information operations during peace and conflict. Not all of these operations use force. The national command authority employs all types of forces in SASO. Army Special Operations Forces (ARSOF) are specially organized, trained, and equipped to conduct special operations. In some types of SASO, MI or an ARSOF unit might be the only Army force supporting the operation. MI personnel must consider these unique requirements when supporting SASO or ARSOF missions.

This chapter describes and sets the doctrinal foundation for IEW support to information operations. The military operations of the future will leverage technology to distort or restrict the adversary's perception of the battlefield while protecting our own. Using all the principles discussed in preceding chapters, IEW will support the commander in winning the information war. The effectiveness of information operations is predicated on a thorough understanding of the enemy, his C^2 system, and his decision making process. At all levels of war, the Intelligence BOS is an operational tool that assesses and exploits the vulnerabilities of the enemy's information and C^2 systems. IEW is an integral player in C^2W and information operations. Its lead role in building information system IPB, developing C^2W COAs and assessing the effectiveness of information operations has taken MI from a support to an operational role in military operations. IEW operations set the conditions for decisive maneuver.

OPERATIONS OTHER THAN WAR

The preceding chapters have described the principles and fundamentals of IEW operations in the context of conflict and war. However, the Army is, and will be in the future, often called upon to execute operations, which promote peacekeeping, law and order, democracy, and humanitarian endeavors. These operations are collectively described as SASO and, while not all require the application of force, most require IEW support.

Fundamentals of IEW Support to SASO:

Although the principles of JEW support apply equally to war and SASO, the needs of the commander in SASO are often quite different from those of the commander in conventional combat operations. Success in SASO is contingent upon the commander possessing a complete understanding of the situation. This understanding often focuses on what were formerly considered nonmilitary topics such as politics, economics, and demographics. In some SASO, understanding the population and its culture may be the commander's keys to mission success. The nature of SASO requires that the Intelligence BOS be fully engaged, flexible, and responsive to the challenges of these operations. Some fundamental aspects of JEW support to SASO are discussed below.

206

Intelligence Preparation of the Battlefield (IPB). IPB analyzes the threat and environment in a specific geographic area. It supports staff estimates, planning, and decision making. The steps of the IPB process remain constant regardless of mission, unit, or echelon. The commander must define the battlefield environment, describe the battlefield effects, evaluate the threat, and determine threat COAs. Application of these steps, however, will vary with each specific situation. The principal difference between IPB for conventional operations and IPB for SASO is the focus and the degree of detail required to support the commanders decision making process. Other major differences include the impact of the political situation, to include such things as legal mandates or terms of reference, and the enormous demand for demographic analysis. New information categories will emerge for the commander as he directs troops and accomplishes missions in the SASO environment.

Collection management.

Collection management in SASO may differ somewhat from collection of intelligence in conventional operations. PIR and IR will be many and varied, as will the collection resources and methods. For these reasons, the "dispersed

battlefield" collection plan format may be the mo effective for operations such as peacekeeping. The dispersed battlefield collection plan format lends itself to situations where there are many diverse PIR and the availability of collection systems is far outweighed by the number of requirements. This type of collection plan assists the commander and G2 (S2) by providing techniques, which carefully prioritize each indicator and SIR, in addition to the supported PIR and IR. For detailed guidance on the dispersed battlefield collection plan, refer to FM 34-2.

Standardized checklists.

Standardized checklists can also enhance the collection effort by focusing attention towards answering PIR and IR even when a situation is unique or personnel are new to the operational environment. The checklists also help to speed the train-up time of intelligence sections and units. Some examples of checklists used during peacekeeping operations in Somalia, in 1993, included the Area Assessment Checklist, Convoy Debrief Checklist, Roadblock Checklist, and the Airfield Security Checklist. Overall aspects and considerations of each checklist will need to be modified to each situation and to the operational environment.

Intelligence disciplines.

All the intelligence disciplines should be employed to the fullest extent possible. The following describes how each discipline contributes to the overall intelligence picture:

- **HUMINT.** HUMIT is the most important discipline in many SASO activities for collecting information and understanding the AO. Whether collected by host nation personnel or US HUMINT, it contributes the most to understanding the population, its culture and needs, and the operational environment. HUMINT in many SASO activities is derived from non-MI military and

207

civilian personnel in the AO. In peacekeeping, information gathered by patrols, observation posts, and roadblocks provides a substantial amount of information for M analysts to evaluate. UN workers are a source of information during humanitarian relief operations. In SASO, every individual is a potential source of HUMINT.

- **IMINT**. IMINT assets should be used to enhance the commander's common picture of the battlefield. Imagery of key facilities, belligerent dispositions, staging areas, obstacles, and potential trouble spots can speed the commander's planning process by greatly reducing the uncertainty involved in the operation. Use assets from all levels, to include those of national and coalition partners, if involved in combined operations. Simple assets such as helicopters and UAVs are excellent for performing short-notice missions, such as route reconnaissance.

- **MASINT**. MASINT systems measure objects or events in order to identify them by their signatures. As in combat operations, MASINT
  systems can provide or enhance coverage of areas not under or beyond the range of visual observation.

- SIGINT. SIGINT assets provide the commander with valuable, often NRT intelligence on threat and belligerent intentions, readiness, and dispositions by intercepting and locating command, maneuver, fire support, reconnaissance and logistics emitters.

- MDCI personnel play an active role in force protection in SASO. MDCI teams provide the commander with information on how well threat forces can see his forces and the commands vulnerability to threat intelligence collection, as well as information regarding the current terrorist threat level.

Dissemination. Dissemination of intelligence products should be conducted using standard report formats. Intelligence personnel should ensure that liaison officers pass intelligence products to all parties requiring them in joint or combined operations. PSYOPS units are also very useful in disseminating peacekeeping operation objectives and ensuring that friendly efforts are hilly understood by belligerent parties and the civilian population.

Stability and Support Operation Activities:

SASO encompasses a variety of activities. Some operations such as show of force, attacks and raid and noncombatant evacuation operations require the IEW support of a combat operation. Humanitarian assistance and support to counter-drug operations are SASO activities that may not involve the use of force, but do require intelligence support to accomplish the mission. Though not an all-inclusive listing of SASO missions, an understanding of the following SASO activities and their IEW support can serve as a basis for planning future SASO.

Support to Domestic Civic Authorities. In times of domestic emergency, the Federal Government may direct the Armed Forces to assist civil authorities.

Within CONUS, the Army has primary responsibility for such assistance. Army units support disaster relief humanitarian assistance, and similar operations. Federal law also authorizes the use of military force to suppress domestic violence or insurrection. Under the provisions of the Posse Comititus Act, though, neither the AC nor the US Army Reserve may execute the law in the place of duly appointed law enforcement officials without specific presidential or congressional approval and direction.

Historical Perspective

Operation Garden Plot

On the afternoon of 29 April 1992, the worst civil unrest since the 1960s erupted in the streets of Los Angeles (LA). Forty-four people died and hundreds were injured before order was restored Property damage reached the billion dollar mark. It began as a small disturbance in south central LA, but quickly escalated and spread rapidly throughout the city and country. The violence initially overwhelmed law enforcement agencies, resulting in the burning of large areas of the city. The governor of California committed the state police and two thousand National Guard soldiers to assist in restoring law and order on 30 April. Following a Presidential Executive Order on 1 May, JTF-LA was formed. The Executive Order federalized unit of the California Army National Guard (CAARNG) and authorized active military forces to assist in the restoration of law and order. JTF-LA formed and deployed within 24 hours. It operated in a unique domestic disturbance environment while working with city, county, state, federal agencies, and the CAARNG. JTF-LA was completely successful in meeting the three objectives defined in its mission statement, which were-assume command and control of federalized National Guard and AC Marine and Army forces, establish liaison with local law enforcement agencies; and conduct civil disturbance operations to restore order in the greater LA area.

A full complement of intelligence analysts was required to support the assault command post (ACP) during Operation Garden Plot. Law enforcement agencies generally have adequate data collection capabilities, but lack the ability to perform detailed intelligence analysis. Considerations for the G2 (S2) in an operation such as Garden Plot may include points similar to the following:

- Conduct the IPB process in an exceptional degree of detail to support the JTF commander's decision making process. This detail will require a full demographic analysis of the area. IPB graphics produced during a terrain analysis of the target area may include a population status overlay, a key facilities and target overlay, and a LOC overlay.
- Evaluate the threat and build an accurate threat model, which will require dependence on information Rom a wide variety of sources and agencies. In Operation Garden Plot, military forces established intelligence exchange with suburban police departments, local city command post, the Los Angeles Police Department (LAPD), the LAPD emergency operations center, the city command center, the sheriffs office, the Federal Bureau of Investigation (FBI), and the

Bureau of Alcohol, Tobacco, and Firearms. Close and effective liaison must be established with all potential sources and agencies. Local law enforcement agencies have access to HUMINT, often unavailable to the military. The intelligence staff of the law enforcement agencies have unparalleled expertise in civil disturbances and gang behavior, while military analysts are in the best position to apply this experience to civil-military operations.

- Analyze threat patterns and activities. Analysts should keep in mind that gangs and other criminal elements may change their normal patterns of activity when military forces are present, making pattern analysis extremely difficult.

- Obtain force protection information. Civil disturbance missions require an especially robust MDCI capability. MDCI personnel can be used to obtain force protection information, but given the restrictions of AR 381-10 on the use of M assets to collect on US citizens it may be more appropriate for military police and other non-M personnel to perform the function.

- Anticipate the need to procure additional communications equipment to support intelligence operations during civil disturbances. During Operation Garden Plot, units used a variety of government-owned, off-the shelf purchased and personally owned equipment to effectively conduct operations. Additional communications equipment included much things as cellular phones, facsimile machines, and police scanners.

- Use imagery assets whenever possible. Aerial photographs of the target area to include key facilities, intersections, rally and staging areas, and potential trouble spots, can be an invaluable aid to commanders and staffs for planning and assessing operations.

Humanitarian Assistance and Disaster Relief. Humanitarian assistance (HA) includes programs conducted to relieve or reduce the results of natural or manmade disasters or other endemic conditions, such as human pain, disease, hunger, or privation that might present a serious threat to life and result in great damage or loss of property. HA, provided by US Forces, is designed to supplement or complement the efforts of the host nation, civil authorities, or agencies that may have the primary responsibility for providing HA. Disaster relief operations fall within the overall context of HA and are conducted in emergency situations to prevent the loss of life and property. Such operations may be in the form of immediate and automatic response by US military commanders or in response to requests from domestic authorities, foreign governments, or international agencies. Army elements are often responsible for supporting the implementation of assistance programs developed by the Office of Foreign Disaster Assistance within the Department of State.

Historical Perspective

Operation Provide Comfort

On 5 April 1991, President Bush announced the beginning of a relief operation in northern Iraq. Operation Provide Comfort combined post-conflict activity with extensive SOF involvement, focused on providing humanitarian assistance and protection to the displaced Kurdish population of Iraq following an unsuccessful attempt by Kurdish rebels to overthrow the Iraqi government. The US responded immediately By 7 April, US aircraft from Europe dropped relief supplies over the Iraq borders. More than 6, 000 soldiers from units which just had participated in Operation Desert Storm eventually redeployed to Turkey and Northern Iraq in support of Operation Provide Comfort. The initial objective of the operation was to reduce the death rate among the 400, 000 Kurdish refugees forced to survive in the mountains. Subsequent objectives included establishing a security zone in northern Iraq so that refugees would feel safe to return setting up refugee camps within the secure zone, and begin repatriating Kurds to the secure zone. There were a number of problems encountered during the operation. The Iraq government hostility towards the Kurds, combined with the continued presence, threats and harassment of Iraqi military, police, and secret police, made many Kurds reluctant to return to their homes. Additionally, the initial security zone did not include the city of Dahuk, which was the origin of most of the refugees

IPB for HA and disaster relief operations must be part of the deliberate planning process. For disasters, as in all no-notice operations, there is always danger. A military presence is often required before IPB can be completed. HA missions are not immune to danger and uncertainty as was evidenced by the destabilizing effects of competing factions in northern Iraq and in Somalia. Considerations for the G2 (S2) in HA operations may include some of the following:

- Collection sources and agencies for the operation include those used in conventional military operations, as well as some that are not normally considered. Potential sources and agencies include news media, liaisons with host nation police, government, and military, as well as liaisons with nongovernment organizations, private voluntary organizations, and international organizations. As in any operation, the standard collection plan format is a valuable aid, but if PIR and IR are many and varied, then the analyst should consider the use of the dispersed battlefield collection plan format.

- Employment of MINT, whenever possible. Use aerial platforms to photograph the extent of damage to the area and to conduct reconnaissance on key supply routes.

- Establish effective liaisons with all parties participating in HA operations.

Support to Counter-Drug Operations. Military efforts in counter-drug operations are directed primarily to support-

- Law enforcement agencies, other US agencies, and cooperating foreign governments to interdict the flow of illegal drugs at the source, in transit, and during distribution.

- Host nations, which include assisting their forces to destroy drug production facilities and collaboration with host nation armed forces to prevent export of illegal drugs.

- Interdiction efforts which center on monitoring and detecting illegal drugs in transit.

- Domestic counter-drug operations which include military planning and training assistance for domestic law enforcement agencies, equipment loans and transfers, use of military facilities and other assistance as requested and authorized.

Historical Perspective

Joint Tasks Force Six

The Secretary of Defense (SECDEF) has made counter-drug (CD) operations a high priority mission for the DOD and consequently, the Department of the Army (DA). In response to DOD guidance, the Secretary of the Army and the Army Chief of Staff signed and distributed the Army Counternarcotics Plan on 17 April 1990 This plan articulates a clear statement of intent and provides major subordinate commanders and DA staff with the broad guidance required to develop COA's. In further defining the DOD role in CD operations, the SECDEF directed all US major commands to draw up plans spelling out how they proposed to assist in the reduction of tugs coming into the US. United States Army Forces Command participation in the plan came with the activation of JFT 6 at Ft Bliss, TX. JFT 6 is designed as a planning and coordinating HQ to provides operational support from the DOD to federal, state, and local law enforcement agencies along the southwest border The southwest border is the principal corridor for moving drugs. Over 50 percent of illegal drugs entering the US cross the international boundary extending from the Gulf of Mexico to the Pacific Coast. Drugs are smuggled via land air, and water. Not only is Mexico a supplier of drugs, it is also a transit country for shipment from other countries It is estimated that in 1991 there were 150-200 organized Mexican groups whose sole purpose was drugs smuggling. MI personnel at JFT 6 are continually working to establish "modus operandi" for the drug smugglers. MI personnel also coordinate with the National Guard off our border states to ensure unity of effort in providing intelligence analysis, detection and monitoring, use of ground sensors, and photo reconnaissance.

Counter-drug IPB, particularly analysis of the terrain combined with knowledge of the drug trafficking organizations, can help to identify the best locations for law enforcement agency response teams and maximize their ability to apprehend large numbers of suspects. Although counter-drug IPB is a successful tool, commanders and intelligence professionals should be cautious not to overemphasize it. Planners should be prepared to adjust all collection assets such as listening and observation posts as experience is gained in counter-drug operations for a particular region. The drug traffickers will adjust their operations in reaction to your presence in the area.

Establishing the "modus operandi" for drug producers and traffickers will require the exchange of information between many sources and agencies. Potential sources of information may include domestic and host nation governments, military, police, the US Border Patrol, the FBI, the Drug Enforcement Agency (DEA), the US Customs Service, and the US Coast Guard.

Drug production and trafficking has a profound influence on the local population, so the analyst must be able to recognize the effects of these influences. Examples can be subtle, such as an unexplained increase in affluence within the population or increased corruption within the government. Domestic and host nation HUMINT sources will be most suited to detect the subtle changes in the population. Other effects may be more pronounced, such as an abrupt change from food crops to drug crops, the transfer of large cash deposits to out-of-country or offshore banks, or the eradication of extradition laws. Effective liaisons with domestic and host nation government agencies, military, and law enforcement agencies will be the key to identifying the effects of the drug trade.

Use IMINT assets to the maximum extent possible. Assets should be used to look for suspected laboratories or their construction cache sites of drugs or materials, and agricultural areas for drug crops. Assets may also be used to look for transshipment of drugs over rugged, isolated areas and the existence of newly-constructed or cut roads or trails which may suggest new transshipment routes, agricultural areas, or drug laboratories.

Anticipate increased capabilities on the part of the drug traffickers. Communications, for instance, may begin as telephone and amateur radio, but could rapidly move to encrypted digital SATCOMS. Money is seldom an issue in drug operations and the traffickers will spend the money to acquire the technology necessary to keep their operations secure. SIGNT collectors can be very useful in supporting counter-drug operations outside US borders, especially at locating remote production or transshipment facilities.

FM 100-5 and FM 34-7 provide more detailed information on SASO activities and IEW support to SASO.

SPECIAL OPERATIONS

ARSOF include Special Forces (SF), Rangers, CA, PSYOPS, and Army Special Operations Aviation (ARSOA) units. All types of ARSOF perform strategic, operational, and tactical missions in war and SASO. SOF operations are conducted during peacetime, conflict, and war independently or in coordination with allied forces. The Intelligence BOS supports the IEW requirements of all ARSOF missions. The five principal missions of special operations are---

- Direct action.

- Special reconnaissance.

- Counterterrorism.

- Unconventional warfare.

- Foreign internal defense.

Direct Action:

Direct action missions are shot duration strikes or small-scale offensive actions, which seize, destroy, or damage specific targets and capture or recover personnel or materiel. Army SF and Rangers conduct direct action missions often against targets deep within enemy controlled territory. The most frequent ARSOA mission is infiltration, exfiltration, and resupply of ARSOF by air. ARSOA supports SF or Rangers in direct action or can conduct direct action missions autonomously. Examples of IEW support include-

- Acquiring detailed knowledge of the target site.

- Identifying routes in and out of the target area.

- Determining the strength and order of battle of any threat forces that may respond.
- Identifying countermeasures to defeat enemy systems.

- Locating and suppressing enemy air threat.

Special Reconnaissance:

Army SF or ARSOA conduct special reconnaissance to obtain information not available by other means. Special reconnaissance complements national and theater collection systems to satisfy intelligence gaps and confirm information in the intelligence database.

Special reconnaissance operations can be broken into two categories: battlefield reconnaissance and surveillance using standard tactics and techniques, and clandestine collection. Clandestine collection is complex and sensitive and may require control of SF teams by the national intelligence community.

Counterterrorism:

Counterterrorism missions involve offensive measures against terrorists including preemptive and punitive actions. Only SF units specially organized, trained, equipped, and designated in theater OPLANS conduct counter-terrorism. They require detailed, responsive intelligence on terrorist personalities, organizations, logistical support, weapons, equipment, training, tactics, and information about any hostages. Counterterrorism mission planners and various national and military agencies must coordinate closely to gather, analyze, and immediately deliver the needed information to the SF unit performing the counterterrorism mission.

Unconventional Warfare:

Unconventional warfare is a broad spectrum of military and paramilitary operations against an established government or occupying power. Unconventional warfare normally involves inserting SF elements into an area controlled by hostile forces. The SF organize, train and equip indigenous forces, and support them in conducting guerrilla warfare or other direct offensive low-visibility operations, as well as indirect operations such as sabotage, subversion, or intelligence collection.

PSYOP missions are designed to influence the attitudes and behaviors of foreign enemy, friendly, or neutral audiences. In unconventional warfare, PSYOP elements try to demoralize hostile forces and reduce their will to fight.

The Intelligence BOS provides detailed all-source intelligence on the geography, targets in the area, the situation within and between partisan groups, and in-country sources of intelligence or support. Examples of IEW support to PSYOP elements include-

- Gathering information on the ethnic or religious makeup of a town or village.

- Determining attitudes and beliefs of the people.

- Identifying enemy activities or plans.
- Locating mobile target groups.

- Locating and jamming threat PSYOP transmitters.

Foreign Internal Defense:

Foreign internal defense missions support the host nation government. These missions may involve-

- SF elements, which conduct actions to strengthen the host countries defense establishment.

- CA elements, which set up a temporary civil administration at the request of the host nation to maintain law and order, and provide life-sustaining services until the host nation can resume normal operations. Examples of other CA actions are supporting NEO, coordinating local resources and facilities, and controlling civilian interference with US military activities.

- PSYOP elements, which act to counterthreat propaganda and weaken the influence of insurgent groups.

- ARSOF elements, which require the same types of EW support for foreign internal defense as well as unconventional warfare. They also need to know the sources of friction within the host country that impact on the acceptability and success of the government.

In addition to the five principal missions listed above, SOF my participate in collateral activities of security assistance, HA, antiterrorism, counter-drug operations, personnel recovery, and special activities with other components.

The Joint Publication 3-series, and FM 34-7 and FM 34-130 provide detailed planning guidance for SASO. FM 34-36 describes IEW support to ARSOF missions.

INFORMATION AGE AND IEW

Operation Desert Storm and other recent operations have shown that the nature of warfare has changed dramatically with the arrival of the information age. The information age is characterized by the proliferation of information systems and the increasing ability to rapidly collect, assimilate, and disseminate information. In the information age, those with access to, or control of these systems can immediately influence public opinion, world commerce, political dialogue, and other issues affecting the security of nations. The impact of the information age on military operations has caused a revolutionary change in the way US Forces conduct operations and the nature of warfare itself. The key to this modern form of warfare is knowledge-based operations.

Thus, the key to successful knowledge-based operations is exploiting and controlling information.

The information age has changed the conduct of IEW operations. Although MI can extend current IEW support to information operations, there are several aspects of information warfare that will generate new or more detailed IEW requirements. MI must-

- Learn and refine the capability to find and identify the vulnerabilities in the critical nodes of an adversary's decision-making system.

216

- Monitor the information warfare capabilities of potential adversaries and assess this capability as a threat to friendly battle command systems.

- Develop the analytical sills necessary to identify, depict, and exploit the information base of the opposing commander's decision making process and the global information environment.

- Ensure IEW operations effectively support the development and maintenance of the commander's common picture of the battlefield.

- Refine the methods to synchronize IEW operations of fully modernized, digitized forces with other forces--our own, other service, and allies.

MI must have a thorough understanding of the enemy C^2 structure and his decision making process to effectively support the development and maintenance of the commander's common picture of the battlefield. Information operations will require new analytic and synthesis techniques that describe the enemy C^2 information infrastructure in terms of the enemy commander's decision making process, and the critical nodes that allow him to exercise effective C^2 of his combat forces. Inherent is the requirement to understand how the enemy commander will be affected by specific C^2W actions and predict his response.

Another impact on the intelligence system is the need to assess the effectiveness of the information operations effort. This "electronic" BDA will allow commanders to adjust their efforts to maximize the effects on the enemy. An important aspect of this "electronic" BDA will be real-time analysis and synthesis to determine when information operations have created a vulnerability in the enemy C^2 structure that can be exploited by fire and maneuver. Information operations pose a unique challenge to BDA because the effects of C^2W on the enemy C^2 may not be in the form of physical damage.

INFORMATION WARFARE

The concept of information warfare states that knowledge is becoming the Army's center of gravity. Technology now allows us to improve our commander's knowledge base while we diminish and degrade the quantity and quality of the enemy commander's knowledge base. A primary measure of effectiveness in this type warfare is the

commander's decision making cycle. The intelligence system plays a vital role on both sides of this equation. On the friendly side, the ability to produce a common, coherent, real-time picture of the battlefield helps to reduce uncertainty and shorten the decision making process while effective CW operations significantly increase and distort the enemy's decision making cycle. Figure 6-1 illustrates some aspects of this new operational environment.

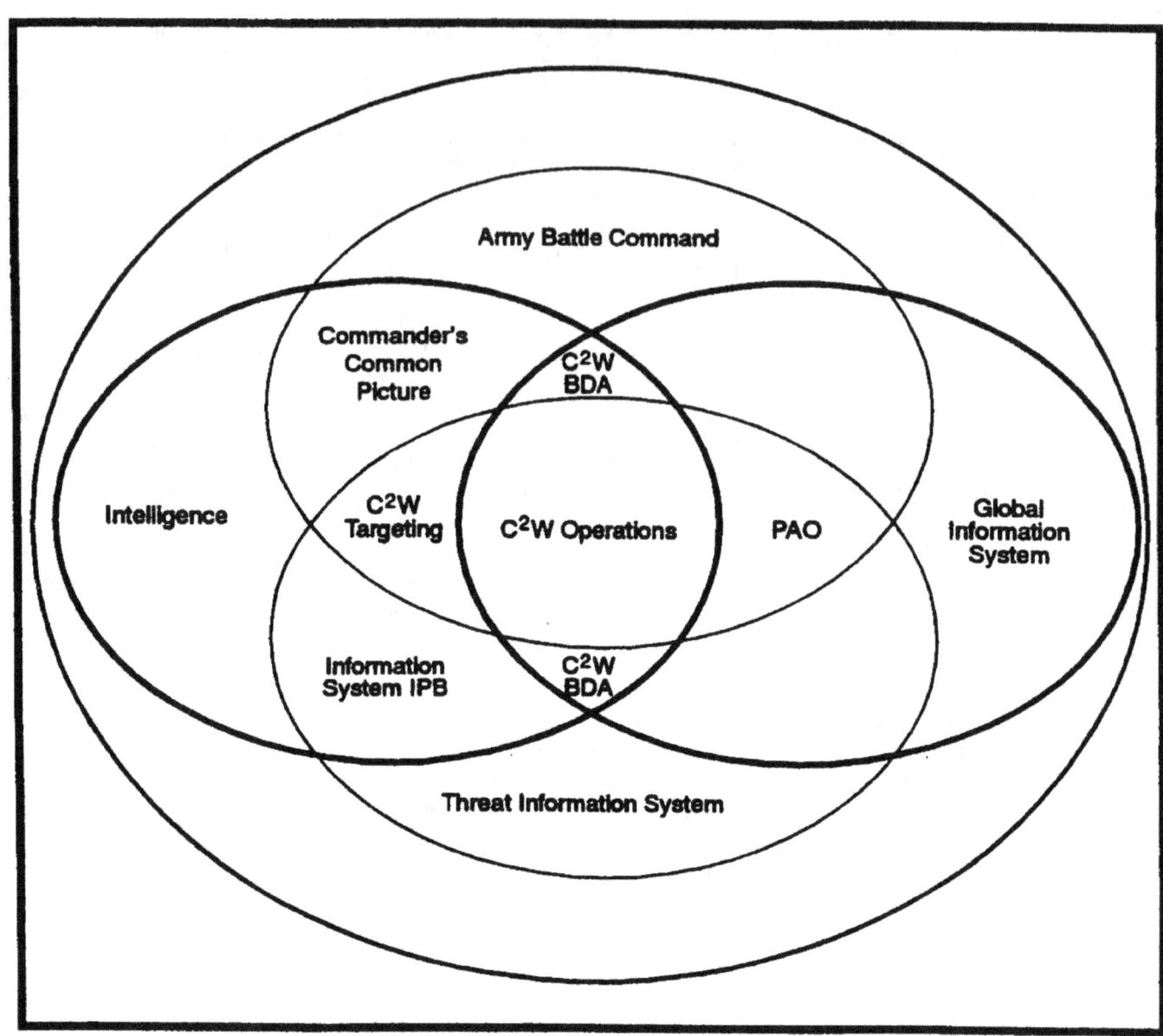

Figure 6-1. Military operations environment.

INFORMATION OPERATIONS

Information operations are the way the Army will prepare and execute knowledge-based warfare across the full range of military operations. Information operations are essential to winning the information war on the future battlefield, and IEW is the key to successful information operations. Information operations enable, enhance, and protect the commander's decision making cycle while influencing an opponents. This is accomplished through effective intelligence, battle command, and C^{2}W operations as an integral part of joint, combined, or interagency operations. Battle command is about imposing control on the compressed dimensions of battle space by achieving and sustaining a high tempo of operations, overwhelming lethality, and superior survivability. Supporting battle command, information operations are conducted across the full range of military operations.

In peacetime, information operations are conducted at various levels of intensity against assorted adversaries. In SASO situations where restraint is often required, nonlethal C^{2}W is used to bring about a desired response from threat forces. In cases where the use of force is unavoidable, all elements of information operations are employed in concert to best achieve the objective. The effective combination of lethal and nonlethal C^{2}W attack on information operation's targets allows the prediction of the impact of the targeting effort on the enemy's ability to react.

The IEW battle space is frequently global as was demonstrated in Operation Desert Storm. The vast array of systems and sources available to the intelligence community will require a universal vision of the battlefield as shown in Figure 6-2. This vision is crucial in providing the analytical perspective required to give commanders a common picture of the battlefield. The commander's ability to increase the quality of his decisions and compress his decision making process is directly related to his ability to visualize current and Suture situations. This common picture binds the intelligence and battle command functions together.

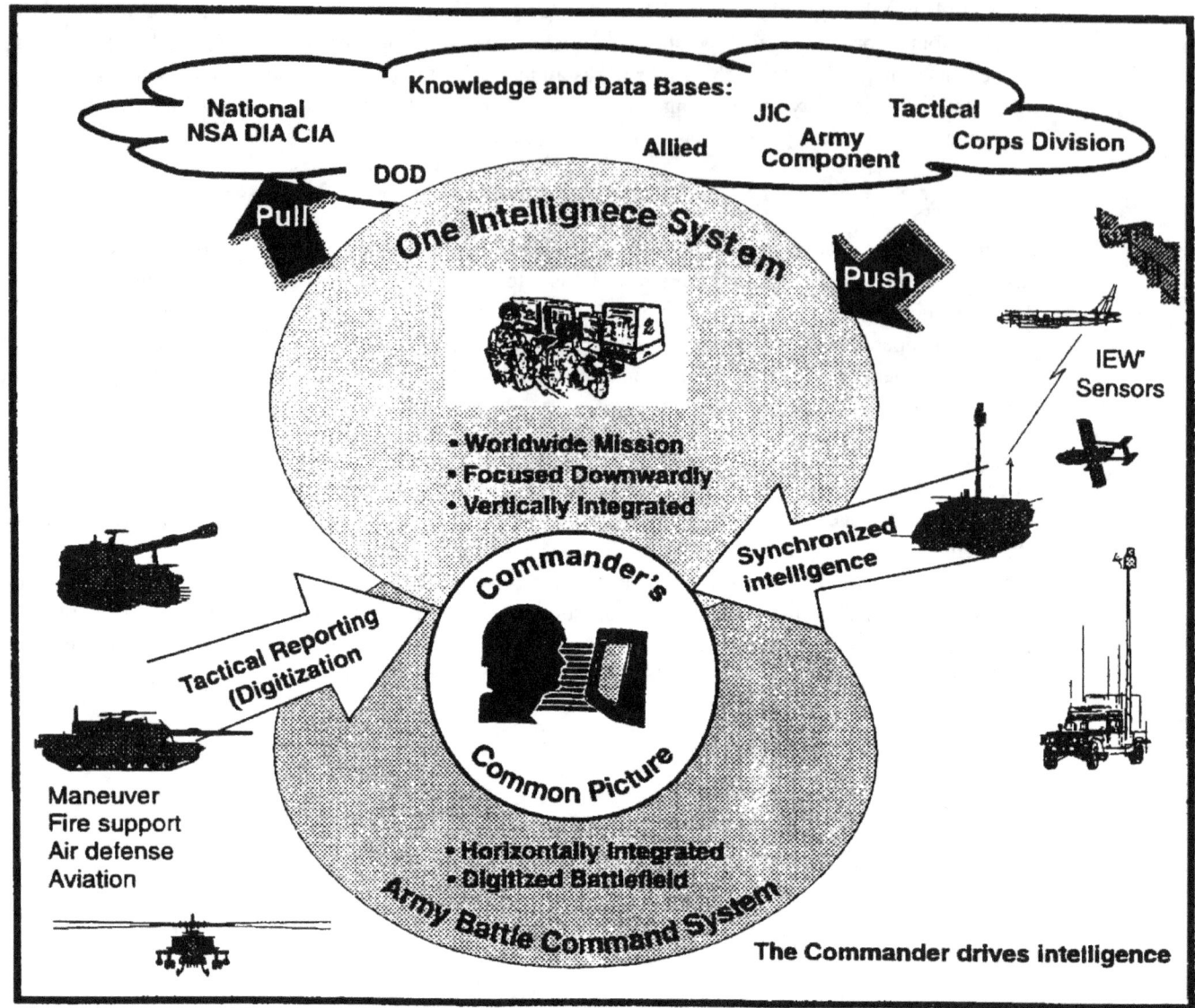

Figure 6-2. IEW battle space.

COMMAND AND CONTROL WARFARE

C²W is knowledge-based and decision oriented. Fast-paced moves and countermoves characterize it by opposing commanders. The HVTs in C²W are the commander's decision-making processes. The objectives in C²W are to allow friendly commanders to make better decisions rapidly (inside the threat commander's decision making cycle), while causing the enemy to make bad decisions or hesitate in making a decision at a critical point in time on the battlefield. See Figure 6-3. C²W integrates OPSEC, military deception, PSYOP, EW, and physical destruction with mutually supported intelligence to deny information and to influence, degrade, or destroy adversary C² capabilities

220

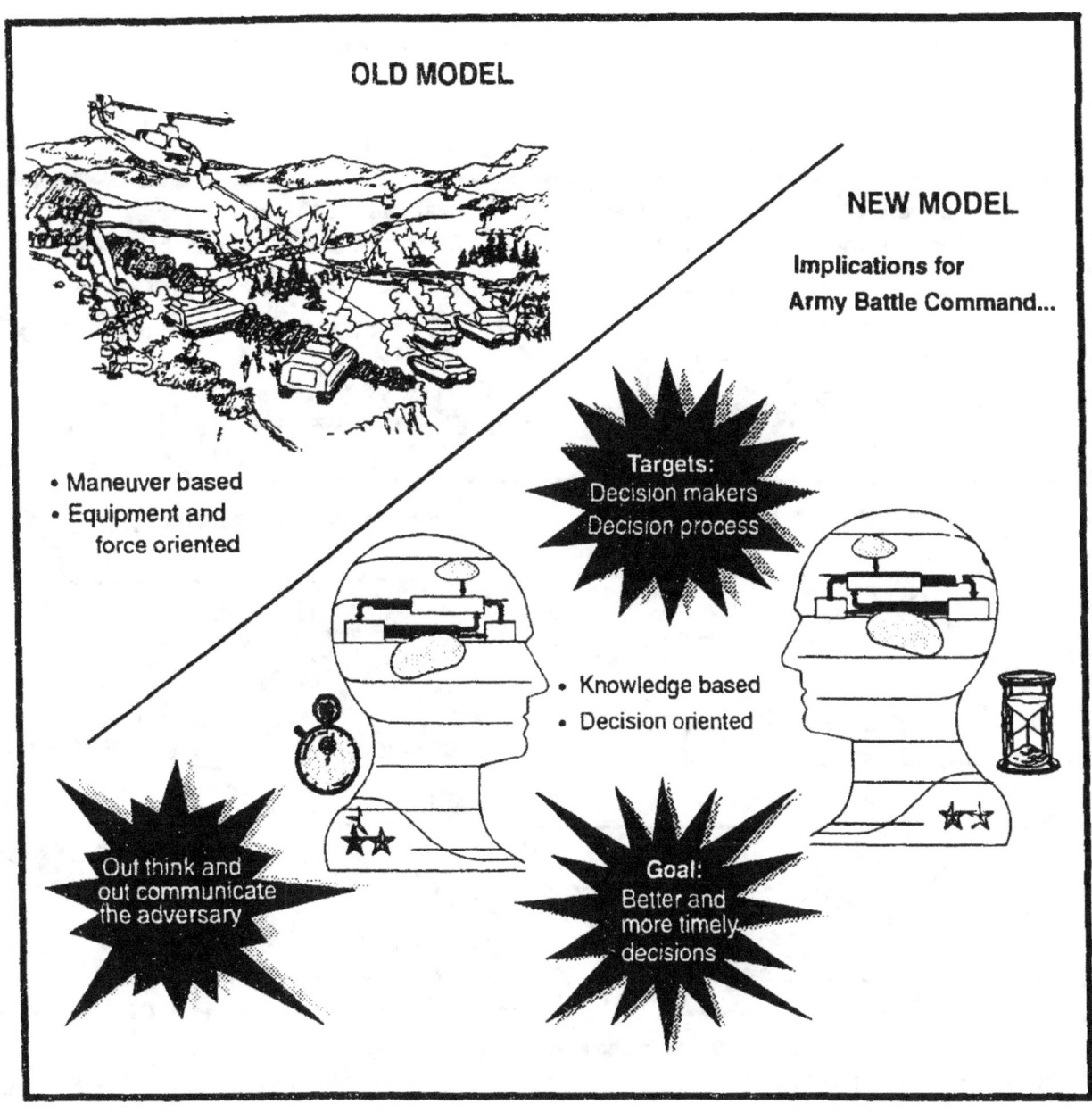

Figure 6-3. C²W objectives.

while protecting friendly C² capabilities. The C²W part of information operations is not a system. It is a strategy that applies the primary C²W components to reduce the adversary's C² capabilities (counter-C²) while protecting friendly C² capabilities (C²-protect). It applies across the full range of military operations and at all levels of war.

C²W is supported by an information system IPB. This form of IPB as shown in Figure 6-4, is the basis for developing C²W COAs and targeting. The process builds upon the standard IPB but requires-

- Understanding the "art" of decision making and leadership.

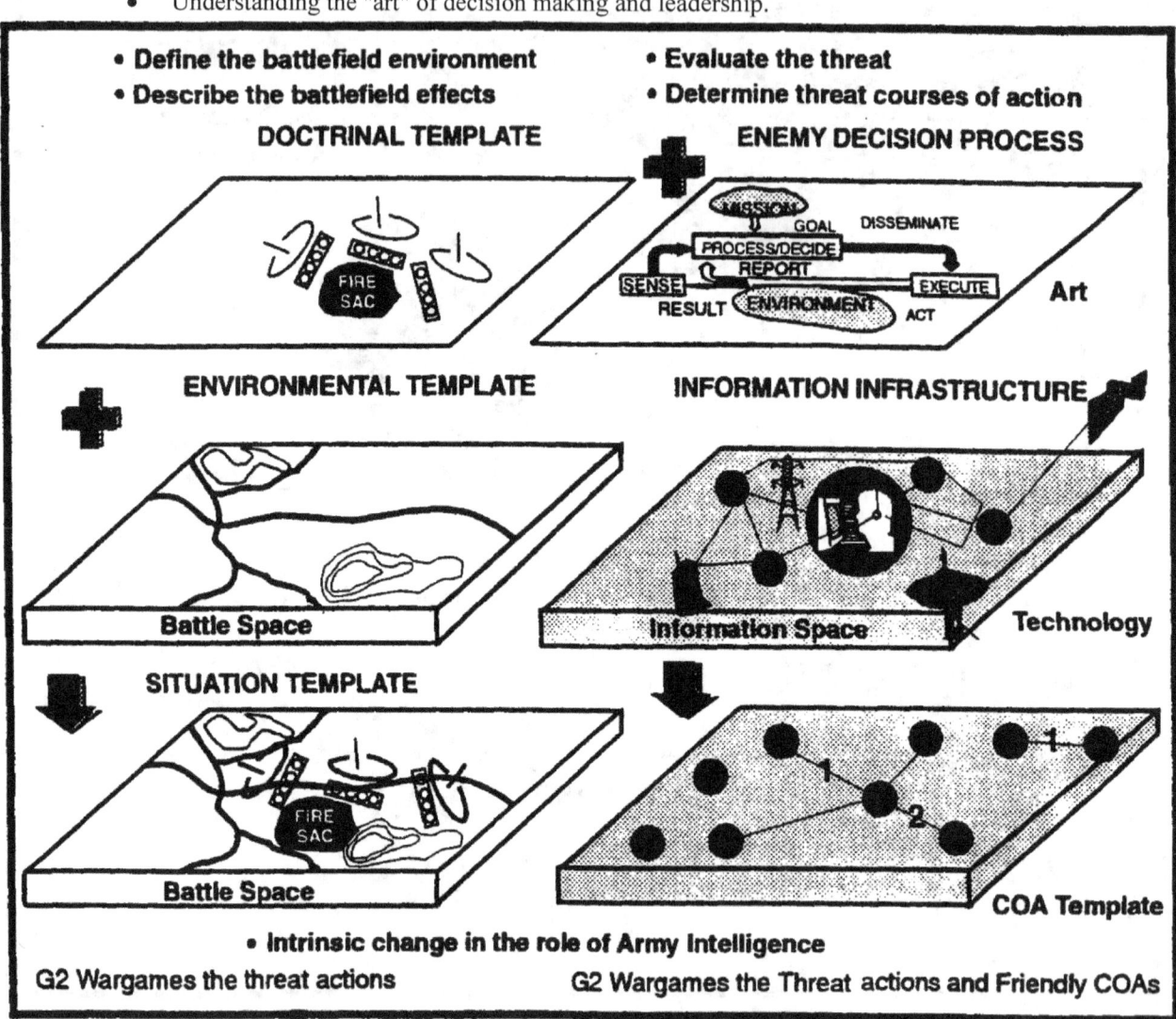

Figure 6-4. IPB of an information system.

- Knowledge of the technical requirements of a wide array of information systems.

- Ability to conduct highly technical processing to produce C²W COA templates.

222

The effectiveness of C^2W operation is predicated on a thorough understanding and assessment of the enemy's capabilities from equipment through his decision making process.

The Intelligence BOS is a operational tool that creates and exploits vulnerabilities in the enemy battle command. IEW is an operator in C^2W and information operations. From conventional and information system IPB, developing C^2W COAs, supporting information operations, and assessing the effectiveness of C^2W operations, IEW has taken on an operational role in military operations.

The more capable Army of the future will still be based on a hierarchical force level command but will be empowered by fully digitized information management systems. The commander will drive information operations just as he drives the intelligence effort. He will use information operations to focus and leverage information to better command his force and apply the elements of combat power.

LESSON 6

PRACTICE EXERCISE

The following items will test your grasp of the material covered in this lesson. There is only one correct answer for each item. When you have completed the exercise, check your answers with the answers with the answer key that follows. If you answer any items incorrectly, study again that part of the lesson, which contains the portion involved.

1. Which of the following is NOT supported by IPB?

    A. staff estimates

    B. mission success

    C. planning

    D. decision making

2. Which of the following is one of the five principal missions of SOF?

    A. antiterrorism

    B. Civil Affairs

    C. Humanitarian Assistance

    D. Direct Action

LESSON 6

PRACTICE EXERCISE

ANSWER KEY AND FEEDBACK

ITEM	CORRECT ANSWER AND FEEDBACK	
1.	B.	page 6-2, para 3)
2.	D.	(page 6-10, para 3)

APPENDICES FOR COUNTERINTELLIGENCE OPERATIONS AND INTELLIGENCE SUPPORT MISSIONS LESSONS

APPENDIX A

CRIME SCENE PROCESSING

Successful crime scene processing depends upon the investigator's skill in recognizing and collecting items and facts that may be valuable as evidence.

When processing a crime scene, the investigator must:

* PROTECT the crime scene from destruction or contamination.

* PRESERVE all items and facts of evidentiary value obtained at the crime scene. This includes making sketches and notes; photographing the scene; collecting trace evidence and fingerprints; questioning suspects, victims, and witnesses; and marking evidence.

* PRESENT the findings made from crime scene processing. This is the purpose of protecting and preserving the crime scene.

The investigator must attempt to reconstruct what actually occurred during the crime, and if testifying in court, be able to logically and positively identify all facts and items obtained during his investigation. The purpose of this appendix is to acquaint the investigator with—

* Searching for collectable evidence.

* Making investigative notes and sketches.

* Photographing the crime scene.

CRIME SCENE PROCEDURE.

Initial Actions.

Depending on the type of crime committed and the location, the crime scene is the area surrounding the location, to include all direct traces of the crime. The investigator should note the name and position of the person notifying him and the time the crime was reported.

Upon arrival at the scene, the investigator should do the following:

* Record the date, arrival time, and weather conditions.

* If an injured person is on the scene, arrange for medical attention, identification, and removal. The scene is disturbed only to the extent necessary to have medical aid rendered to the injured or to have a doctor examine a deceased victim. Consideration should be given to providing a searched pathway to the victim.

* If the offender is at the scene, apprehend him.

- If the scene is not fully protected, ensure its protection by using MP or other responsible persons to keep curious persons away from the scene and keep witnesses, suspects, and victims present from disturbing the scene. It may be necessary to reroute traffic or take other action to prevent any disturbance of the scene until a complete examination is made.

Evidence. The body of a deceased victim should not be covered until thoroughly processed for evidence. Premature covering could result in destruction or alteration of valuable trace evidence.

Immediate action is taken to protect items of possible evidentiary value that may be destroyed by rain, snow, fire, or other causes. For example, a raincoat or piece of canvas may be used to cover impressions in the earth that are exposed to rain. Wooden or paste board boxes may be placed over impressions in snow. Items that will melt must be shielded from the sun or other heat sources. Objects such as food and blood should be covered to protect them from contamination.

Witnesses. Determine and record the names of persons at the scene who may be witnesses and separate them. These persons should be removed from the immediate area of the scene as soon as practicable.

Conduct preliminary questioning of witnesses, suspects, and victims to determine in general the extent of the incident or crime. Record all movements made at the scene and what items persons have touched.

Note the names of all persons present. Those present within the immediate area of the scene should be only the minimum needed to assist the investigator. It may be necessary to request military or other officials present to refrain from examining or disturbing objects or aspects of the scene.

Investigating personnel must maintain CONTROL and SECURITY of the crime scene.

RECORDING.

The investigator begins the process of recording pertinent facts and details of the investigation the moment he arrives at the crime scene.

He writes down identification of persons involved and what he initially sees. He also draws a rough sketch of the crime scene and takes an integrity photograph. This is accomplished to ensure that an image of the crime scene is recorded before the scene is disturbed. The recording continues for the duration of the crime scene processing. Techniques for recording sketches and investigative notes are discussed later.

SEARCHING FOR EVIDENCE.

Each crime scene is different, according to the physical nature of the scene and the crime involved. Consequently, the scene is processed to develop essential evidentiary facts pertinent to the offense. A general survey of the scene is always made, noting the location of obvious to the offense. A general survey of the scene is always made, noting the location of obvious traces of the action, probable entry and exit point used by the offender(s), and the size and shape of the area involved.

In rooms, buildings, and small outdoor areas, a systematic clockwise circle search for evidence is often initiated. (A counterclockwise or any other systematic movement may be just as effective in the search. However, in the interest of uniformity, it is recommended the clockwise movement be used).

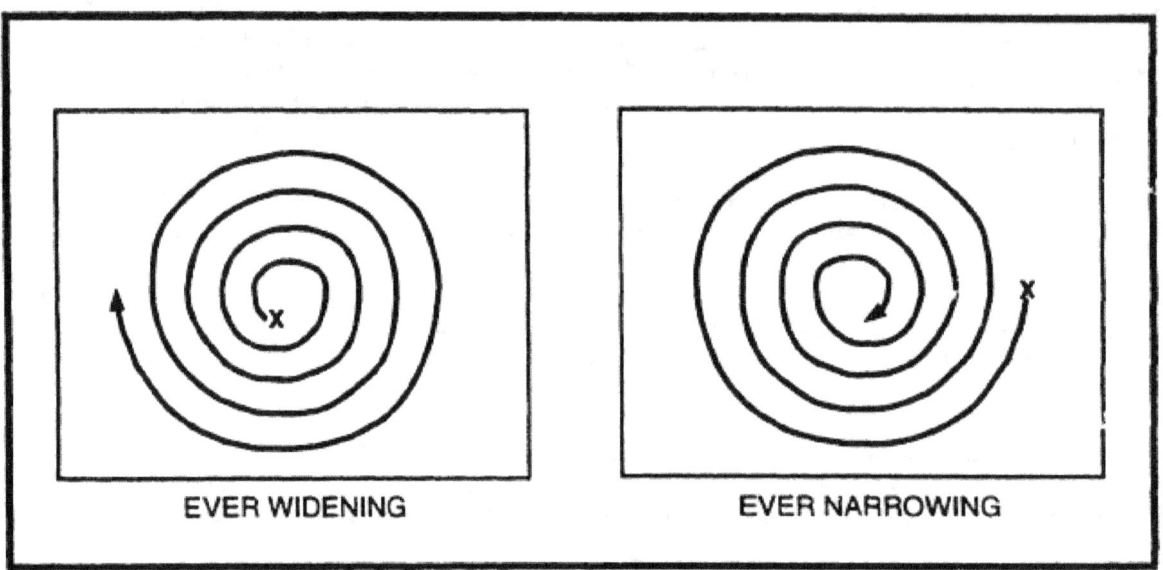

EVER WIDENING   EVER NARROWING

Figure A-1. Circle Search.

The investigator examines each item encountered at the scene to locate anything that may be of evidentiary value. He should accomplish the following:

* Give particular attention to fragile trace evidence that may be destroyed or altered if it is not collected immediately.

* If any doubt exists as to the value of an item, treat it as evidence until proven otherwise.

* Ensure each item or area where latent fingerprints may be present is closely examined and action taken to develop the prints.

* Carefully protect any impressions of evidentiary value in surfaces conducive to making casts or molds. Photograph the impression and make a cast or mold.

* Note stains, spots, and pools of liquid within the scene and treat them as evidence.

- Note any peculiar odors emitting from the scene.

- Treat as evidence all other items, such as hairs, fibers, and earth particles foreign to the area in which they are found. This includes scrapings under the victim's fingernails. (Small bags, used to cover the hands of deceased victims, would prevent loss or destruction of trace evidence.)

- Continue systematically and uninterruptedly to the conclusion of the processing of the scene. The search for evidence is initially completed when, after a thorough examination of the scene, the rough sketch, necessary photographs, and investigative notes have been completed and the investigator has returned to the point from which the search began. Further search may be necessary after the evidence and the statements obtained have been evaluated.

In large outdoor areas, it is advisable to divide the area into strips about 4 feet wide. The search starts at one end and moves back and forth across the area from one side to the other. A grid search takes place after a strip search is completed. It covers the area in a similar manner, but from end to end.

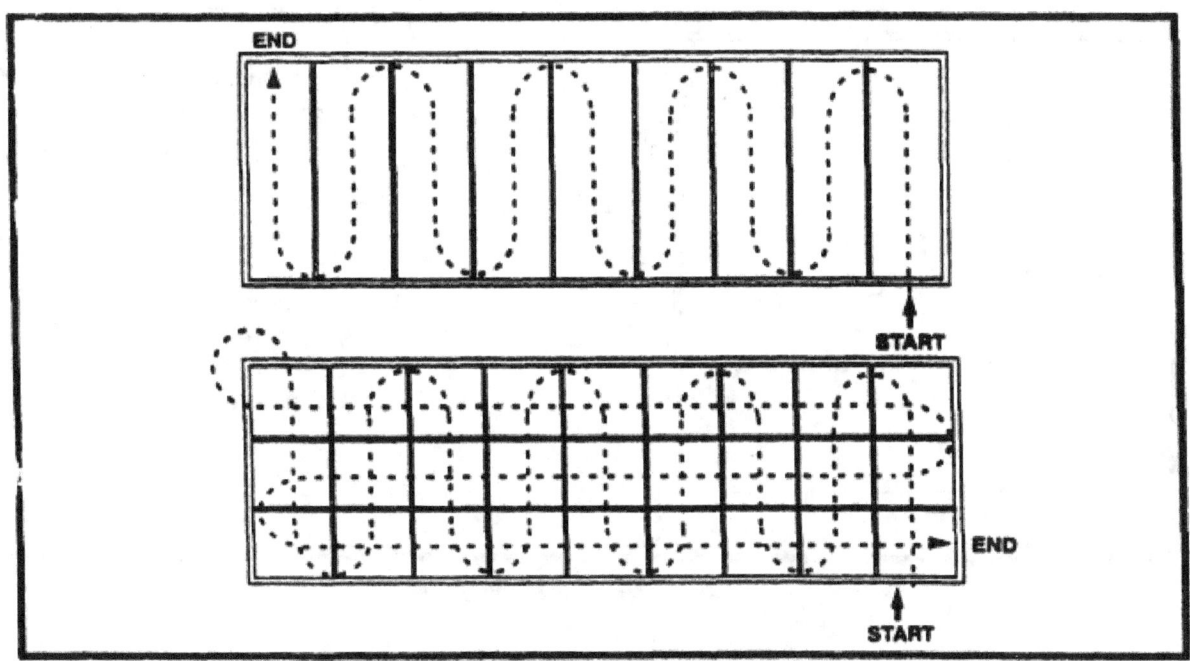

Figure A-2. Strip Search and Grid Search.

Indoor or outdoor areas may also be divided into zones or sectors, which are searched as individual areas (see two examples in Figure A-3).

It may be advisable to make a search beyond the area considered to be the immediate scene of the incident. If so, persons needed to accomplish the search may be secured from an MP or other available unit.

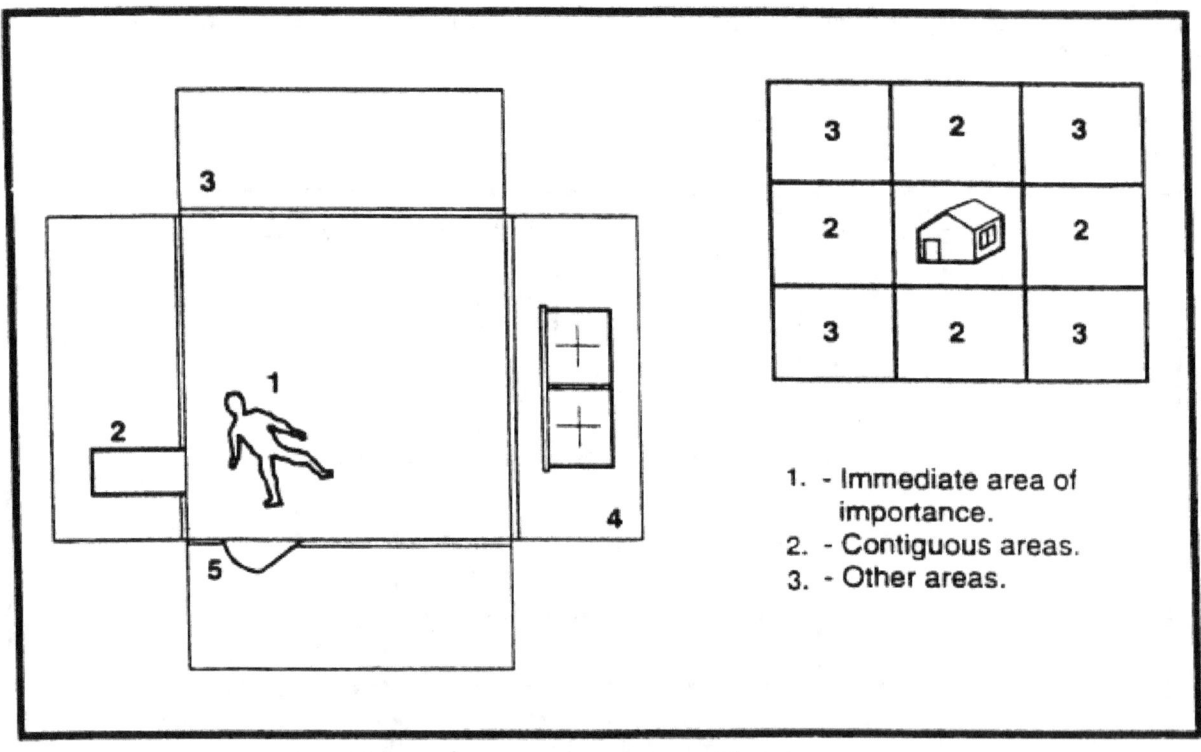

Figure A-3. Zone or Sector Search.

1. - Immediate area of importance.
2. - Contiguous areas.
3. - Other areas.

All persons participating in the search must be thoroughly briefed as a minimum on the following points:

First: A full description of the item(s) being sought.

Second: All information available as to how the item(s) may have been hidden or discarded.

Third: The action to be taken when the item(s) is/are found. The searchers should be emphatically informed that when they discover an item believed to be the one being sought, or one similar, they should immediately notify the investigator in charge of the search, refrain from touching or moving the item and protect the area until the investigator arrives.

After completing the search of the scene, the investigator examines the object or person actually attacked by the offender. For example, a ripped safe or desk drawer that has been opened would be processed after the remainder of the scene has been examined for traces of the offender.

COLLECTING EVIDENCE

Collecting evidence at a scene is usually accomplished after the search has been completed, rough sketch finished, and photographs taken. It may be advisable under certain conditions to collect various fragile items of evidence as they are found. Those items that would impede further search should be collected when they are located and depicted on the sketch. The essential factor is that evidence be carefully and properly collected.

The investigator must handle evidence as little as possible. Rubber gloves may be used. See table 1 for recommended methods of handling specific items that may be collected at a scene.

Table I. Recommended Methods for Handling Crime Scene Items.

Items	Method
Handguns	Use your fingers on the knurled grip. Do not touch smooth grips of smooth metal parts. Use the tip of the grips. Do not touch the magazine base of pistols. Place in a box bracing the weapons at the front and rear.
Paper, money, documents, paper	Use tweezers. Do not place tweezers over any obvious smudge. Place each item in a clean envelope or bag.
Broken glass	Use your fingers on the edges of larger pieces. Do not touch flat surfaces. Use tweezers on pieces too small for your fingers. Do not grasp at points of any obvious smudges. Wrap pieces individually in clean tissue, place in a rubbing box, and stabilize to prevent rubbing, shifting, or breakage.
Dried stains on smooth surface furniture	Collect portions of furniture bearing surfaces of of furniture stain in original patterns, if possible, otherwise, scrape with pocket knife or putty knife, removing as little of the finished surface as possible.
Bottles, jars, drinking glasses	Insert two or more fingers into large mouth vessels. Place the index fingers on the top and bottom of small mouth vessels. Do not contaminate or spill any substance in the vessel that may be of evidentiary value.
Bullet	Use your fingers or tweezers with taped ends. Avoid damage to rifling marks on the circumference. Place in a pillbox.
Cartridge case	Pick up at the open end with tweezers. Avoid scratching. Place in a pillbox.
Dried stains on a floor	Collect portion of floor bearing stain in original pattern, if possible; otherwise, remove by gouging deeper than the stain with putty knife, wood chisel, or other necessary tool. Place in pillbox or larger similar container.

If the investigator touches a piece of evidence in a manner that leaves his fingerprints on the article, he indicates this fact in his notes and informs the laboratory personnel if they make an examination of the evidence. The investigator's and the victim's fingerprint cards should be forwarded with latent prints to decrease delay of latent identification.

It may be necessary to damage, partially destroy, or otherwise decrease the effectiveness of an article to collect important evidence. For example, it may be necessary to cut the upholstery on a piece of furniture to obtain an area stained with blood or to cut out a section of a wall to collect fingerprints that cannot be collected by other means. Such action is based on the merits of the individual case. A door or window may be removed from a building to have it processed at a laboratory or held as evidence.

The investigator should ensure necessary measures are taken to protect the contents of a building or room from which a door or window is removed.

When collecting evidence at the scene for laboratory analysis, the amounts needed will depend upon the type of evidence and the test to be conducted.

For proper evaluation of a stain by laboratory technicians, control samples should be submitted in addition to the collected stains. For example, a stain, soil, or porous surface is collected by dipping or gouging beneath the stain. Unstained portions are also collected and identified as control samples. The integrity of control samples is preserved as carefully as that of evidence.

Marking Evidence for Identification.

The investigator places his initials, date and time of discovery of each item of evidence, so it can be identified by him at a later date. These marks should be placed on the item of evidence as soon after discovery as is feasible and in a place least likely to affect the appearance, monetary, or evidentiary value of the item. Evidence that cannot be marked should be placed in a suitable clean container, sealed, and the identifying marks placed on the container. The investigator makes appropriate notes, to include a description, in his notebook at the time the evidence is marked.

In instances in which several items with the same appearance are collected, the investigator places an identifying number on each item and indicates, by that number, in his notes and on the sketch where each item was found.

If a bullet, a knife, or other item on which the investigator would normally place his initials cannot be marked in the recommended manner, the item is placed in a suitable container and the container is marked for identification.

Additional information on marking evidence can be found in lesson 3 of this subcourse.

GENERAL EVIDENCE PROCESSING.

Tagging evidence. Physical evidence the investigator obtains must be tagged prior to its submission to the evidence custodian. This action should take place at the scene of the crime when the evidence is collected, at the place of receipt, or as soon thereafter as possible. The tag serves as an aid in the processing and storage of evidence (see lesson 3).

Evaluating evidence. Frequently, the successful conclusion of an investigation depends on an accurate evaluation of the evidence. Each item of evidence must be evaluated in relation to all other evidence, individually and collectively.

The investigator's evaluation of evidence begins with the first information received concerning the incident or crime and continues until the investigation has been satisfactorily concluded or discontinued by proper authority. The evaluation may include a discussion of the evidence with supervisors, other investigators, laboratory technicians, or other experts in a given field.

Preserving evidence. It is the investigator's responsibility to ensure every precaution is exercised to preserve physical evidence in the state in which it was received until it is released to the evidence custodian.

Preservation includes security and chain of custody. A key-type field safe should be made available to the investigator for temporary storage of evidence during other than normal duty hours (see lesson 3).

Releasing evidence. Once in the investigator's possession, evidence is released only to the evidence custodian or another person designated by the investigator's supervisor.

Releasing the scene. The scene is not released until all processing has been completed. The release should be affected at the earliest practicable time, particularly in instances in which an activity has been closed or its operations curtailed.

Sketches and Investigative Notes.

Properly prepared sketches may be used to question witnesses, suspects, and victims; to prepare a report of investigation; and to present information in court.

They are also valuable sources of information for both trial and defense counsels. Sketches are frequently introduced in court as evidence and used to acquaint the court with crime scenes and help witnesses orient themselves as they testify. Sketches and notes made during an investigation become DA property and are not retained or used as personal property.

Notes or sketches used to refresh the investigator's memory during a court appearance may be reviewed by the court. Appropriate attention is given to ensure all notes and sketches are legible and project clear, meaningful facts. Lack of organization in notes or sketches could adversely influence the weight given to the investigator's testimony by a court.

Sketches. A sketch which graphically portrays the scene of a crime and items within the crime scene is of interest to the investigation. The sketch, crime scene photographs, and investigative notes are complementary and necessary to effectively process the crime scene.

The sketch provides the best means of portraying distances between objects at the scene. There are two basic kinds of sketches, the rough sketch and the smooth sketch (scaled drawing). Both types of sketches contain the same general information, but differ according to the technique of presenting the information.

To cover items of interest to the investigation, crime scene sketches must, as a minimum, depict the following:

- Locations of approaches, such as roadways, paths, entrances, exists, windows, and skylights.

* Size of the area or building.

* Exact locations and relative positions of all pertinent evidence found at the scene.

* Camera locations.

In depicting the above, the sketch should:

* Each sketch should have a caption to identify the illustration. (eg. "Rough sketch showing camera positions and distances.)"

* Reflect accurate measurements verified by another person.

* Indicate compass direction of north. (Located on top of the scale bar)

* Designate the scale (for scaled drawing only). If no scale is used, state this fact. (Located in bottom center)

* Use a conventional system of measurement (English or metric system). Paces or steps are not used.

* Must contain a legend located in lower left position that explains all symbols or letters used to identify objects on the sketch. Military symbols are used where practicable.

* Each sketch must have a sketch title block, located in the lower right portion that depicts the report or incident number, offense alleged, name and rank or title of the victim, scene (portrayed - citing room number, bldg number, and type of building, location (citing complete name of installation, city, state, zip code, date and time the sketch was started, and the name and rank or title of the persons who made and verified the sketch.

Rough sketch. The purpose of a rough sketch is to portray information accurately, not necessary artistically. A rough sketch is usually not drawn to scale. But it must show accurate distances, dimensions, and relative proportions. The rough sketch is filed with the copy of the report retained by the originating office.

More than one sketch can be made of a particular scene. One may reflect measurements; another camera positions; and a third may be required to show locations of items of physical evidence at the scene. In some instances, separate sketches may be the best way to record multiple scenes contained within a larger area of investigative interest, or to provide detailed depictions of isolated locations within a relatively small crime scene. Conditions may necessitate the sketching of a limited area within the crime scene.

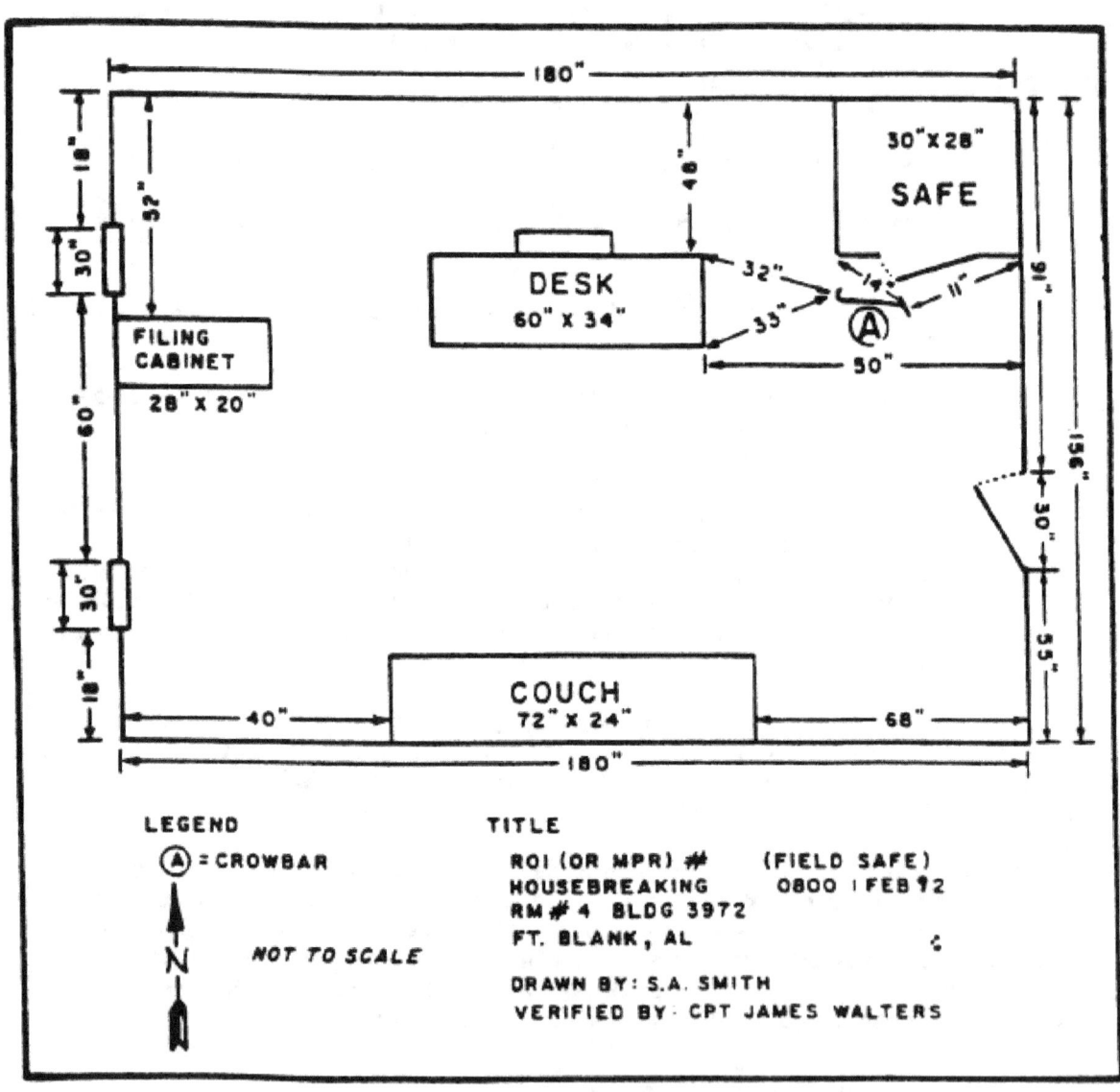

Figure A-4. Rough Sketch, Showing Evidence
Measurements and Triangulation.

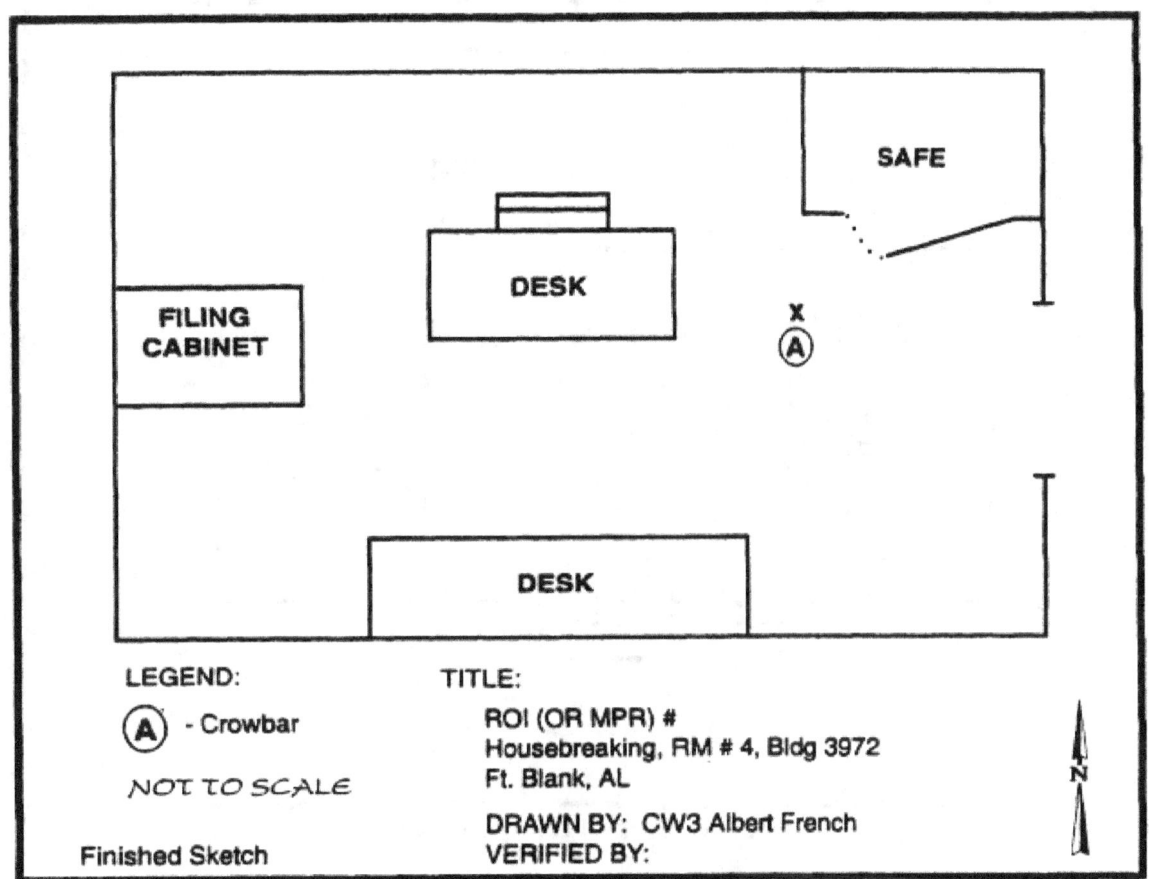

LEGEND:

(A) - Crowbar

NOT TO SCALE

Finished Sketch

TITLE:

ROI (OR MPR) #
Housebreaking, RM # 4, Bldg 3972
Ft. Blank, AL

DRAWN BY: CW3 Albert French
VERIFIED BY:

N

Figure A-5. Smooth Sketch.

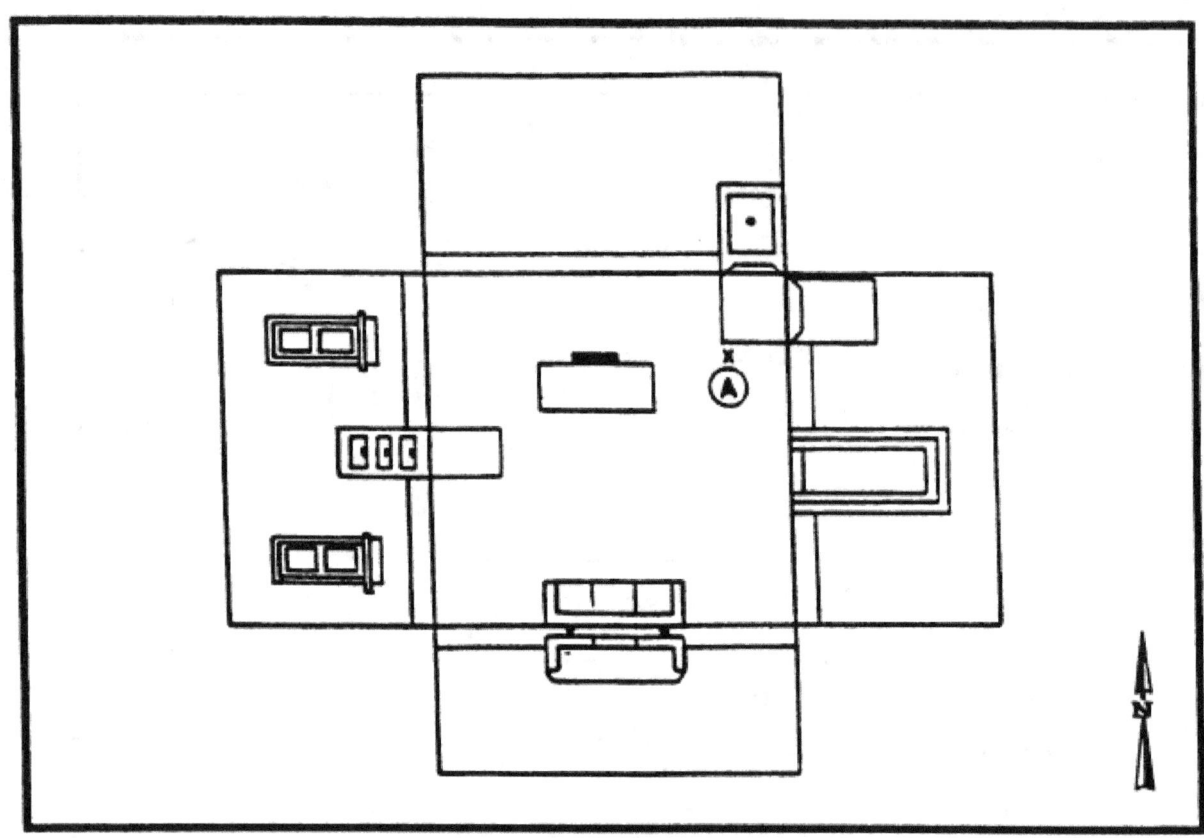

Figure A-6. Cross-Projection Sketch.

Items necessary to prepare a rough sketch are as follows:

* Soft lead pencil.

* Bond paper or graph paper.

* Several thumbtacks to hold one end of the steel tape down when you're working alone.

* Clipboard large enough to form a back for the paper.

* Steel tape (at least 100 feet long).

* A straightedge ruler.

* A magnetic compass.

Smooth sketch. A smooth finished sketch is a more finished version of a rough sketch, using the information provided in the rough sketch. A smooth sketch need not be drawn by the same person who draws the rough sketch. But whoever draws the rough sketch must verify the accuracy of the smooth sketch if made by an experienced draftsman. When drawn to scale, the sketch need not include figures to show distances. If not drawn to scale, this fact should be indicated on the sketch and distances should be shown as on a rough sketch. A copy of the finished sketch is appended to each copy of the investigative report.

If the finished sketch is prepared by investigative unit personnel, the following materials are considered necessary:

* Drawing board or table.

* Draftsman T-square.

* Pencil and ink drawing compass.

* Ink ruling pen.

* Lettering and drawing pens.

* Black india ink.

* Drawing and tracing paper.

* Architect scale.

* Art gum and ink erasers.

* Engineer or architect triangles.

* Drawing pencil.

* French curve.

Projection Sketch. A cross-projection sketch may be used to add another dimension to sketches. It is useful when items or locations of interests are on or in wall surfaces in an enclosed space. The walls, windows, and doors in a cross-projection sketch are drawn as though the walls had been folded out flat on the floor (see Fig A-6).

Methods to Establish Location and Measurement.

Various sketch methods may be used to locate evidence and other important items at the scene. The simplest form of a sketch is a two-dimensional presentation of a scene as viewed directly from above. Evidence is located on this type of sketch by triangulation. Triangulation is used for indoor and outdoor sketches having fixed reference points. Objects are located by creating, a triangle of measurements from a single, specific, identifiable point on an object to two fixed points, all on the same plane, at the scene. If movable items are to be used as reference points, they must first be "fixed" themselves. Do not triangulate evidence to evidence. Do not triangulate under or through evidence. Do not take a line of measurement through space. Measure your line along walls, or table top: In the interest of clarity, keep the angle of triangulation measurement between 45 and 90 degree on the sketches.

Regulator shaped items are fixed by creating two separate triangles of measurements. Each originates at opposite points on the object and ends at two fixed points, in the same plane, at the scene.

Pliable objects are fixed by creating a single triangle of measurement from the center of mass of the object to two fixed points, on the same plane, at the scene. You also measure the longest and widest dimension of the object.

Inhibited outdoor areas usually have easily defined, fixed reference points such as buildings, edges of roads, and sidewalks. When these are present, the triangulation method can be used to establish the location of objects. But uninhabited or remote areas may not have easily defined, fixed points will have to be located by using the intersection-resection method taught in map reading. See FM 21-26 for more discussion on intersection-resection.

INVESTIGATIVE NOTES.

Investigative notes are prepared for use in recalling places, events, incidents or other pertinent facts. They are filed with the copy of the report retained by the originating office.

Basic Principles of note taking are:

* Notes should be printed or made in legible handwriting, preferably in ink. The ink should not smudge easily.

* Each page of notes should be identified with the investigator's name, the case number (when known), and the date.

* Short phrases should be used; single words or shorthand notes may not be meaningful at a later date or to other persons.

* The first notes recorded after a complaint is received should include the date and time the complaint or information was received, name of the person reporting the information, names of the accused or suspected person(s), exact location of the incident, and a brief account of the details received. A complete identity of each person should be recorded when he is first mentioned.

Notes should be made when an action is taken, when information is received, and when an event is observed. However, the investigator should not allow his note taking to adversely affect the questioning of a person who may be distracted by such action and subsequently withhold information.

Notes should indicate a detailed description of any item considered to be pertinent to the investigation. This includes:

* Unusual or peculiar marks of identification.

* The exact location where the item was found and the relative distances separating various items.

* Trade names, and serial and model numbers.

* The recording of all identifying marks placed on the item.

Notes should indicate action taken by the investigator that may have a bearing on evidence obtained or significantly affect the investigation.

Notes should identify each photograph taken of a scene. They should be accurate and complete, since they form the basis for the preparation of the formal investigative report. The investigator may also use the notes to refresh his memory if he appears as a witness in a court proceeding.

Notes should not be edited or erased. If a mistake is made, the entry should be lined out, initialed, and then rewritten.

Crime Scene Photography.

One of the most valuable aids to a criminal investigation is provided by photographs. When properly taken, photographs supplement notes and sketches, clarify written reports, provide identification of personnel, and provide a permanent record of fragile perishable evidence.

The most important rule in crime scene photography is to photograph all evidence or possible evidence before anything is moved or touched.

General Considerations. Maintaining perspective is the most important consideration in crime scene photography. Photographs that nearly duplicate the exact scene with respect to scope, position, color, and form are the most useful.

Time is also an important consideration. Fragile trace evidence subject to nature (such as a footprint in the rain and fingerprints) should be photographed prior to any other processing.

There should not be any extraneous objects in the photographs such as investigators, their clothing, or equipment. Notes should be taken of the type of camera and film used, photographs taken, and any information necessary for the photographers to be able to answer "Yes" to the question, "Does this photograph represent the scene as you saw it?"

If it has been determined an explosive was used and there is residue of explosives in the area, a flash attachment should not be used.

When necessary, all objects should be photographed from different angles to ensure complete coverage. Evidence flags are useful in marking the location of small items of evidence for a photograph.

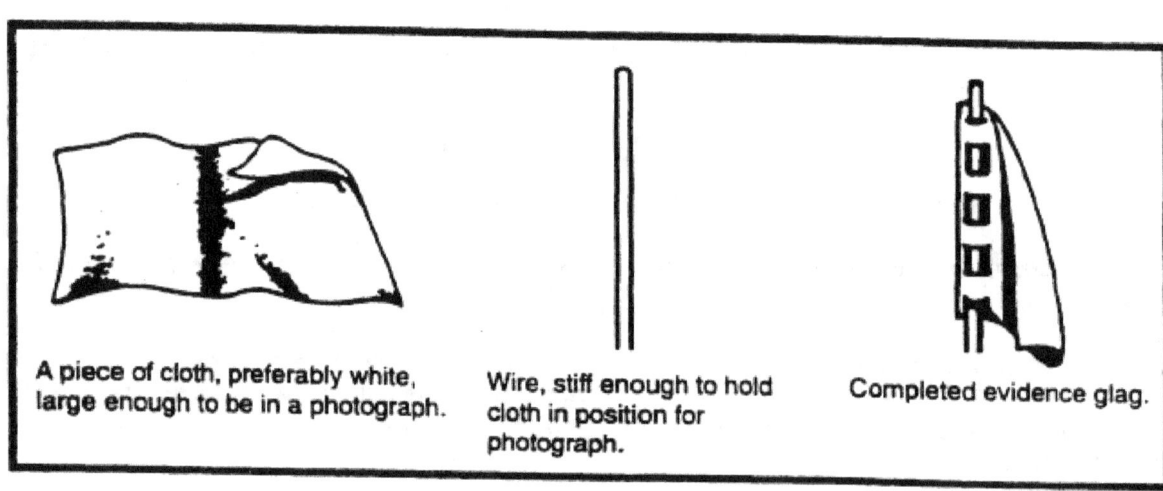

A piece of cloth, preferably white, large enough to be in a photograph.

Wire, stiff enough to hold cloth in position for photograph.

Completed evidence glag.

Figure A-7. Evidence Flag.

When pertinent, photographs should be taken of the general scene, approaches to the crime scene, surrounding areas, closeups of the entrance and exit locations, or those routes most likely used.

Special Considerations.

Arson scenes. There are several special considerations in photographing a fire. The photographer should seek out various possible angles from which to take photographs, attempting to keep out of smoke-filled areas.

Photographs of the entire structure should be made first. Color film should be used to show the color of the smoke, flames, and vapors. A series of photographs taken at intervals of several minutes may show the intensity and direction of the fire. Photographs should be made of any spectators at a fire, because the perpetrator may be present watching the results of his efforts.

After the fire, the entire exterior of the structure should be photographed. Following this, all affected interior areas should be photographed, to include any evidence discovered. Suspected points of origin should be photographed in detail. Since the photographer cannot rely on his exposure meter when trying to photograph charred wood, two or three stops overexposure will be required.

```
                    ARSON:  DURING FIRE

    o  Various angles

    o  Color photo of entire structure first (include
       smoke, flames, and vapor)

    o  Series taken at intervals of several minutes

    o  Spectators

                    ARSON:  AFTER FIRE

    o  Entire exterior

    o  Affected interior areas

    o  All evidence

    o  Suspected points of origin
```

Figure A-8. Photographing the Arson Scene.

Other evidence. Various items of evidence should be specifically photographed. This evidence should normally be located in an overall view of the crime scene. Next, a medium-range shot should be taken of the object to show its surrounding area. A third, closeup shot of the object should be made to show any peculiarities, followed by the same shot with a ruler in the picture area.

crime scene, surrounding areas, closeups of the entrance and exit locations, or those routes most likely used.

Special Considerations.

Arson scenes. There are several special considerations in photographing a fire. The photographer should seek out various possible angles from which to take photographs, attempting to keep out of smoke-filled areas.

Photographs of the entire structure should be made first. Color film should be used to show the color of the smoke, flames, and vapors. A series of photographs taken at intervals of several minutes may show the intensity and direction of the fire. Photographs should be made of any spectators at a fire, because the perpetrator may be present watching the results of his efforts.

After the fire, the entire exterior of the structure should be photographed. Following this, all affected interior areas should be photographed, to include any evidence discovered. Suspected points of origin should be photographed in detail. Since the photographer cannot rely on his exposure meter when trying to photograph charred wood, two or three stops overexposure will be required.

Counterintelligence Operations

Appendix B

SPECIMEN	MARKING	DETERMING AMOUNT		PRESERVING	PACKAGING	TRANSMITTING
		STANDARD	EVIDENCE			
Abrasive, including carborundum, emery, sand, metal filling, and so on.	Label and tag container. Show type of material, date obtained, investigator's name, or initials, case and evidence number.	Call lab for guidance.	Send all evidence.	No special instructions.	Use ctonainers such as ice cream box, metal pill box, or powder box. Seal to prevent any loss. Seal small amounts in folded paper packet, the place in container.	Send by Registered Airmal, RR, or Air Express.
Acids.	Same as above.	Send up to 1 qt, but at least 15cc (1/2 ounce) if available.	Send up to 1 pint.	No special instructions.	Call lab for guidance. Label "Acids", Glass", "Corrosive".	R.R. Express only.
Adhesive tape.	Same as above.	Send up to one foot.	Send all evidence.	No special instructions.	Place on waxed paper or cellophane. Pack in pill, or powder box, paper container, or druggiar's fold. Seal edges	Send by registered mail.
Alkalines (like Caustic soda, potash, ammonia.)	Same as above.	Send up to one quart liquid, 1 lb solid.	Send up to one quart or 1 lb but on less 15cc or (1/2 oz). If available, send up to five rds. Cite specification and lot number if available.	No special instruction.	Call lab for guidance. Label "Alkali, Glass, corrosive"	Send by RR Express only.

SPECIMEN	MARKING	DETERMING AMOUNT		PRESERVING	PACKAGING	TRANSMITTING
		STANDARD	EVIDENCE			
Ammunition	Same as above.	If standard make usually not necessary to send any. Otherwise submit two rounds.	Send up to five rds, cite specification and lot number if available.	No special instructions.	Pack in cotton, soft cloth in small container to prevent frction, shifting and contac while in transit. Place in wooden box. Label "Explosive".	Send by RR express.
Blasting caps	Place label and tag on outside of container. Note type of material, date obtained, investigator's name or initials, case and evidence number.	No special instructions.	Send all evidence.	CONSULT WITH LAB FOR GUIDANCE	CONSULT WITH LAB FOR GUIDANCE.	CONSULT WITH LAB FOR GUIDANCE.
Blood (liquid)	On adhesive tape on outside of test tube, write none of victim or subject, date taken, doctor's name, investigation name, case and evidence number.	Submit 5cc (I/5 ounce) collected in a sterile test tube or sheppard (vac tube).	Send all evidence.	Use sterile tube only. No preservation, no refrigerant.	Wrap in cotton, soft paper, place in mailing tube or strong mailing carton to prevent breakage and spillage.	Send by registered mail.
		For small quantities, collect using sterile gauze.	Send all up to 1/5 ounce.	Air dry gauze	Place in envelope seal.	
		For drowning cases, send two speci- mans, one from each side of heart.	Send all evidence	Consult laboratory if preservation is required.	No special instructions.	

SPECIMEN	MARKING	DETERMING AMOUNT		PRESERVING	PACKAGING	TRANSMITTING
		STANDARD	EVIDENCE			
Blood Solid (dried)	Place scrapings on paper and use duggist fold. Note type of specimen, date secured, investigator's name, case and evidence numer on outside of folded paper.	Submit 5cc (l/5 ounce) blood collected from persons related to case (see instruc-tion for liquid blood). Also send a control speciman of material (soil, porous matter) from which stain collected.	Send as much as possible.	Keey dry, or if partly dried, dig completely under natural conditions.	Seal top, ends, and all folds to prevent leakage.	Send by registered mail.
Blood stained clothing, fabric	Use property tag and/or mark directly on clothes. Note type of specimen, date secured, investigor's name, case and evidence number.	Submit 5cc (l/5 ounce) of blood collected from persons related to case (See instruc-tions for liquid blood).	Send all evidence.	If wet when found, dry under natural conditions. Use no excessive heat to dry. Ue no preservaives.	Wrap each article separately and identify on outside of package. Place in a strong box packed to prevent shifting of contents.	Send by registered mail.
Body organs	Label or mark outside of container. Note victim's name, date of death, date of autopsy, name of doctor, investigator's name, case and evidence number.		CONSULT	WITH LAB	FOR GUIDANCE	

IT 0735

| SPECIMEN | MARKING | DETERMING AMOUNT | | PRESERVING | PACKAGING | TRANSMITTING |
		STANDARD	EVIDENCE			
Bullets	On outside of container mark investigator's initials, date secured, case and evidence number.	No special instructions.	Send all evidence.	No special instructions.	Place bullet on cotton or soft paper. Place in pill, powder, or match box. Pack to prevent shifting in transit.	Send by registered mail.
Cartridges (live rounds)	Identify as directed above.	Send two rounds.	Send all evidence.	No special instructions.	Same as above.	Send by UPS or by military transportation.
Cartridges (empty shells)	Identify as directed above.	Send any found.	Send any evidence.	No special instructions.	When fingerprint evidence possible, place in test tube, seal, and label.	Send by registered mail.
Charred or burned paper	On outside of container note type of material, date obtained, investigator's name or initials, case, and evidence number.	No special instructions.	Send any evidence.	Keep dry. Do not add moisture with atomizer or otherwise.	Pack in rigid container between layer of cotton. If fragile and brittle, consult for guidance.	Consider hand-carrying. If necessary, send by registered mail.
Check protector, rubber stamp, and date stamp sets, known standards.	Place case and evidence number, investigator's name or initials, date secured, name of make and model, and so on sample impressions.	Obtain several copies in full word order of each questioned checkwriter impression. If unable to forward stamps, prepare numerous	Send all evidence.	Do not change the ribbon or alter the inking. See also typewriter specimens.	Wrap securely to prevent shifting or damage. (For transmitting standards, see documents).	Send by registered mail.

| SPECIMEN | MARKING | DETERMING AMOUNT | | PRESERVING | PACKAGING | TRANSMITTING |
		STANDARD	EVIDENCE			
Clothing Fabric	Attach property tag and/or mark directly on material. Note type of evidence, investigator's name, date, case, and evidence number.	samples with different degrees of pressure. No special instructions.	Send all evidence.	Leave clothing whole. Do not cut out stains. If wet, air dry before packing. For gun powder residue, avoid shaking.	Wrap each article individually. Identify article on outside of package. Place in strong container. For gun powder residue, fold fabric flat, placing clean paper between folds and wrap so no residue is lost through friction.	Send by registered mail.
Documents Anonymous letter, codes, cipher, extortion letters, fraudulent checks, questioned and secret writing, hand written and printed speciman, handwriting, handprinting, and forgeries. Know standards or exemplars (See also charred or burned papers.)	Place in paper envelope, seal and place investigator's initials, case and evidence number on envelope.	Submit as many samples as possible of suspect's handwriting, including samples of words used in questionned letters if possible. For checks, obtain genuine cancelled checks. Submit finger-print cards for all persons known to have handled documents.	Send all evidence. Include original envelopes. Advise if letter should be treated for latest finger-prints. Advise which parts are questioned and which are known.	Do not handle with bare hands	Place in paper envelope inside manila envelope after insert stiff backing to prevent bending or folding. Seal and mark for identification. Wrap securely. If burned and/or brittle, call lab for guidance.	Send by registered mail.

| SPECIMEN | MARKING | DETERMING AMOUNT | | PRESERVING | PACKAGING | TRANSMITTING |
		STANDARD	EVIDENCE			
Drugs: Liquid	Label or mark bottle in which found with investigator's name, date obtained, case and evidence number.	No special instructions.	Send not less than 15 cc (l/2 ounce); if available.	No special instructions.	If bottle does not have stopper, transfer contents to screw-topped bottle and seal with adhesive tape. Mark "fragile." Ensure against breakage.	Send by registered mail or RR or air express.
Drugs: powder pill, and solids.	Label or mark outside of pillbox with investigator's name, date obtained, case and evidence number.	No special instructions.	Send all evidence.	Guard against pill breakage.	Seal with tape to prevent spillage.	Send by registered mail or RR or air express.
Dynamite other explosives.	Call lab for guidance.			Send all evidence. Do not forward until advised to do so by the lab. Packing instructions will be given at that time.)		
Firearms	Attach property tag with identifying data. Mark investigator's initials and date on barrel, frame, and slide or cylinder.	No special instructions.	Send all evidence.	Keep from rusting. Unload all weapons before shipping. Do not unload magazines. Identify location of each round	Wrap each piece separately in paper and identify contents on package. Place in card board box or wooden box. Pack to prevent shifting while in transit. Label "firearm".	Send by registered mail.

SPECIMEN	MARKING	DETERMING AMOUNT		PRESERVING	PACKAGING	TRANSMITTING
		STANDARD	EVIDENCE			
Fuze (safety)	Attach property tag and/or gummed paper label with investigator's name, date, case, and evidence number.	Send a one foot section.	Send any evidence.	on revolver cylinder. Advise if firearms are to be examined for fingerprints. No special instructions.	Place in manila envelope, box, or suitable retainer.	Send by registered mail, or RR or Air Express.
Gasoline	Label or mark outside of all metal container; note type of material, investigator's name, date, case, and evidence number.	Send up to one quart.	Send up to 1 gallon.	Use only a fireproof container.	Use a metal container packed in wooden box.	RR Express only.
Glass Fragments	Separate questioned and known. Mark investigator's name, date obtained, case and evidence number on outside of sealed containers.	Submit finger-print cards for all persons known to have handled glass.	Send all evidence.	Avoid chipping.	Wrap each piece separately in paper. Pack in a strong box to prevent shifting and breakage. Identify contents. Mark "Fragile".	Send by registered mail.

SPECIMEN	MARKING	DETERMING AMOUNT		PRESERVING	PACKAGING	TRANSMITTING
		STANDARD	EVIDENCE			
Hair and fibers	Label or mark outside of container. Note type of material, date, obtain investigator's name, case and evidence number.	Submit about 15 pulled hairs from each part of head or body in question. Keep hairs from various parts separate.	Send all evidence.	Do not use envelopes.	Wrap specimen in paper using druggist fold. Seal edges and openings with scotch tape or adhesive tape. Place in container and seal.	Send by registered mail.
Impressions: Plaster casts, tire treads, footprints.	On back of cast before plater hardens, place investigator's initials and date.	No special instructions.	Send up to 2 ft.	No special instructions.	Wrap each cast in soft paper or cotton, surround with packing material in box to prevent shifting or breakage. Label "Fragile".	Send by registered mail.
Indented writing	(See also documents)	Original writing, if available.	Send all evidence.	See charred papers.	See charred papers.	Send by registered mail.
Matches	Mark or label outside of container. Note type of material, date obtained, investigator's name, case, and evidence number.	Send one to two books of paper matches. One full box of wooden matches.	Send all evidence.	Keep away from fire.	Pack in metal container. Pack in larger envelope to prevent shifting. Label "Keep Away From Fire."	Send by Registered mail, RR or air express.
Metal	Identify as directed above.	Send up to one lb or l ft.	Send all evidence up to l pound or 1 foot. Provide melt number, heat treatment, and other	Keep from rusting.	If metal is solid, wrap in paper. Use paper boxes or containers for fillings. Seal, pack in strong wooden box or paper.	Send registered mail, RR or Air Express.

SPECIMEN	MARKING	DETERMING AMOUNT		PRESERVING	PACKAGING	TRANSMITTING
		STANDARD	EVIDENCE			
Oil	Identify as directed above.	Send up to one quart.	specifications of _____ if available. Send all evidence up to 1 quart.	Keep away from fire.	Place in metal container with tight screw on top. Pack in strong box using excelsior or similar material.	Send by RR Express.
Paint: Liquid	Label or mark outside of container; note type of materials, origin if known, date obtained, investigator's name, case, and evidence number.	Send up to l quart.	Send all evidence up to 1 quart.	No special instructions.	Use a friction-top paint can or large mouth screw-top jars. If glass, pack in heavy corrogated paper or wooden box to prevent breakage.	Send by registered mail, RR or air express.
Paint: Solid (dried)	Identify as directed above.	Send at least 1/2 square inch if available.	Send all evidence. If paint is on small object, send object.	Wrap object with smears or chips to prevent paint from coming off. Do not pack paint chips in cotton or secure with scotch tape or adhesive.	Wrap chips of paint in paper using druggist fold. Seal to prevent spillage. Do not use envelopes.	Send by registered mail or RR or air express.

| SPECIMEN | MARKING | DETERMING AMOUNT | | PRESERVING | PACKAGING | TRANSMITTING |
		STANDARD	EVIDENCE			
Rope, twine, cordage	Tag and/or mark container : type of material, date obtained, investigator's name, case, and evidence number.	Send up to two ft.	Send all evidence up to 2 ft or more.	No special instructions.	Wrap securely in clean paper. If strands or fibers, use druggist's fold in pillbox. Seal edges and openings with scotch or adhesive tape.	Send by registered mail.
Safe insulation or soil	Label or mark outside of container: Note type of material, date obtained, investigator's name, case, and evidence number.	Send at least 1/2 cupful. Also send "alibi" standards.	Send all evidence up to 1 pound.	Avoid use of glass containers.	Pack in an ice cream box, pillbox, powder box, or the like. Seal edges and corners to prevent any spillage.	Send by registered mail or RR or Air Express.
Semen stains	Tag and/or mark article, note type of material, date obtained, investigator's name, case, and evidence number.	No special instructions.	Send entire article.	Air-dry. Avoid friction with stained area. Do not roll item. Do not fold or cleanse stained area. (See blood stained clothing).	Fold carefully, protect area with clean paper. Pack to prevent shifting in transit.	Send by registered mail.
Tools	Label and/or tag tool, note type of tool, investigator's name, or initials, case and evidence number.	Send the tool.	Send all evidence.	No special instructions.	Wrap each tool in paper. Pack strong cardboard or wooden box to prevent shifting.	Send by registered mail or RR or Air Express.

Appendix B

| SPECIMEN | MARKING | DETERMING AMOUNT | | PRESERVING | PACKAGING | TRANSMITTING |
		STANDARD	EVIDENCE			
Toolmarks	Tag and/or mark objects on the opposite end and from where toolmark appears. Note investigator's name, date obtained, case and evidence number.	Send the tool.	Send all evidence.	Cover ends of object bearing toolmarks with soft paper, and wrap with string paper to protect ends. Keep questioned specimans separate from known standards.	After marks have been protected, wrap in strong wrapping paper, place in a strong box, and pack to prevent shifting.	Send by registered mail, RR, or Air Express.

IT 0735

Counterintelligence Operations

Appendix C

APPENDIX C

ACRONYMS

APO	Army Post Office
ATF	Alcohol, Tobacco, and Firearms Division
BW	Biological Warfare
CBW	Chemical, Biological Warfare
CCF	Central Personnel Security Clearance Facility
CI	Counterintelligence
CII	Counterintelligence Investigation
CIDC	Criminal Investigation Division Command
CINCUSAREUR	Commander in Chief, United States Army, Europe
CONUS	Continental United States
CW	Chemical Warfare
DCSINT, DA	Deputy Chief of Staff for Intelligence, Department of the Army
DIS	Defense Investigative Service
DPDO	Defense Property Disposal Office
EUSA	Eighth US Army
EW	Electronic Warfare
FBI	Federal Bureau of Investigation
FCA	Foreign Counterintelligence Activity
INSCOM	Intelligence and Security Command
ISEW	Intelligence, Security, and Electronic Warfare
MACOM	Major Army Command
MP	Military Police
MPRJ	Military Personnel Records Jacket
MPR	Military Police Report
NBC	Nuclear, Biological, and Chemical
NCIS	Naval Criminal Investigative Service
ODCSINT	Office of the Deputy Chief of Staff for Intelligence
OSI, IG	Office of Special Investigations, Inspector General
PSI	Personnel Security Investigation
SCI	Sensitive Compartmented Information
SJA	Staff Judge Advocate
SOP	Standing Operating Procedures
UCMJ	Uniform Code of Military Justice
USACIL	US Army Criminal Investigation Laboratory
USAIRR	US Army Intelligence Records Repository
USAREUR	United States Army, Europe
USSS	US Secret Service

☆U.S. GOVERNMENT PRINTING OFFICE: 2003-528-075/80336

Intelligence and Electronic Warfare Operations

Appendix A

APPENDIX A

SECTION I - GLOSSARY

SECTION II - TERMS

GLOSSARY

Section I. Abbreviations and Acronyms

A

ABCA	American, British, Canadian, and Australian
AC	Active Component
ACE	analysis and control element
ACP	assault command post
ACR	Armored Cavalry Regiment
ACT	analysis control team
ADP	automatic data processing
AEB	aerial exploitation battalion
AI	area of interest
AM	amplitude modulation
ammo	ammunition
AMOPES	Army Mobilization and Operations Planning and Execution System
AO	area of operation
AR	Army regulation
ARFOR	Army force
ARM	antiradiation missile
ARNG	Army National Guard
ARSOA	Army Special Operations Aviation
ARSOF	Army Special Operations Forces
ASARS	Advanced Synthetic Aperture Radar System
ASAS	All-Source Analysis System
ASC	Army service component
ASL	authorized stockage list

B

BCV	battle command vehicle
BDA	battle damage assessment
bde	brigade
bn	battalion
BOS	Battlefield Operating System

C

C²	command and control
C²W	command and control warfare
C³I	command, control, communications, and intelligence
CA	Civil Affairs
CAARNG	California Army National Guard
cav	cavalry
CCIR	commander's critical information Requirement
CD	counter-drug
CENTCOM	Central Command
CGS	common ground station
CI	counterintelligence
CIA	Central intelligence Agency
CINC	Command in Chief

CIO	Central Imagery Office
CICS	Chairman, Joint Chiefs of Staff
CIS	Commonwealth of Independent States
CMISE	Corps MI Support Element
co	company
COA	course of action
COMINT	communications intelligence
comms	communications
CONUS	continental United States
CP	command post
C-RISTA	counterreconnaissance, intelligence, surveillance, and target acquisition
CS	combat support
CSG	cryptologic support group
CSS	combat service support

D

DA	Department of the Army
DCI	Director, Central Intelligence
DCSINT	Deputy Chief of Staff, Intelligence
DEA	Drug Enforcement Agency
DF	direction finding
DIA	Defense Intelligence Agency
DISE	Deployable Intelligence Support Element
DIVARTY	division artillery
DOCC	Deep Operations Coordination Cell
DOD	Department of Defense
DP	decision point
DS	direct support
DSNET3	Defense Secure Network 3
DST	decision support template

E

EA	electronic attack
EAC	echelons above corps
ECB	echelons corps and below
ELINT	electronic intelligence
EMCON	emission control orders
EP	electronic protection
EPDS	Electronic Processing and Dissemination System
EPW	enemy prisoner of war
ES	electronic warfare support
ETUT	enhanced tactical users terminal
EW	electronic warfare
EWO	electronic warfare officer

F

FA	field artillery

FBI	Federal Bureau of Investigation	JCMEC	Joint Captured Materiel Exploitation Center
FIS	foreign instrumentation signals	JCS	Joint Chiefs of Staff
FISINT	foreign instrumentation signals Intelligence	JDEC	Joint Document Exploitation Center
FM	frequency modulation; field manual	JDISS	Joint Deployable Intelligence Support System
FRAGO	fragmentary order	JIC	Joint Intelligence Center
freq	frequency	JIF	Joint Interrogation Facility
FSE	fire support element	Joint STARS/	
FSO	fire support officer	JSTARS	Joint Surveillance Target Attack Radar System
FTX	field training exercise	JTF	joint task force

G

L

G2	Assistant Chief of Staff, G2 (Intelligence)	JWICS	Joint Worldwide Intelligence Communications Systems
G3	Assistant Chief of Staff, G3 (Operations and Plans)	LA	Los Angeles
GBCS	ground-based common sensor	LAN	local area network
GEN	general	LAPD	Los Angeles Police Department
GPS	Global Positioning System	LOC	lines of communication
GRCS	GUARDRAIL Common Sensor	LOS	line of sight
GS	general support	LRS	long-range surveillance
GSM	ground station module	LRSU	long-range surveillance unit
GSR	ground surveillance radar	LST	lightweight satellite terminal
GS-R	general support-reinforcing	LTIOV	latest time information is of value
GUARDRAIL	AN/USD-9A or 9B		

H

M

HA	humanitarian assistance	MASINT	measurement and signature Intelligence
HPT	high-payoff target	MDCI	multidiscipline counterintelligence
HQ	headquarters	METL	Mission Essential Task List
HTF	how to fight	METT-T	mission, enemy, troops, terrain and Weather, and time available
HUMINT	human intelligence		
HVT	high-value target	MI	military intelligence

I

I&W	indications and warnings	MICAT	Military Intelligence Combat Assessment Tables
IDB	integrated data base	MIIDS	military intelligence integrated data base system
IEW	intelligence and electronic warfare		
IMETS	Integrated Meteorological System	MITT	Mobile Integrated Tactical Terminal
IMINT	imagery intelligence		
INSCOM	United States Army Intelligence and Security Command	MOS	military occupational specialty
		MOUT	Military Operations on Urbanized Terrain
Intel	intelligence		
INTREP	intelligence report		
INTSUM	intelligence summary		

N

IPB	intelligence preparation of the Battlefield	NAI	named area of interest
		NATO	North Atlantic Treaty Organization
IPDS	Imagery Processing and Dissemination System	NBC	nuclear, biological, chemical
		NEO	noncombatant evacuation operation
IPW	prisoner of war interrogation	NGIC	National Ground Intelligence Center
IR	information requirements	NIST	National Intelligence Support Team
ISE	intelligence support element	NMJIC	National Military Joint Intelligence Center

J

J2	Intelligence Directorate	NRO	National Reconnaissance Office
		NRT	near-real time
		NSA	National Security Agency

NSC	National Security Council

O

obj	objective
OCONUS	outside continental United States
OEM	original equipment manufacturer
OOTW	operations other than war
OPCON	operational control
OPLAN	operation plan
opns	operations
OPORD	operation order
OPSEC	operations security

P

PAO	public affairs office
PIR	priority intelligence requirement
PLL	prescribed load list
POD	port of debarkation
PSYOP	psychological operations
Pub	publication

Q

QSTAG	Quadripartite Standardization Agreement
QUICKFIX IIB	AN/ALQ-151(V)2

R

R	reinforcing
RAOC	Rear Area Operations Center
RC	Reserve Components
REDTRAIN	Readiness Training
REMBASS	Remotely Monitored Battlefield Sensor System
rep	representative
ret	retired
RII	request for intelligence information
ROE	Rules of Engagement

S

S2	Intelligence Officer (US Army)
S3	Operations and Training Officer (US Army)
S&TI	scientific and technical intelligence
SANDCRAB	airborne jamming system
SATCOM	satellite communication
SCI	sensitive compartmented information
SEAD	suppression of enemy air defenses
SECDEF	Secretary of Defense
SF	Special Forces
SHF	super high frequency
SIGINT	signals intelligence
SIR	specific information requirements
SOF	special operations forces
SOFA	Status of Forces Agreement
SOR	specific orders and request
SPIRIT	Special Purpose Intelligence Remote Integrated Terminal

spt	support
SSO	special security office
STANAG	Standardization Agreement
SUCCESS	Synthesized UHF Computer Controller Enhanced Subsystem
survl	surveillance
SWA	Southwest Asia

T

TAA	tactical assembly area
TAI	target area of interest
TB	technical bulletin
TBP	to be published
TC	training circular
TCAE	technical control and analysis Element
TEB	tactical exploitation battalion
TECHINT	technical intelligence
TENCAP	Tactical Exploitation of National Capabilities
TOC	tactical operations center
TPL	time phase line
TRAC	tactical radar correlator
TRACK-WOLF	AN/TRQ-152
TRADOC	United States Army Training and Doctrine Command
TROJAN	AN/FSQ-144V
TTP	tactics, techniques, and procedures

U

UAV	unmanned aerial vehicle
UHF	ultra high frequency
UN	United Nations
US	United States (of America)
USAR	United States Army Reserve
USSID	United States Signal intelligence Directive

W

WAN	wide area network
WARM	wartime reserve modes

Section II. Terms

Area of Interest - The geographical area from which information and intelligence are required to permit planning or successful conduct of the command's operation. The AI is usually larger than the command's AO and battlespace. The AI includes any threat forces or characteristics of the battlefield environment that will significantly influence the accomplishment of the command's mission.

Area of operations - That portion of an area of conflict necessary for military operations. AOs are geographical areas assigned to commanders for which they have responsibility and in which they have the authority to conduct military operations.

Battle command - The art of battle decision making, leading, and motivating soldiers in their organizations into action to accomplish missions. Includes visualizing current state and future state, then formulating concepts of operations to get from one to the other at least cost. Also includes assigning missions; prioritizing and allocating resources; selecting the critical time and place to act; and knowing how and when to make adjustments during the fight.

Battle damage assessment - The timely and accurate estimate of damage resulting from the application of military force, either lethal or nonlethal, against an objective or target.

Battle space - Components determined by the maximum capabilities of a unit to acquire and dominate the enemy; includes areas beyond the AO; it varies over time according to how the commander positions his assets. It depends on the command's ability to both acquire and engage targets using its own assets or those of other commands on its behalf.

Battlefield operating system - The major functions performed by the force on the battlefield to successfully execute Army operations in order to accomplish military objectives. BOS form a framework for examining complex operations in terms of functional operating systems. The systems include maneuver, fire support, air defense, C2, intelligence, mobility and survivability, and CSS.

BOS synchronization matrix - A written record of wargaming. The BOS synchronization matrix

depicts the criteria that generate each anticipated friendly decision and the resulting action by each friendly BOS. Other information required to execute a specific friendly COA may also be included.

Branch - A contingency option built into the basic plan for changing the disposition, orientation, or direction of movement of the force.

Capability - The ability to successfully perform an operation or accomplish an objective. The evaluation of capabilities includes an assessment of a force's current situation as well as its organization, doctrine, and normal TTPs. Capabilities are stated in terms of broad COAs and supporting operations. Generally, only capabilities that will influence accomplishment of the friendly command's mission are addressed.

Center of gravity - The hub of all power and movement upon which everything depends. That characteristic, capability, or location from which enemy and friendly forces derive their freedom of action, physical strength, or the will to fight.

Command and control - The exercise of authority and direction by a properly designated commander over assigned or attached forces in the accomplishment of the mission. C^2 functions are performed through an arrangement of personnel, equipment, communications, computers, facilities, and procedures employed by a commander in planning, directing, coordinating, and controlling forces and operations in the accomplishment of the mission. C^2 refers to the information systems the commander and staff use to conduct operations.

Command and control-protection - The division of C2W that seeks to deny, negate, or turn to friendly advantage of adversary efforts to destroy, disrupt, and deny information in the US and allied C2 system, including it s supporting communications, information, and intelligence activities.

Command and control system - The combination of personnel, equipment, communications, computers, facilities, and procedures employed by the commander in planning, directing, coordinating, and controlling forces and operations in the accomplishment of the mission. The basic functions of a C^2 system are sensing valid information about events and the environment, reporting information, assessing the situation and associated alternatives for action, deciding on an appropriate COA, and ordering actions in correspondence with the decision.

Command and control warfare - The integrated use of OPSEC, military deception, PSYOP, EW, and physical destruction mutually supported by intelligence, to deny information to, influence, degrade or destroy adversary C^2 capabilities, while protecting friendly C^2 capabilities against such action. C^2W applies across the full range of military operations and all levels of war.

Common understanding of the battlefield - How the commander and staff perceive the battlefield environment. It includes the sum of all that is known or perceived of friendly and threat forces and the effects of the battlefield environment.

Counter-command and control - Those measures taken to prevent effective C^2 of adversary forces by denying information to, influencing, degrading, or destroying the adversary C^2 system.

Course of action - A possible plan open to an individual or commander that would accomplish or is related to accomplishment of the mission. A COA is initially stated in broad terms with the details determined during staff wargaming. To develop COAs, the staff must focus on key information and intelligence necessary to make decisions. COAs include five elements: WHAT (the type of operation), WHEN (the time the action will begin), WHERE (boundaries, axis, etc.), HOW (the use of assets), and WHY (the purpose or desired end-state).

Critical node - An element, position, or communications entity whose disruption or destruction immediately degrades the ability of a force to C^2, or effectively conduct combat operations.

Decision point - The point in space and time where the commander or staff anticipates making a decision concerning a specific friendly COA. DPs are usually associated with threat force activity or the battlefield environment and are therefore associated with one or more NAIs. DPs also may be associated with the friendly force and the status of ongoing operations.

Decision support template - A graphic record of wargaming. The DST depicts DPs, timelines associated with movement of forces and the flow of the operation, and other key items of information required to execute a specific friendly COA.

Delaying operation - An operation usually conducted when the commander needs time to concentrate or withdraw forces, to establish defenses in greater depth, to economize in an area, or to complete offensive actions elsewhere. In the delay, the destruction of the enemy force is secondary to slowing his advance to gain time. Delay missions are delay in sector, or delay forward of a specified line for a specified time or specified event.

Doctrinal template - A model based on postulated threat doctrine. Doctrinal templates illustrate the disposition and activity of threat forces and assets (HVTs) conducting a particular operation unconstrained by the effects of the battlefield environment. They represent the application of threat doctrine under ideal conditions. Ideally, doctrinally templates depict the threat's normal organization for combat, frontages, depths, boundaries and other control measures, assets available from other commands, objective depths, engagement areas, and battle positions. Doctrinal templates are usually scaled to allow ready use on a map background. They are one part of a threat model.

Event matrix - A description of the indicators and activity expected to occur in each NAI. It normally cross-references each NAI and indicator with the times they are expected to occur and the COAs they will confirm or deny. There is no prescribed format.

Event template - A guide for collection planning. The event template depicts the NAIs where activity (or its lack) will indicate which COA the threat has adopted.

Electronic warfare - Consists of three subcomponents: electronic attack (EA), electronic warfare support (ES), and electronic protection (EP).

Global information systems - Non-DOD information systems (media, government agencies, nongovernmental organizations, international organizations, foreign governments, and industry) which collect, process, and disseminate information about operations. These systems largely operate autonomously and are not subject to control by the Army. The information they publish is accessible to all interested parties and can significantly impact decision making and execution.

High-payoff target - Targets whose loss to the threat will contribute to the success of the friendly COA.

High-value target - Assets that the threat commander requires for the successful completion of a specific COA.

Indications and warnings - One of the six IEW tasks.

Indicators - Positive or negative evidence of threat activity or any characteristic of the AO which points toward threat vulnerabilities or the adoption or rejection by the threat of a particular COA, or which may influence the commander's selection of a COA. Indicators may result from previous actions or from threat failure to take action.

Information - In intelligence usage, unevaluated material of every description that may be used in the production of intelligence.

Information requirement - An intelligence requirement of lower priority than the PIR of lowest priority.

Information systems - A term generally applicable to all installations, fabrications, or facilities for originating, transferring, processing, and storing data which may be used for the support and control of military forces or government.

Information systems security - A composite of means to protect telecommunications systems and automated information systems and the information they process.

Intelligence preparation of the battlefield - The systematic, continuous process of analyzing the threat and environment in a specific geographic area. IPB is designed to support the staff estimate and military decision making process. Most intelligence requirements are generated as a result of the IPB process and its interrelation with the decision making process.

Intelligence requirement - A requirement for intelligence to fill a gap in the command's knowledge and understanding of the battlefield or threat forces. Intelligence requirements are designed to reduce the uncertainties associated with successful completion of a specific friendly COA; a change in the COA usually leads to a change in intelligence requirements. Intelligence requirements that support decisions which affect the overall mission accomplishment, such as choice of a COA, branch, or sequel, are designated as PIR. Less important intelligence requirements are designated as IR.

Intelligence support base - Intelligence support base described the principal organization in a split-based operation from which a deployed commander pulls intelligence. Located in CONUS or at a location outside the AO, the intelligence support base performs collection management; produces and disseminates tailored intelligence products; and maintains accessible intelligence data bases needed to support the deployed commander. It may possess the capability of collecting and processing information on the AO. In most cases, the intelligence support base will provide the follow-on IEW assets which deploy to the AO.

Lines of communications - All the routes (land, water, and air) that connect an operating military force with one or more bases of operations and along which supplies and military forces move. Note that not all roads, or rails are LOCs. Some are unsuited, others may be suitable, but not used. Note also that is this context, a communications center is an area where LOCs coverage, such as transshipment points or hub-pattern cities (for example, Bastogne, Belgium).

Latest time information is of value - The time by which information must be delivered to the requestor in order to provide decision makers with timely intelligence. Sometimes the LTIOV is the expected time of a decision anticipated during staff wargaming and planning. If someone other than the decision maker must first process the information, the LTIOV is earlier than the time associated with the DP. The time difference accounts for delays in processing and communicating the final intelligence to the decision maker.

Mission, enemy, troops, terrain and weather, and time available - Used to describe the factors that must be considered during the planning or execution of a tactical operation. Since these factors vary in any given situation, the term "METT-T dependent" is a common way of denoting that the proper approach to a problem in any situation depends on these factors and their interrelationship in that specific situation.

Military Intelligence - A branch of the United States Army.

Named area of interest - The geographical area where information that will satisfy a specific information requirement can be collected. NAI are usually selected to capture indications of threat COAs but also may be related to conditions of the battlefield.

Nuclear, biological, chemical - Used to denote weapons or operations which depend on NBC warheads or agents for their casualty-producing effects; or which protect or defend against or react to their use.

Order of battle - Intelligence pertaining to identification, strength, command structure, and disposition of personnel, units, and equipment of any military force. The order of battle factors form the framework for analyzing military forces and their capabilities, building threat models, and hence developing COA models.

Possible - Information or intelligence reported by only one independent source is classified as "possibly true." The test for independence is certainty that the information report of a source was not derived from some other source, usually resulting in reliance on original reporting. A classification of "possibly true" cannot be based on analytical judgment alone.

Priority intelligence requirement - An intelligence requirement associated with a decision that will affect the overall success of the command's mission. PIR are a subset of intelligence requirements with a higher priority than information requirements. PIR are prioritized among

themselves and may change in priority over the course of the operation's conduct.

Probable - Information or intelligence reported by two independent sources is classified as "probably true." The test for independence is certainty that the information report of one source was not derived from the other source, usually resulting in reliance on original reporting. Analytical judgment counts as one source. Ensure that no more than one source is based solely on analytical judgment.

Reconnaissance - A mission undertaken to obtain information by visual observation, or other detection methods, about the activities and resources of an enemy or potential enemy, or about the meteorologic, hydrographic, or geographic characteristics of a particular area. Reconnaissance differs from surveillance primarily in duration of the mission.

Retrograde - An organized movement to the rear or away from the enemy. It may be forced by the enemy or may be made voluntarily. Such movements may be classified as withdrawal, retirement, or delaying operations.

Sequel - Major operations that follow an initial major operation. Plans for sequel are based on the possible outcome—victory, stalemate, or defeat — of the current operation.

Situation template - Depictions of assumed threat dispositions, based on threat doctrine and the effects of the battlefield, if the threat should adopt a particular COA. In effect, they are the doctrinal template depicting a particular operation modified to account for the effects of the battlefield environment and the threat's current situation (training and experience levels, logistic status, losses, dispositions). Normally the situation template depicts threat units two levels of command below the friendly force as well as the expected locations of HVTs. Situation templates use TPLs to indicate movement of forces and the expected flow of the operation. Usually, the situation template depicts a critical point in the COA. Situation templates are one part of a threat COA model. Models may contain more than one situation template.

Specific information requirement - Specific information requirements describe the information required to answer all or part of an intelligence requirement. A complete SIR describes the information required, the location where the required information can be collected, and the time during which it can be collected. Generally, each intelligence requirement generates sets of SIRs.

Specific order or request - The order or request that generates planning and execution of a collection mission or analysis of data base information. SORs sent to subordinate commands are orders. SORs sent to other commands are requests. SORs often use system-specific message formats but also include standard military operations and FRAGOs.

Surveillance - The systematic observation of airspace or surface areas by visual, aural, photographic, or other means. Surveillance differs from reconnaissance primarily in duration of the mission.

Target area of interest - The geographical area where HVTs can be acquired and engaged by friendly forces. Not all target areas of interest (TAIs) will form part of the friendly COA; only TAI associated with HPTs are of interest to the staff. These are identified during staff planning and wargaming. TAIs differ from engagement areas in degree. Engagement areas plan for the use of all available weapons; TAIs might be engaged by a single weapon.

*U.S. Government Printing Office: 2003 — 528-075/80106

www.ingramcontent.com/pod-product-compliance
Lightning Source LLC
Chambersburg PA
CBHW081323310526
45789CB00018B/2285